Dream Telepathy

Dream Telepathy

Experiments in Nocturnal ESP

SECOND EDITION

Montague Ullman
and
Stanley Krippner
with
Alan Vaughan

ORIGINAL FOREWORD BY GARDNER MURPHY

McFarland & Company, Inc., Publishers
Jefferson, North Carolina, and London

British Library Cataloguing-in-Publication data available

Library of Congress Cataloguing-in-Publication Data

Ullman, Montague.
   Dream telepathy / by Montague Ullman, Stanley Krippner, Alan
Vaughan.
     p. cm.
     Bibliography: p. 229.
     Includes index.
     ISBN 0-89950-349-7 (lib. bdg.; 50# acid-free natural and
     70# enamel gloss papers) ∞
     1. Dreams. 2. Telepathy. 3. Divination. 4. Psychical research.
I. Krippner, Stanley, 1932– . II. Vaughan, Alan. III. Title.
BF1091.U43 1989
135'.3 – dc19   88-39093
                                                   CIP

Printed in the United States of America.

McFarland & Company, Inc., Publishers
  Box 611, Jefferson, North Carolina 28640

To the memory of Gardner Murphy,
distinguished scholar, colleague, and friend

Contents

FOREWORD TO THE REVISED EDITION   ix

FOREWORD TO THE FIRST EDITION   xi

PART I—SPONTANEOUS TELEPATHIC DREAMING

1. *Cicero's Complaint*   3
2. *Sifting the Evidence*   9
3. *ESP on the Couch*   22
4. *The Alcoholic Cat*   35

PART II—EXPERIMENTAL STUDIES

5. *Early Explorations: From "Raf" to Ralph*   45
6. *Moving Eye Witnesses*   58
7. *A Dream Comes to Life*   66
8. *A Dream Grows in Brooklyn*   74

Between pages 84 and 85 there are 20 plates

9. *"Color His Wounds Red"*   85
10. *Women's Night*   97
11. *"The Prince of the Percipients"*   106
12. *One-Night Stands*   119
13. *Long-Distance "Sensory Bombardment"*   130
14. *Dreaming of Things to Come*   138
15. *Finding Out More About ESP*   145

PART III—THEORETICAL IMPLICATIONS

16. *What Does It Mean?*   159
17. *Sleep, Psyche, and Science*   173

APPENDICES

Appendix A — Erwin's Nocturnal Tour of the French Quarter   183

Appendix B — Psychology and Anomalous Observations: The Question of ESP in Dreams (by Irvin L. Child)   191

Appendix C — ESP in Dreams: Comments on a Replication "Failure" by the "Failing" Subject (by Robert L. Van de Castle)   209

Appendix D — A Group Approach to the Anomalous Dream   217
(by Montague Ullman)

REFERENCES

229

INDEX

245

Foreword to the Revised Edition

There are several reasons for the appearance of the revised edition of *Dream Telepathy*. Perhaps the most important is the ever-growing interest in dreams, a phenomenon we have observed among researchers, clinicians, and the general public. In addition, we have noticed a curiosity concerning possible telepathic effects in dreams, especially dreams that seem to be "shared" by clients and therapists, by husbands and wives, and by friends and lovers. In fact, there is considerably greater interest on the part of the public in these matters than existed at the time this book first appeared.

Following the initial publication of *Dream Telepathy* in 1973, a number of reports appeared in the psychological literature that were critical of our approach. This current edition has provided us with the opportunity to discuss the issues raised by our critics and to respond to them. We are pleased to include in this volume a separate and in-depth response to these criticisms by a distinguished colleague, Professor Irvin Child of Yale University.

We believe that our work at the Maimonides Medical Center established a sound experimental base linking dreams and telepathy. The implications of this relationship are far-reaching, both for the scientific understanding of dreams and for the penetration of such anomalous phenomena as presumptive telepathic effects. It is our hope that the appearance of the present edition will be a timely reminder of the need to take cognizance of these strange phenomena and to further explore their nature where they may appear — be it clinically in the consulting room, experimentally in the laboratory, or as they emerge spontaneously in our lives.

MONTAGUE ULLMAN, M.D.,
STANLEY KRIPPNER, PH.D.,
ALAN VAUGHAN.

Foreword to the First Edition

This volume takes a giant step into the unknown. A prominent psychiatrist, a versatile and ingenious psychologist, and a collaborator in the laboratory from which their work has come present us with a broad, clear, specific, and highly challenging approach to the telepathy of the dream. Dreams can carry a message through channels other than the channels of the senses. This has long been suspected. Indeed, it has been the subject of both theory and practice from the ancient civilizations of China and Egypt to the period of modern parapsychology. For several decades, attempts to study telepathy in the dream have appeared in the research of psychiatrists and psychologists. Sigmund Freud, having introduced the scientific world to the obscure and intriguing messages of the dreams of his patients, his colleagues, and himself, referred at times to the problem of telepathy in the dream, and a considerable body of psychoanalytic studies of dream telepathy is scattered through reports of his clinical work with patients.

In recent years the need for an experimental method has clearly been shown. Dreams are so complicated, their symbolism so involved, that the likelihood of coincidence of dreams with actual events is very great, and no "master key" is likely to open the fortress of scientific incredulity *but* planned experiments. The authors give us, after their extensive historical survey of dream studies, a detailed and disciplined account of the experimental methods they have developed over the years at the Dream Laboratory of the Maimonides Medical Center in Brooklyn. Over a hundred published studies have shown the real payoff which follows from a strict experimental method in which normal, genuine, real dreams of ordinary human beings are studied with full attention to the rigorous techniques of electrophysiology.

In such studies, it is necessary to bring an experimental subject to the laboratory in the evening to become familiar with the setting and with the procedure to be followed. The subject prepares for sleep, and electrodes are fastened to his scalp. He goes to sleep; he dreams—as is shown both by the rapid eye movements and the brain-wave changes which go with the sleeping process. When the records show he has been dreaming, he is awakened. He tells what he dreamed and gives free associations to what he has reported. A distant experimenter, nearly a hundred feet away and beyond three closed doors, has been attempting to guide the course of the sleeper's dream thoughts in accordance with a randomly chosen target, following a procedure which would exclude any possibility of the subject's normal knowledge of what was being beamed to him.

Later the data are evaluated by comparing the contents of the subject's dreams with the contents of the message which was beamed to him. Results have demonstrated that the resemblances are significantly greater than would be expected by chance. Along the lines of an improved method of evaluating successes and failures much more work remains to be done. Enough, however, has been done to show that in a span of a half-dozen years with over a hundred subjects, there is a significant relation between what is "sent" and what is "received." This has been reported in various technical publications but two additional steps have now been taken: First, the integration of all these reports into one coherent readable whole, and second, the conversion of scientific terminology and scientific ways of presenting data into a form more suitable for the general reader. The reader can now get the whole essence of the scientific procedure with abundant exemplification of actual cases, and with frequent stops along the road to permit evaluation of what has been discovered and what remains to be done. This book, in my judgment, is a very important addition both to scientific and general literature in the field of modern parapsychology.

It is difficult to imagine today a study more important, more nearly central to our fundamental problems in parapsychology: Can we adapt to the experimental and quantitative requirements of the laboratory, the vast floating psychological energies of the living human mind, so complex, so challenging, so full of both inspiration and terror — as we see its conscious and unconscious expressions in civilization and in the forces which tear civilization apart? Can parapsychology move from the world of the bizarre, absurd, and occasionally demonic to the realm of verifiable and intelligible expression of latent human nature? What are these hidden forces at work within us? Our seventeenth-century ancestors know that blankets gave off sparks in cold weather. But what was electricity "good for"? Today, electricity drives our machines, lights our halls, monitors our studies of man. Dream telepathy, dealing with the individual's efforts to make contact with distant reality and with the social nature of man's unconscious powers, is likely to be among the sparks which will be made into a science within the next century. We cannot afford to ignore such sparks. Rather, let us be grateful that there are men whose work aims to understand and control those deep forces which occasionally express themselves in the far ranging scientific study of the dream.

GARDNER MURPHY

PART ONE
SPONTANEOUS TELEPATHIC DREAMING

CHAPTER 1

Cicero's Complaint

The anomalous dream that seems to transcend time and space remains no less controversial today than it was in the days of Cicero, the great Roman orator, who complained that dream divination was sheer superstition.

Now, however, dreams that seem to capture information from afar are interpreted by parapsychologists as possible examples of extrasensory perception — in particular, of telepathy. The propensity of scientists to interpret dream telepathy as something occult, magical, or divine has dwindled to the point where psychological, medical, and psychiatric journals now publish authenticated accounts of scientifically controlled experiments in dream telepathy. It is the account of the *spontaneous* telepathic dream that is seldom printed in journals, yet it does happen — such dreams apparently do occur — to ordinary people in everyday life.

An experience of one of the authors, Alan Vaughan, is a case in point. He watched one of his favorite writers, Kurt Vonnegut, Jr., on a television talk show one night, and had a dream about him two nights later. He wrote about the dream to Vonnegut on March 13, 1970. "...you appeared in a dream I had this morning. We were in a house full of children. You were planning to leave soon on a trip. Then you mentioned that you were moving to an island named Jerome. (As far as I know there is no such place, so perhaps the name Jerome or initial 'J' has some related meaning.)"

Vonnegut's answer was dated March 28, 1970. "Not bad. On the night of your dream, I had dinner with Jerome B. [an author of children's books], and we talked about a trip I made three days later to an island named England."

The experience had all the markings of the spontaneous telepathic dream: A pair of unusual details mixed capriciously into a bizarre dream concoction in which talking with Jerome about going to an island becomes transformed into going to an island named Jerome.

It is difficult to make comparisons between dreams of the modern and those of the ancient world since we know little about the daily dream life of average ancient people. The writings and the traditions that have survived dwell mostly on the dreams of great men and women—the kings, queens, pharaohs, and other important personages. Reflecting their strong religious beliefs that rulers were divine beings or children of gods, the ancient peoples would have scorned a term as secular and insignificant as "spontaneous dream telepathy"; rather, they spoke in reverence of "a divine dream from the gods."

The story of one such dream is told on a stone tablet erected by Pharaoh Thutmes IV about 1450 B.C. in front of the Great Sphinx of Gizeh in Egypt.

> . . . it happened when the Prince Thutmes was come on his wandering about the time of mid-day, and had stretched himself to rest in the shade of the great god, that sleep overtook him.
>
> He dreamt in his slumber at the moment when the sun was in the zenith, and it seemed to him as though this great god spoke to him with his own mouth. . .
>
> "Behold me, look at me, thou, my son Thutmes. I am thy father Hormakhu, Khepra Ra Toom. The kingdom shall be given to thee. . . . The earth shall be thine in its length and in its breadth . . . plenty and riches shall be thine . . . long years shall be granted thee as thy term of life. . . . I will give the best of all things.
>
> "The sand in the district in which I have my existence has covered me up. Promise me that thou will do what I my heart wish; then will I acknowledge that thou art my son, that thou art my helper. . . ."[1]

When Thutmes IV came to the throne as Pharaoh, he cleared away the sand that had drifted up about the Sphinx sacred to Hormakhu, and, as the dream had promised, the reign of Thutmes IV was long and fruitful.

More familiar are the dreams recorded in the Bible. The most famous of these is the Pharaoh's dream interpreted by Joseph as predicting seven years of plenty and seven years of famine. Joseph's dream interpretation fits into the general category of *oneiromancy,* or interpreting dreams to foretell future events. The dream itself was held to come from God.

Only rarely does the Bible tell of telepathic dreams between individuals, and even then, there is always a divine element, such as in the well-known dream of Nebuchadnezzar. King Nebuchadnezzar awoke one morning having forgotten a dream but feeling strongly that the dream must have been divinely inspired. He sent word to wise men, astrologers, and dream interpreters that they must tell him what his dream had been and then interpret it. If they failed he threatened to execute them. Their reply was, "If you tell us the dream, we'll interpret it." "No," insisted the King, "you must first tell me the dream as I have forgotten it." Naturally this caused grave consternation among the dream interpreters. When Daniel heard of this he prayed that God would reveal to him the King's dream. It is said that that night Daniel received a "night vision" of the King's dream. When Daniel went to the King and told him the dream, the King apparently recognized it as being also his own, for he then asked Daniel to interpret the dream's meaning with regard to the future. This Daniel did to Nebuchadnezzar's satisfaction and to the great relief of the other dream interpreters.

Another classic example of a dream held to come telepathically from a divinity is one attributed to Alexander the Great while he was besieging the Phoenician city of Tyre (*Tyros* in Greek). Alexander dreamed of a satyr dancing on a shield. This was recognized as a pun by the dream interpreter Aristander. He told Alexander that the Greek word for satyr (*satyros*) could also mean "Tyre is yours" (*Sa Tyros*). Inevitably (otherwise we would not know the story today), Alexander succeeded in capturing Tyre.

The lack of documentation for these unusual dream experiences would tend to put such tales into the category of myths that grow up around great men. The modern reader is as skeptical of Alexander's prophetic dreams as he might be of the story that Alexander was fathered by a divine snake. Alexander's tutor, Aristotle, also doubted that such dreams came from the gods. Rather, he rationally contended that some dreams brought their own fulfillment while other dreams might come true simply by coincidence — an argument that we shall meet again.

Better documented is the ancient world's use of dreams in diagnosing and even in curing illnesses. Plaques in praise of gods who brought healing dreams crowded the sanctuary walls of the temple precincts of such gods as Asclepius. The ill person was put to sleep on a couch in the temple and was told that a god would appear to him in a dream that would give him the remedy for his disease. This practice, called "incubation," was, if the plaques are to be believed, often successful. Modern medicine would interpret the mechanism in a different way, much as Aristotle did in suggesting that the dreamer might be aware in sleep of symptoms he had ignored in the waking state.

Oneiromancy, or dream interpretation, continues to fascinate people today as it did in ancient times. The techniques of interpretation, however, are much transformed. The first "bible" of oneiromancy is the work of Artemidorus of Daldis, who assembled a catalog of dream symbols with ready-made interpretations. As psychiatrist Jan Ehrenwald remarks, "The mercenary spirit of the dream interpreters of the time is illustrated by Artemidorus' admonition to his son and successor in the mantic arts to limit the copies in circulation of his *magnum opus* so as to preserve their market value for the benefit of his heirs."[2]

Artemidorus' interpretative recipes still survive in the various dream books published in the United States and Europe, reflecting an underground subculture that persists despite negative criticism from eighteenth-century rationalism and even twentieth-century technocracy. Today a person can still buy paperbound books that promise to instruct the reader in interpreting his dream so as to pick the right number in a lottery. Although Artemidorus' heirs lost their corner on the market several centuries ago, the commercial value of dream books is as great as it ever was.

In the eighteenth century adherents of the Age of Reason derided claims made for the prophetic nature of dreams. Dreams were caused only by indigestion or cold drafts. But despite what the scholars thought, odd dreams continued to occur — such as this dream described in his journal by Charles Dickens.

> I dreamed that I saw a lady in a red shawl with her back towards me.... On her turning round, I found that I didn't know her and she said, "I am Miss Napier."
>
> All the time I was dressing next morning, I thought — what a preposterous thing to have so very distinct a dream about nothing! and why Miss Napier? For I have never heard of any Miss Napier. That same Friday night I read. After the reading, came into my retiring-room Miss Boyle and her brother, and *the* lady in the red shawl whom they present as "Miss Napier"![3]

Although Dickens testified that "These are all the circumstances exactly told" the psychical researcher would be skeptical. After all, Dickens apparently did not write down the dream until *after* Napier's red-shawled introduction, and memory can play tricks even on famous men. But we shall leave attempts to verify such paranormal dreaming by psychical researchers to the next chapter.

A dream of a lady in red took on a symbolic meaning in a dream interpreted by the American psychic Edgar Cayce on March 5, 1929. The dreamer was a member of the New York Stock Exchange, who asked Cayce for an interpretation of this dream: "Dreamed we should sell all our stocks including box stock (one considered very good). I saw a bull following my wife, who was dressed in red."

Edgar Cayce's psychic dream interpretation said that "this is an impression of a condition which is to come about, a downward movement of long duration.... Dispose of all held, even box...."

Hugh Lynn Cayce, Edgar Cayce's son, comments that the red dress might signify danger and that the bull suggests a "bull market," which was leaving. Also, the stockbroker's wife asked him for a divorce a few months later.

A dream a month later seemed even more ominous for Wall Street in its interpretation by Cayce. "There must surely come a break where there will be panic in the money centers, not only of Wall Street's activities but a closing of the boards in many other centers...."

The stock market crash of the fall of 1929 seemed to fulfill Edgar Cayce's dream interpretation. Was it prophecy? Or could the dreamer and Cayce somehow have unconsciously assessed where the practices of Wall Street at that time would lead? The believer will answer one way, the skeptic the other.[4]

Skepticism about such unusual dreams has existed as long as recorded history, even, it seems, when the skeptic is alleged to have had a paranormal dream himself. Falling into this category is none other than the illustrious silver-tongued orator of ancient Rome, Marcus Tullius Cicero. Here is the tale of one of his dreams coming true.

> On the first day of the new year Cicero accompanied Caesar, as Consul, to the Capitol. As it chanced he told his companions of a dream he had had the previous night. He had seen a noble-looking youth, let down on a chain of gold from the skies, standing at the door of the temple. At that very instant Cicero's glance fell on Octavius, who, known by sight to very few of the participants in the ceremony, had been brought there by his great-uncle, Caesar. Cicero exclaimed at once, "But there is the actual boy I dreamed of!"[5]

Octavius, of course, took the more familiar name of Augustus when he succeeded Caesar as emperor of Rome and ushered in Rome's Golden Age. Cicero, unfortunately, was unable to enjoy those years as he was put to death the year before. We don't know if he had been warned of his fate by other prophetic dreams or by dream interpreters. If he was warned, we can assume that he most likely ignored it having had his fill of the quack dream interpreters, astrologers, and near–Eastern diviners who crowded into Rome to make a quick denarius with glibly said sooths. Cicero attacked them with his famous essay "On Divination," which argued against taking dreams seriously.

> But the defenders of divination reply . . . that a long continuance of observations has created an art. Can, then, dreams be experimented on? And if so, how? for the varieties of them are innumerable. Nothing can be imagined so preposterous, so incredible, or so monstrous, as to be beyond our power of dreaming. And by what method can this infinite variety be either fixed in memory or analyzed by reason?
>
> . . . those very persons who experience these dreams cannot by any means understand them, and those persons who pretend to interpret them, do so by conjecture, not by demonstration. And in the infinite series of ages, chance has produced many more extraordinary results in every kind of thing than it has in dreams; nor can anything be more uncertain than that conjectural interpretation of diviners, which admits not only of several, but often of absolutely contrary sense.
>
> Let us reject, therefore, this divination of dreams, as well as all other kinds. For, to speak truly, that superstition has extended itself through all notions, and has oppressed the intellectual energies of all men, and has betrayed them into endless imbecilities.[6]

Cicero's complaint was doubtless a minority voice scarcely heard above the swirling crowds of Roman citizens eagerly buying their amulets and

magic potions from turbaned diviners from the East and anxious to know if
their dreams meant good fortune or ill. It was a time when no public
ceremony could be performed without first consulting the entrails of animals
for propitious signs. The Roman public, much like that of India today,
believed implicitly in divination and astrology. Superstition was a way of life,
and the occult arts were ways of dealing with the unknown.

Not until the mid–twentieth century did Cicero's complaint find ears
ready to listen. It is only comparatively recently that we have found ways to
answer the excellent questions that Cicero posed more than two millennia
ago:

> Can dreams be experimented on?
>
> And if so, how?
>
> And by what method can this infinite variety be either fixed in memory or
> analyzed by reason?

And what about chance?

It is in answer to Cicero's complaint that the present volume is offered.

CHAPTER 2
Sifting the Evidence

Cicero's complaint finds persuasive restatement in our own time. It is echoed even by parapsychologists such as Dr. Leonid L. Vasiliev. Vasiliev, who died in 1966, was one of the Soviet Union's most distinguished physiologists and founder of Russia's first parapsychology laboratory at the University of Leningrad in 1959. Writing in the tradition of Pavlov, Vasiliev updated the classic case against paranormal dreaming.

One would assume that all false explanations of dreams had long ago been consigned to archives, but they still prevail, even among educated men, if they are not fully cognizant of the achievements of modern natural science.

Anyone who has not yet discarded all superstition is especially amazed by the fantastic aspect of dreams. How often, on awakening, we ask ourselves: "Why did I dream this? Nothing like it exists. I have never heard, read, or conceived anything in the least like it!" Indeed, why do dreams so often bear no resemblance at all to anything that we can recall from our personal experience? The question is complicated, but science has an exhaustive answer...

It must be remembered once and for all that, however wondrous, incomprehensible, and mysterious dreams may seem, they contain only what we have experienced, consciously or unconsciously, at least once in our waking state. Dreams are nothing more than the reprocessing by a partially awake brain of erratically tangled fragments and traces of some past experience of what we, at one time or another, had seen, heard, thought, or read...

For many, the alleged prophetic and oracular purport of dreams remains their most mysterious aspect even today ... Prophetic dreams are more often founded simply on misunderstanding. Nearly everyone has dreams, sometimes many dreams in one night. In a week, a month, a person accumulates tens, if not hundreds, of dreams. Do many of them materialize? Of course not. Dreams as a rule do not materialize; only in exceptional cases do they coincide, more or less, with future events. According to the theory of probability this is as it should be: many dreams, many events — some of them must inevitably coincide. There is nothing wonderful in this...

Parapsychologists do not concur in the assertion that in dreams it is possible for the sleeper to see only fragments and traces of what he has personally experienced, only that which he at one time or another saw, heard, thought, or read. Avowing the existence of telepathic and telesthetic (clairvoyant) phenomena, they assume that some dreams may be conditioned by parapsychological abilities, which are intensified during the natural and hypnotic sleep.

. . . one cannot exclude the possibility of two totally unrelated events coinciding by chance. Consequently, such incidents are not in themselves sufficient proof of the existence of telepathic and clairvoyant perceptions or dreams. Accounts of such occurrences will become truly significant only when telepathic and telesthetic phenomena are confirmed by repeated experiments. . . . [1]

Vasiliev's analysis was first published in Russia in 1958, four years before experimental work in dream telepathy was first mapped out by the Maimonides Dream Laboratory team. Yet the study of spontaneous dream telepathy goes back to the 1880s during the early years of England's Society for Psychical Research, which was founded to "examine without prejudice or prepossession and in a scientific spirit those faculties of man, real or supposed, which appear to be inexplicable on any generally recognized hypothesis."

In 1886 three of the society's founders produced a monumental study of cases of spontaneous paranormal experiences titled *Phantasms of the Living,* including over 1,300 pages of case histories organized according to the type of paranormal phenomena reported. Most of the work was done by the critical investigator Edmund Gurney, with great help from Frederic W. H. Myers, later the society's President, and Frank Podmore, an equally astute investigator.

The word *telepathy* was coined by Myers in 1882 to describe "fellow-feeling at a distance," including not only thought transference between distant persons but also emotions and less definable impressions. Of most interest to us is the modestly titled chapter, "Example of Dreams Which May Be Reasonably Regarded as Telepathic." The authors noted that telepathic dreams are comparatively rare: "The grotesque medley which constantly throng through the gate of ivory thrust into discredit our rarer visitants through the gate of horn." Both Gurney and Myers were classical scholars, and they were alluding to Homer's gates of ivory, through which come "false" dreams, and those of horn, through which come "true" dreams.

Over half of the 149 cases of dream telepathy described in the book dwelled on the same macabre theme: death. Perhaps dreams of death are very common, and the skeptic might answer that sooner or later one particular dream will correspond with an actual death.

This objection was noted:

Millions of people are dreaming every night; and in dreams, if anywhere, the range of possibilities seems infinite; can any positive conclusion be drawn from such a chaos of meaningless and fragmentary impressions?... Are any valid means at hand for distinguishing between a transferred impression and a lucky coincidence?... And what proportion of striking correspondences are we to demand before we consider that the hypothesis of chance is strained in accounting for them?[2]

To answer these questions the Society sent out questionnaires to 5,360 persons asking the group if they had had in the last twelve years a vivid dream of the death of someone known to them. Only about one out of every twenty-six persons questioned replied in the affirmative. The authors' arithmetic showed that telepathic dreams of death occurred far more often than chance would allow. A weakness in this procedure relates to the word "vivid." It may well be that unless the dreamed death actually occurs dreams of death go unremembered. In that case the powerful emotion engendered in the dreamer will make the dream seem "vivid" in retrospect. It might be argued that such a questionnaire would be valid only if it were given to persons who had recorded their dreams during a specific control period.

The second largest category of telepathic dreams contained those in which the presumed "agent" or "target person" of the dream (the person dreamed about) was in distress or danger. Here is a classic example of a "death or distress" dream that turns out to be telepathic. The "percipient" (dreamer), Mrs. Morris Griffith, at the time she wrote her account (1884) was living at 6 Menai View Terrace, Bangor, North Wales.

On the night of Saturday, the 11th of March, 1871, I awoke in much alarm, having seen my eldest son, then at St. Paul de Loanda on the south-west coast of Africa, looking dreadfully ill and emaciated, and I heard his voice distinctly calling to me. I was so disturbed I could not sleep again, but every time I closed my eyes the appearance recurred, and his voice sounded distinctly, calling me "Mamma." I felt greatly depressed all through the next day, which was Sunday, but I did not mention it to my husband, as he was an invalid, and I feared to disturb him. We were in the habit of receiving weekly letters every Sunday from our youngest son, then in Ireland, and as none came that day, I attributed my great depression to that reason, glad to have some cause to assign to Mr. Griffith rather than the real one. Strange to say, he also suffered from intense low spirits all day, and we were both unable to take dinner, he rising from the table saying, "I don't care what it costs, I must have the boy back," alluding to his eldest son. I mentioned my dream and the bad night I had had to two or three friends, but begged that they would say nothing of it to Mr. Griffith. The next day a letter arrived containing some photos of my son, saying he had had fever, but was better, and hoped immediately to leave for a much more healthy station, and written in good spirits. We heard no more till the 9th of May, when a letter arrived with the news of our son's death from a fresh attack of fever, on the night of the 11th of March, and adding that just before his death he kept calling repeatedly for me. I did not at first connect the date of my son's death with that of my dream until reminded of it by the friends, and also an old servant, to whom I had told it at the time....

With characteristic thoroughness, the authors asked for more details from Mrs. Griffith, who answered:

> I have never in all my life, before or since, had any such distressing dream, nor am I ever discomposed in any way by uncomfortable dreams.
>
> I never remember at any time having any dream from which I have had any difficulty in knowing at once, whilst awakening, that I had been dreaming, and never confuse the dream with reality.
>
> I also unhesitatingly assure you that I have never had any hallucination of the senses as to sound or sight.[3]

Although most of the cases reported in *Phantasms of the Living* were contributed by the English upper class, the authors cast their investigative nets into America as well. The following case, which appeared first in a letter to the *Religio-Philosophical Journal,* was reported by Dr. Walter Bruce of Micanopy, Florida, and rivals the tales of Edgar Allan Poe.

February 17th, 1884

> On Thursday, the 27th of December last, I returned from Gainesville (12 miles from here) to my orange grove, near Micanopy. I have only a small plank house of three rooms at my grove, where I spend most of my time when the grove is being cultivated. There was no one in the house but myself at the time, and being somewhat fatigued with my ride, I retired to my bed very early, probably 6 o'clock; and, as I am frequently in the habit of doing, I lit my lamp on a stand by the bed for the purpose of reading. After reading a short time, I began to feel a little drowsy, put out the light, and soon fell asleep. Quite early in the night I was awakened. I could not have been asleep very long, I am sure. I felt as if I had been aroused intentionally, and at first thought someone was breaking into the house. I looked from where I lay into the other two rooms (the doors of both being open) and at once recognised where I was, and that there was no ground for the burglar theory; there being nothing in the house to make it worth a burglar's time to come after.
>
> I then turned on my side to go to sleep again, and immediately felt a consciousness of a presence in the room, and singular to state, it was not the consciousness of a live person, but of a spiritual presence. This may provoke a smile, but I can only tell you the facts as they occurred to me. I do not know how to better describe my sensations than by simply stating that I felt a consciousness of a spiritual presence. This may have been part of the dream, for I felt as if I were dozing off again to sleep; but it was unlike any dream I ever had. I felt also at the same time a strong feeling of superstitious dread, as if something strange and fearful were about to happen. I was soon asleep again or unconscious, at any rate, to my surroundings. Then I saw two men engaged in a slight scuffle; one fell fatally wounded — the other immediately disappeared. I did not see the gash in the wounded man's throat, but knew that his

throat was cut. I did not recognise him, either, as my brother-in-law. I saw him lying with his hands under him, his head turned slightly to the left, his feet close together. I could not, from the position in which I stood, see but a small portion of his face; his coat, collar, hair or something partly obscured it. I looked at him the second time a little closer to see if I could make out who it was. I was aware it was someone I knew, but still could not recognise him. I turned, and then saw my wife sitting not far from him. She told me she could not leave until he was attended to. (I had got a letter a few days previously from my wife, telling me she would leave in a day or two, and was expecting every day a letter or telegram, telling me when to meet her at the depot.)

My attention was struck by the surroundings of the dead man. He appeared to be lying on an elevated platform of some kind, surrounded by chairs, benches, and desks, reminding me somewhat of a school-room. Outside of the room in which he was lying was a crowd of people, mostly females some of whom I thought I knew. Here my dream terminated. I awoke again about midnight; got up and went to the door to see if there were any prospects of rain; returned to my bed again, and lay there until nearly daylight before falling asleep again. I thought of my dream and was strongly impressed by it. All strange, superstitious feelings had passed off.

It was not until a week or 10 days after this that I got a letter from my wife, giving me an account of her brother's death. Her letter, which was written the day after his death, was mis-sent. The account she gave me of his death tallies most remarkably with my dream. Her brother was with a wedding party at the depot at Markham station, Fauquier County, Va. He went into a store near by to see a young man who kept a bar-room near the depot, with whom he had some words. He turned and left the man, and walked out of the store. The bar-room keeper followed him out, and without further words deliberately cut his throat. It was a most brutal and unprovoked murder. My brother-in-law had on his overcoat, with the collar turned up. The knife went through the collar and clear to the bone. He was carried into the store and laid on the counter, near a desk and show case. He swooned from loss of blood soon after being cut. The cutting occurred early Thursday night, December 27th. He did not die, however, until almost daylight, Saturday morning. . . .[4]

Dr. Bruce's account continues with reference to another dream about that time, reported by his sister-in-law, Mrs. Stubbing, who was visiting her cousins in Kentucky. Here is Mrs. Stubbing's account of her dream:

. . . I saw two persons — one with his throat cut. I could not tell who it was, though I knew it was somebody that I knew, and as soon as I heard of my brother's death, I said at once that I knew it was he that I had seen murdered in my dream; and though I did not hear how my brother died, I told my cousin, whom I was staying with, that I knew he had been murdered. This dream took place on Thursday or Friday night, I do not remember which. I saw the exact spot where he was murdered, and just as it happened.[5]

The vividness of Dr. Bruce's account seems to vouch for its authenticity, but his case would probably receive little attention today because it lacks an essential qualification: It was not recorded or told to anyone prior to his hearing of the murder. His sister-in-law's dream, while given in less detail, had been told to her cousin before news of the murder arrived.

In the overwhelming majority of dream telepathy cases recorded in *Phantasms of the Living,* the agent and percipient are either related to each other or are friends. Typically, dreamers did not regard themselves as "psychic" in any way but reacted to the telepathic dream experience as something quite extraordinary and puzzling. It was likely to be a once-in-a-lifetime experience, vividly remembered even after many years. While the great majority of these telepathic dreams could be categorized as "terrible," there is also a smaller but intriguing group we could call "trivial." It is quite possible that trivial dreams occur much more frequently than reported — after all, how many people will take the trouble to write to a psychical research society about a dream like the following? The letter was written to the Society by Jean Eleanora Fielding.

> *Yarlington Rectory, Bath, 19th May, 1886*
>
> I sleep badly, and on Monday night it was 2 o'clock when I slept. I had, for half-an-hour before going off, fixed my mind upon every turn and corner of my girlhood's home (where I have not been for above 20 years) in Scotland. My father, a squire, had a neighbor squire, called *Harvey Brown.* In my whiling away the night, I dwelt upon him, and his house and family, *particularly.* My husband knew him *only* by name, but of course, knew my home, and loves it as much as I do. He and I awoke at 6. Before *a word* of any kind was said, he said to me, "I have had such a strange dream about Harvey Brown, and been at the old home, wandering about it." What made it seem stranger is that Harvey Brown is a man we never spoke of in our lives, or for 20 years have ever thought of, till Monday night in idleness I went over old meetings with him; and I was wide awake and my husband asleep; he had slept heavily all the night after a 12 mile walk; so there was no possibility of my leading his mind near Scotland, in any conversation even, before he slept.[6]

Fielding was doubtlessly more alert to the possibilities of such telepathic dreaming than the average person, having written to the Society previously, in November 1885, with an account of simultaneous dreams that she and her husband had in which they both dreamed of a woodsman at a house they had lived in seventeen years before.

While numerically small in the annals of spontaneous dream telepathy, such trivial cases will assume importance later in the analogy they make to the laboratory induction of dream telepathy; for murder and mayhem cannot be visited upon experimental subjects. Smaller, more subtle effects must suffice in the laboratory.

An account of the first known attempt to induce telepathic dreams by experimental means was published by Dr. G. B. Ermacora, an Italian psychical researcher who edited an Italian journal named *Rivista di Studi Psichici*. Ermacora's "Telepathic Dreams Experimentally Induced" was first published in England in the Society for Psychical Research's *Proceedings* in 1895. Ermacora had concentrated on experiments with a mental medium in Padua, Signorina Maria Manzini, who apparently showed great talent at telepathy. As with most mediums, Manzini had a trance personality, or control, a child named Elvira. When Angelina, Manzini's four-year-old cousin, arrived from Venice to stay with her, the stage was set for what certainly must be one of the most bizarre experiments in the history of psychical research.

According to Manzini's testimony in her letters to Ermacora, it began when little Angelina began to dream about Manzini's control, Elvira. When Ermacora went to see her, Manzini purportedly entered an altered state of consciousness that allowed Elvira to write through her. Elvira promised to appear in a dream to little Angelina carrying a beautiful doll and wearing a pink dress. The next evening Manzini said that she had elicited from Angelina a dream report of Elvira carrying a doll but dressed in blue instead of pink.

Ermacora's complete trust in the medium's honesty was doubtlessly chivalrous but perhaps misplaced in the intricate world of psychical research. Yet there were no obvious signs that the medium embroidered on little Angelina's dream reports. By Experiment No. 7, Ermacora was suggesting to Elvira the theme of the dream "she" should try to induce telepathically in Angelina.

> I proposed that Elvira, dressed in red and with a large straw hat on, should accompany Angelina to the Piazza San Marco at Venice, and should find it turned into a garden with grass and many flowers. The companile should have vanished, and there should be a very large tree in its place. Many children, dressed in white, should be running and playing with young goats. A peasant on the great tree should saw off a branch, and Angelina should hear the saw make the sound *zin-zin*. [7]

Elvira's answer was "It is rather long. It is possible for me, but I don't know if the child will remember all that. However, we will try."

Unfortunately, as it turned out, Professor William James arrived from the United States to see how the experiment was getting on. Apparently, like a talking bird on a television show, nothing happened. And one must credit Ermacora for at least including in his account every failure as well as success.

By Experiment No. 14, it occurred to Ermacora that he should introduce some scientific controls. The medium's mother, Signora Annetta, had arrived, and it was she who then questioned the child in the morning before the medium awoke. The dream that Ermacora proposed to Elvira the night before was: "Angelina is with me in the church of S[an] Marco at

Venice. Elvira, dressed in pink and with a white handkerchief round her head, comes to meet us, and all three go to the Riva degli Schiavoni, and go into a tent, where we are shown a fine tiger."

Angelina told the following dream to Signora Annetta in the morning. "She was with me at Venice in the church of [S]an Marco. A little girl entered dressed in pink, with a white handkerchief on her head. We all went together to a little house, where there was an animal like a cat, but larger, and not really a cat."

It sounds almost too good to be true. Yet Ermacora was convinced that the child had not been given any verbal suggestion (by the medium?) because the images were visual and Elvira was not recognized.

By Experiment No. 16, Ermacora resolved to use as target material something unknown to Angelina. He proposed as a dream that Angelina would be in the house of Professor B., unknown to Angelina, but known to the medium, and that Ermacora would bring the child some figs.

The next day Ermacora found the medium and the child at home. Angelina's dream report mentioned a certain gentleman "handsome, tall, rather stout, with beautiful long moustaches" and, later, figs. Ermacora then produced seventeen photographs of middle-aged men, including the target professor. He asked Angelina to select her "dream gentleman." While the medium looked on, Angelina hesitated without choosing one. Dr. Ermacora "watched Signorina Maria to see if she influenced Angelina by an unconscious sign."

When the medium's mother returned, Ermacora asked her to persuade Angelina to choose the photograph when the medium was not present. Ermacora wrote,

> When I returned in the evening, Signora Annetta assured me that her daughter had not seen the photographs since I left, and that the child had made her choice while Signorina Maria was out of the house. She then showed me two photographs that the child had selected, adding that she preferred one of the two. Now, the portrait preferred as most resembling the gentleman in the dream is precisely that of Professor B.... I should add that the choice was made among 27 portraits instead of 17; I added 10 more when I left.

Had Ermacora at last found an evaluation system that was foolproof? Or, as an unchivalrous skeptic might suggest, did the medium, while Ermacora was away, tell her mother and the child which photograph was actually that of Professor B.? Perhaps the idea would not occur to an Italian gentleman of the late nineteenth century, but, unfortunately, it too readily leaps into the mind of more suspicious contemporary mentalities. Especially suspect is the child's initial reluctance to make a choice, contrasted with her later choice of two photographs, the second choice also closely resembling Professor B.

Our suspicions increase by reading the report of Experiment No. 24, in which another gentleman friend of Ermacora's, also known to the medium, is used as a target person. When the doctor showed the child twenty pictures from which she was to choose her "dream man," again she could not recognize him until "a later occasion."

Ermacora ingenuously comments, "From time to time, as the child told her story she turned towards Signorina Maria for approbation, as if she were convinced that Signorina Maria had been present at the scene; and this shows how easily she confounds her dreams with reality." Ermacora footnotes that statement with what seems to us a less than convincing defense. "I believe myself in a position to reject as an absurdity the hypothesis that the child's story is a comedy taught her by Signorina Maria, and that consequently she turned ingenuously to the latter for suggestions; and it is besides disproved by the later successes under stricter conditions."

We look in vain for these "stricter conditions." Ermacora recounts that his later experiments included making use of illustrations in various catalogs and scientific books. He always showed them to the medium for at least half a minute, and the medium always had access to the child before the trusting doctor arrived to question her about her dream. Little Angelina's incredible accuracy in these tests far surpasses any results obtained under modern experimental conditions.

By Experiment No. 59, Ermacora became even more adventurous. He showed the medium a word in a book—a very odd word, *Guglielmeide,* written in large characters. He asked her to make Angelina dream that she could read [remember, Angelina is only four]. The next day, the good doctor wrote,

> I sent to fetch Angelina from school, and showed her the book open at the page where the word *Guglielmeide* was written, and told her to look for the word she had seen in her dream. As I saw she was too timid to pay attention, I sent her away with Signora Annetta (the medium's mother) and the book. They soon returned, and Angelina showed me the word *Guglielmeide,* but could not pronounce it. . . .
>
> From these experiments, which unfortunately were not followed up, I drew a hope, which will certainly be realised later on by others, of the possibility of teaching reading by means of telepathy.

Ermacora's effort, with all its faults and shortcomings, did represent the first serious investigation into the question of dream telepathy. His experience, in retrospect, illustrates the by now well-known hazard of relying on the social virtue of honesty in people who make their bread and butter by impressing others with their "supernatural" abilities.

The exhaustive two-volume work by F. W. H. Myers, *Human Personality* (1903),[8] does not mention Ermacora's telepathy experiment. Instead, Myers in his chapter on "Sleep" concentrates on spontaneous cases that were better researched. Myers gives several examples of cases that first appeared to be paranormal dreams, but on closer investigation, could be traced to subliminal memories, that is, things not consciously noticed but remembered by the unconscious. For instance a woman described how she found a missing brooch because of a dream that showed it shut up in a certain magazine on a certain page. She had been looking at that magazine at her hairdresser's. When she returned to the hairdresser's shop and told the staff of her dream, they found her brooch in the named magazine.

To Myers it was all too evident that the woman's subliminal memory had registered the loss of the brooch between the pages of the magazine and that the dream was therefore not paranormal.

Ruling out all normal alternate hypotheses was a task that the early English researchers pursued vigorously with methodical investigations. In doing so, they brought to light many extraordinary powers of the unconscious or subliminal mind that until then had been unrealized.

In the cases that Myers classifies as true telepathy the percipients were often persons of good reputation who had witnesses of the dream telepathy experience. However good such evidence might be in a court of law, it still remains inadequate for formulating any valid hypotheses. Dreams are notoriously difficult to remember — especially over a span of several years — and the skeptic's point is valid if he suggests that tricks of memory, of either the dreamer or the witness, can embroider a fragmentary dream impression to a vividly detailed story that matches exactly a distant event. To sift the evidence with a finer sieve requires that the dream be written down *before* the dreamer learns of the event that corresponds with his dream.

A case that seems to meet that criterion, at least partially, is reviewed by the English psychical researcher G. N. M. Tyrrell in his book *Science and Psychical Phenomena*. It is, as Tyrrell remarks, a case "of a curious kind." We would point out that theoretically it could be considered clairvoyant, telepathic, or precognitive, depending on which way it is viewed. Often such experiences are classified merely as "general extrasensory perception." The dreamer, Dudley Walker, felt only that it was "no ordinary dream." In his dream of June 27, 1928, Walker felt that he was actually involved in the scene that he describes.

> I was in an overhead signal-box, extending over a railway-line I had never seen before. It was night, and I saw approaching what I knew was an excursion train, full of people, returning from some big function. I knew it was my duty to signal this train through, which I did, but at the same time I had a feeling that the train was doomed. (I have nothing to do with railway work.)
>
> In my dream I seemed to hover in the air, and follow the express as it slowed to round a loop line. As it approached a station I saw, to my horror, another small train on the same line. Although they seemed both travelling slowly, they met with terrible impact. I saw the express and its coaches pitch and twist in the air, and the noise was terrible. Afterwards, I walked beside the wreckage

in the dim light of dawn, viewing with a feeling of terror the huge overturned engine and smashed coaches. I was now amid an indescribable scene of horror, with dead and injured people, and rescue workers everywhere.

Most of the bodies lying by the side of the track were those of women and girls. As I passed with some unknown person leading me, I saw one man's body in a ghastly state, lifted out and laid on the side of an overturned coach.

I distinctly heard a doctor say: "Poor chap, he's dead." Some other voice said: "I believe I saw his eyelids move." Then the doctor said: "It's only your nerves; he has been dead some time."

I was quite upset on getting up, and felt too unwell to eat any breakfast. All day at business I have been thinking about this dream.

On coming home, you can imagine my feelings when I beheld the placards [of a newspaper headline] announcing the accident.[9]

The train accident had occurred just before midnight of June 27 at a city some miles distant. A newspaper report contained several details that corresponded with Walker's dream:

It was an excursion train. It collided with another train. Eight people were killed — a man, six women, and one little girl. An engine was derailed. "One gruesome sight was that of a man's body lying on top of one of the carriages."

Mr. Walker had given a detailed account of the dream to his mother and to his boss at work before the news was known, and, importantly, he had written a short note about the dream in his diary at work. When he was questioned by an investigator from the Society for Psychical Research, Walker could give no reason why he should have dreamed about that particular accident. As a class of dreams, Walker's dream resembles precognitive dreams of disaster in which the percipient has a dream about a news event that he reads about soon after.[10] The extraordinarily close correspondence of details demonstrates that a dream can be a most accurate conveyor of ESP — a finding made by reviewing thousands of spontaneous ESP cases.

Attempting to verify a spontaneous case beyond all reasonable doubt is a formidable task, for few people keep dream diaries or are so attuned to psychical research as to send parapsychologists their accounts of dreams that they feel might turn out to be paranormal. In a recent issue of the *Proceedings* of the American Society for Psychical Research, Dr. Ian Stevenson of the University of Virginia Parapsychology Division devotes six pages to his investigation of Case 35 in which a woman had a presumably telepathic dream about the death of her best friend's brother-in-law.[11] The woman had written Dr. Stevenson's colleague, Dr. J. G. Pratt, in 1965 about the dream that she had had in 1963. Dr. Stevenson asked her for a detailed account in 1969, and in fact received three letters from her. Dr. Stevenson also corresponded with the chief witnesses to the dream experience, the woman's husband and her best friend. Dr. Stevenson then checked out further details by telephone conversations with the woman and also elicited a statement from the dead man's wife. With admirable thoroughness, Dr. Stevenson also obtained a photostat of the death certificate.

The dream itself was in symbolic rather than realistic form. The dead man was seen with an owl, but the dreamer awakened with the impression that this meant death for him. She learned of his death that afternoon. On awakening she had told her husband of her impression of the death, leaving out details of the dream. But she had told the dream to her aunt that morning and telephoned the sister-in-law to inquire after the man's health. As Dr. Stevenson points out, the dream itself was not unusually vivid, but the strong emotion that followed its interpretation by the conscious mind resulted in a "frightened feeling in the pit of my stomach."

Although we can be fairly certain that the dreamer did indeed have a telepathic impression of the man's death, the actual details of the experience emerge as very much more complicated than those suggested by the dreamer's original letter. ("I had a dream about him and when I awoke between 7 and 7:30 A.M. I knew he was dead.") As to the details of the dream itself, it is difficult to suppose that a person can remember perfectly in 1969 a dream that occurred in 1963 — a lapse of six years. As we will show in later chapters, a person's memory of a dream can change considerably from the time he wakes from the dream to a few hours later in the morning when he is asked to recapitulate it. How much can it change over a period of years? If a dreamer's memory is anything like that of a fisherman, we would expect the tale's marvelous qualities, like those of the fish, to increase with years of telling.

Grabbing the telepathic dream while it is still on the hook would seem to be necessary if Cicero's complaint is to be answered. We will leave to Part II — Experimental Studies — our attempt to answer Cicero.

Despite the difficulties in investigating and assessing spontaneous cases of dream telepathy, meaningful patterns do emerge when large collections of these experiences are examined. Of over 7000 spontaneous cases of ESP studied in the United States, nearly two-thirds of the cases were dreams, and a similar proportion holds true in one thousand cases examined in Germany. In a British study of 300 cases, 40 percent were dream experiences. A survey of school children in India showed that about half of their ESP experiences were dreams.[12]

As we have said earlier, death and distress are by far the most common themes in spontaneous cases of dream telepathy. The greater reporting of these types may be due to the emotional significance attached to such dreams. Certainly, most people would feel foolish in reporting a telepathic dream experience about some minor or trivial circumstance.

Emotional bonds seem to be the most binding ties for telepathic dreams. Yet if a person dreamed about a stranger it is most likely that he would not be in a position of hearing that his dream corresponded with the stranger's situation. The case cited in Chapter 1 of the dream about the novelist Kurt Vonnegut, Jr., was in this rare category since the percipient (Alan Vaughan) and Vonnegut had never met. The link in that case was apparently brought about by viewing Vonnegut on television — a category of linkage, of course, not thought of by the early psychic researchers.

Another category not then considered is that of the special bond between the psychoanalyst and his patient. As we shall see in the next section, dreams "say the damnedest things." For, like children, dreams have a way of expressing a truth that is often embarrassing — especially when it is telepathic.

CHAPTER 3
ESP on the Couch

For a generation that regards psychoanalysis as an important part of established orthodoxy in the treatment of mental illness, it is well to recall that the founder of psychoanalysis, Sigmund Freud, had to struggle relentlessly for recognition of his highly unorthodox ideas. His book *Interpretation of Dreams* was published November 4, 1899 (dated 1900), but it took eight years to sell out its limited edition of 600 copies. When a second edition was finally due, Freud cautiously remarked, "My psychiatric colleagues do not seem to have taken any trouble to overcome the initial suspicions which my new conception of the dream produced in them."

It was with considerable courage, then, that Freud dared to appear even more unorthodox in taking up a subject guaranteed to produce even more suspicions: paranormal dreams. It can scarcely be said that Freud rushed in with a believer's zeal: Doubt, ambiguity, even denial characterized his early approach to what he called the "occult." In his *Psychopathology of Everyday Life* (1904), he cites several pseudo-paranormal experiences, implying that all reputed paranormal experiences can thus be explained.

For instance, while walking down a street one day, shortly after having received the title of Professor, Freud was engaging in a "childish revenge fantasy" against a couple whom he felt had been disrespectful to him. He fantasized the couple begging him to take a case, while he archly replied: "Now that I have become a professor, you have confidence in me. The title has made no change in my ability; if you could not use me when I was instructor, you can get along without me now that I am a professor."[1]

At that moment, his thoughts were interrupted by a loud, "Good evening, Professor," and there was the couple on whom he had visited his fantasy revenge. Startled at first, Freud then realized that he must have unconsciously noticed them approaching him, and that this had triggered his fantasy. This incident apparently took place in 1902, a year before the publication of F. W. H. Myers' *Human Personality* in which such pseudo-paranormal experiences were recognized as a class of phenomena due to subliminal perception.

As Freud's psychoanalytic ideas gained greater acceptance, his excursions into the "occult" became bolder, although his feelings on the subject remained ambivalent. He reported his mixed feelings in a paper on "Psychoanalysis and Telepathy" that he prepared in 1921 but which was not published until 1941, two years after his death. Freud wrote

> It is probable that the study of occult phenomena will result in the admission that some of these phenomena are real; but it is also likely that a great deal of time will elapse before one will be able to formulate an acceptable theory accounting for these new facts.... My personal attitude toward such material remains one of reluctance and ambivalence.[2]

In a more cautious paper, "Dreams and Telepathy," that Freud delivered before the International Psychoanalytic Congress in 1921,[3] the reader finds one basic reason for Freud's reluctance to accept telepathic dreams: He had never had one himself. Yet he was intrigued by the possibility of their existence when he heard of a case in which his psychoanalytic theories seemed to demonstrate that telepathy occurring in dreams is distorted in much the same way as material in ordinary dreams. A middle-aged man wrote that he had dreamed vividly of his wife giving birth to twins. Soon after, he received a telegram from his daughter's husband with the news that his daughter had given birth to twins on the same night as his dream. The birth was one month premature, and only one child had been expected.

What aroused Freud's interest was the substitution in the dream of the man's wife for his daughter. Because the dreamer's erotic feelings toward his daughter would be repressed from conscious thought, the *wife* would be substituted for the *daughter* to be acceptable to the dreamer's conscience.

"In our example," says Freud, "it is evident how the message, with the help of a lurking repressed wish, becomes remodeled into a wish fulfillment."

The tracing of telepathic elements in dreams led Freud to the view that it was an "incontestable fact that sleep creates favorable conditions for telepathy," a view upheld by surveys of spontaneous cases of ESP. Freud later conjectured that telepathy

> may be the original archaic method by which individuals understood one another, and which has been pushed into the background in the course of phylogenetic [evolutionary] development by the better method of communication by means of signs apprehended by the sense organs. But such older methods may have persisted in the background, and may still manifest themselves under certain conditions....[4]

In 1935, three years before his death at age 82, Freud was asked by the Hungarian writer Cornelius Tabori about his views on paranormal phenomena. Freud said, "'The transference of thoughts, the possibility of sensing the past or the future cannot be merely accidental. Some people say,' he smiled, 'that in my old age I have become credulous. No ... I don't think so. Merely — all my life I have learned to accept new facts, humbly, readily.'"[5]

In summing up Freud's contribution to parapsychology, the contemporary psychiatrist and parapsychologist Dr. Jule Eisenbud said, "One of the greatest advances — to my mind the greatest — in the study of telepathy and allied phenomena occurred when Freud made the simple observation that psychoanalysis was capable of unmasking a telepathic event which otherwise could not be recognized as such."[6]

Dr. Sandor Ferenczi, a favorite disciple of Freud who shared his interest in the "occult," corresponded with Freud at length about various psychic adventures.[7] Ferenczi's literary executor, Dr. Michael Balint, revealed to the late Nandor Fodor one of Ferenczi's experiments that comes under the category of "ESP on the couch."

> Once, I think it must have been before 1914, a clairvoyant pestered Ferenczi to make some experiments with him. After some resistance, Ferenczi agreed that at a given time immediately after lunch, he would think concentratedly of something and the thought reader would read his thoughts.
>
> On arriving at his consulting room at the given time, Ferenczi picked up a statue of an elephant, lay on his couch for ten or fifteen minutes, holding the elephant in his hands.
>
> A few minutes later he was rung up by his friend, Robert Barany [Bereny], telling him that he had just had a terrifying dream in which he saw Ferenczi in a jungle, fighting with all sorts of wild animals, among them an elephant.
>
> In due course, the letter of the thought reader appeared, containing utter rubbish.[8]

Although this secondhand account does not pull any weight as scientific evidence, we may speculate as to Freud's probable reaction when Ferenczi recounted this experiment to him. Elephants are a rarity in Hungary — especially dream elephants molesting Ferenczi just after lunch. The clairvoyant's failure and the friend's unwitting dream success in telepathy fits into a pattern found over and over again in psychical research: The most interesting results are often the unexpected.

There are few incidents of the unexpected that have had more influence than the mysterious explosive noises that occurred in 1909 and that signaled the break between Freud and his disciple Carl G. Jung. Jung and Freud were engaging in a heated argument on paranormal phenomena, especially precognition, which Freud vehemently rejected. A loud report erupted from a nearby bookcase, alarming both men. Jung said it was an example of "so-called catalytic exteriorization phenomena." Freud said it was bosh, but Jung predicted that there would be another such noise. Another detonation immediately occurred. Freud was aghast.

Jung felt that this psychokinetic* phenomenon was triggered in him by the archetype of the son breaking with the father or, as in this case, by the

---

*The purported movement of objects through no known physical agency.

pupil breaking with the master. To such unexplainable effects Jung gave the name *synchronicity*. Both physical and mental paranormal events seemed to Jung to cluster around such archetypal, emotion-laden circumstances. In his essay "Synchronicity: An Acausal Connecting Principle" (1952), Jung gives examples of both prophetic and telepathic dreams that arose in archetypal situations. Jung writes,

> An acquaintance of mine saw and experienced in a dream the sudden death of a friend, with all the characteristic details. The dreamer was in Europe at the time and the friend in America. The death was confirmed next morning by telegram, and ten days later a letter confirmed the details. Comparison of European time with American time showed that the death occurred at least an hour before the dream. The dreamer had gone to bed late and not slept until about one o'clock. The death occurred at approximately two in the morning. The dream experience is *not synchronous* with the death. Experiences of this kind frequently take place a little before or after the critical event.[9]

Jung's observation that crisis telepathy is often not immediate in time — the experience occurring either just before or after an event — is supported by spontaneous cases collected by parapsychologists. Interestingly, Freud acknowledged that telepathic dreams often appear in the dreamer's consciousness later than the event, after a so-called latency period; but he categorically rejected the verified observation that such dreams often occurred just before the event. The concept of precognition evoked such great distrust and anxiety in Freud that he often cited cases in his lectures of clairvoyant prophecies going wrong or seemingly prophetic dreams being due to unconscious memory.

Jung, on the other hand, apparently had experienced prophetic dreams himself, and he was more open to that puzzling aspect of ESP. He writes,

> In all these cases, whether it is a question of spatial or of temporal ESP, we find a simultaneity of the normal or ordinary state with another state or experience which is not causally derivable from it, and whose objective existence can only be verified afterwards. This definition must be borne in mind particularly when it is a question of future events. They are evidently not synchronous but are *synchronistic*, since they are experienced as psychic images *in the present*, as though the objective event already existed.[10]

Well aware of the logical difficulties of his argument, Jung states that in all these cases

> there seems to be an *a priori*, causally inexplicable knowledge of a situation which is at the time unknowable. Synchronicity therefore consists of two factors: a) An unconscious image comes into consciousness either directly (i.e., literally) or indirectly (symbolized or suggested) in the form of a dream, idea, or premonition. b) An objective situation coincides with this content. The one is as puzzling as the other. How does the unconscious image arise, and how the coincidence? I understand only too well why people prefer to doubt the reality of these things.[11]

Although Jung's hypothesis of synchronicity was developed over a period of many years, he did not publish his ideas on ESP phenomena until the early 1950s. Consequently, this hypothesis has gained few adherents outside of the Jungian school of psychiatry. How the theory is put to use may be seen in an example offered by the Jungian psychiatrist M. L. von Franz.

> A woman with a very strong power complex, and a "devouring" attitude toward people, dreamt of seeing three tigers seated threateningly in front of her. Her analyst pointed out the meaning of the dream and through causal arguments tried to make her understand the devouring attitude she thus displayed. Later in the day the patient and her friend, while strolling along Lake Zurich, noticed a crowd gazing at three tigers in a barn — most unusual inhabitants for a Swiss barn![12]

The three tigers were in the barn because a circus was spending the night in town. However, as Franz points out, "the highly improbable coincidence of the inner and outer tigers in this woman's life . . . inevitably struck her as 'more than mere chance' and somehow as 'meaningful.'" That is, a synchronicity. We can imagine that the patient must have taken the analyst's interpretation of her "devouring attitude" to heart when she came face-to-face with the tigers, her dream symbols made real. Of course, a parapsychologist would merely have registered this incident as a precognitive dream — an interpretation that apparently did not occur to the analyst.

However one views such a coincidence between dream and event, one is struck by the meaningful relationship of the percipient's inner psychic state with the objective event that serves as a dream symbol. The paranormally perceived scene does not seem to be selected at random, but rather it is conditioned by the percipient's own inner needs and reflects emotionally laden anxieties and conflicts. Jung would have used the term "archetypal situation."

"Rubbish" is probably the term that Alfred Adler would have used. As the third founding father of the psychoanalytic movement, Adler was the one most concerned with the significance of the social scene in relation to individual psychopathology. To Adler, paranormal events were to be grouped together with superstition and mysticism and even self-deception and fraud. He scoffed at those who took paranormal events seriously, for such "superstitious folklore" hindered realistic grappling with life's problems.

In conventional psychoanalytic thinking, personal dream symbols are derived from things seen and experienced in the past. That dream symbols should also be derived from future experiences or someone else's experience is an assertion accepted by only a small minority of analysts. But it is to that minority that we turn for examples of telepathy in the analytic situation, or ESP on the couch.

Psychoanalysis in the Freudian tradition can produce extraordinarily explosive situations. Patients can feel threatened, abused, revengeful, and loved, and often show strong emotions toward their analyst. In a case of apparent dream telepathy cited by the analyst Geraldine Pederson-Krag, a woman patient classified as suffering from that Freudian malady "penis envy," apparently tried in a dream to show up her analyst's own anxietal shortcomings.

> I dreamed I had company coming to dinner . . . I was at my wits' end. A mean ruthless man associated with my father was there. There were a lot of guests. I discovered I had not set the table. At least one leaf was missing from the table in the middle, and I put a tray in its place. *I put my silver knives, forks, etc., on the tray. The silver was all a mess. Was there enough?* This important mean man looked down scornfully at my table.[13]

The patient's associations were: "The table with the tray between two leaves was like the laundry tubs in my old home. In the middle one, my Christmas presents were always placed. I wanted a Christmas tree but never had one. *I don't know why I worried about my silver. I had several sets of it and more than I can use.*"

The analyst comments that the patient's strong penis envy was "shown by her desire that was never satisfied for a Christmas tree, the missing leaf in the middle of her table, and the feeling that the fatherly man despised her because of her unpreparedness. Her transference was an identification with me, while denying any relationship between us. . . ."

Only the analyst knew that there was indeed a relationship between her and her patient's dream. The analyst had invited some friends to her home the night before but started to worry that she wouldn't have enough silverware. She anxiously debated whether to replace the expensive silver or "use inferior cutlery." The problem caused her undue consternation.

It seemed almost that the patient's telepathic dream of the situation was a rebuttal to the analyst's diagnosis. The patient's dream associations seem to say: "I may never have gotten my Christmas tree (penis), but I certainly don't have to worry about having enough silver like you do. So there."

Dr. Pederson-Krag relates dreams of still other patients who eavesdrop on her private life in their dreams. A male patient dreamed the following one night. "I was taking my girl to dinner. *She ate about seven dollars' worth of food and my meal only came to two dollars.* I was rather mad but said nothing about it."

We don't know what color Pederson-Krag blushed as her patient was telling that dream, but she does record what she was doing the night of his dream. "My children and I met a colleague for dinner in a restaurant. He wished to pay for the entire party. I insisted on paying my share which came to a little over six dollars, and his was only two dollars. I disliked the situation because of certain implications and soon forgot them."

The analyst pointed out that the patient's dreams often reflected his disappointment that women did not give him enough. "In each dream he used a current suppressed disturbance of mine to declare a feeling he usually denies." Again, the patient seemed to be sneaky in finding ways of making the analyst feel uncomfortable—a patient's revenge by ESP.

Pederson-Krag observed that telepathic dreams occurred especially when she had a "slightly suppressed eagerness" to find telepathic dreams. The patients' dreams related mostly to unpleasant, suppressed situations in the analyst's life that dovetailed with the patients' own anxieties. And, characteristically, "the incidents occurred in the patients' dreams at exactly the same time I was trying to avoid them."

While Pederson-Krag's examples of dream telepathy between herself and her patients seem fairly straightforward, the possibilities for more elaborate and more complexly interrelated dreams and events were realized by at least two more parapsychologically-oriented psychoanalysts, Nandor Fodor and Jule Eisenbud. Fodor's career had carried him through journalism, spiritualism, psychical research, and finally, psychoanalysis. To savor the full flavor of Fodor's wide-ranging and subtle interpretations of Freudian relationships via dream telepathy, one must read his own accounts.[14] To read the accounts, however, it helps if the reader is a psychoanalyst of Freudian persuasion himself, for otherwise the maze of symbolic repressed sexuality combined with mystical interpretations of numbers may be hard to follow, much less believe.

To relate fully to Eisenbud's masterly contributions to dream telepathy, it helps again to have a Freudian point of view. But that in itself doesn't guarantee the reader will end up believing in telepathy. For several years in the late 1940s, psychoanalytic journals raged with the "Eisenbud–Pederson–Krag–Fodor–Ellis Controversy."[15] Dr. Albert Ellis was a well-known psychologist who was not buying telepathy, dream or otherwise. He attacked the pro-telepathy group's findings on the grounds that they were already disposed toward the ESP hypothesis, that they may have given their patients clues of what to dream about, and that chance coincidence would account for the observed oddities of correspondence between dreams and events.

Echoing Cicero's complaint, Ellis objected that

> inadequate, uncontrolled research techniques and observational methods were employed. . . . The hypothesis of telepathic occurrence as an explanation of the reported coincidental dream sequences is only one of several equally (or more) plausible alternative hypotheses. Telepathic dream sequences *may* possibly occur as a result of psychoanalytic therapy; but, thus far, no *scientific* evidence has been offered in support of this hypothesis.[16]

One thing that bothered Ellis in particular was that many of the alleged telepathic dreams did not occur simultaneously. In an example given by Eisenbud, two patients reported to him strikingly similar dreams of a person being caught in a heavy downpour and seeking shelter, one in a mansion and the other in a shack. The only connection between the two patients was that they both had Dr. Eisenbud as an analyst. The two patients had not met each

other and their dreams occurred a night apart. The particularly odd coincidence that Eisenbud noticed was that the name of the first patient was practically the same as the name of the person seeking refuge in the second
patient's dream, a similarity like Selma and Selda.

Eisenbud called it telepathy, Ellis called it chance coincidence, and a
Jungian analyst would undoubtedly have called it a *meaningful* coincidence,
or synchronicity.

As Eisenbud was finishing a rebuttal to Ellis, another patient reported
to him a dream that once again brought up the theme of rain. In an imaginative analysis running to many pages, Eisenbud shows how the dream's
latent content (the thoughts behind the dream symbols) dovetailed with his
own private life, involving in part his conflict with Ellis.

When this further reply of Eisenbud's was published, Ellis made yet
another reply, entitled "Reanalysis of an Alleged Telepathic Dream." Taking
the dream example offered by Eisenbud's patient, Ellis used a similar technique to show how the dream dovetailed a) with his own life; b) with the life
of another analyst's patient; and c) with the protagonist of a recent novel. Was
this "the most stupendous, colossal, miraculous, quadruple-threat telepathic
phenomenon of all time?" Ellis thought not.

Yet, to some, Ellis's reply did not convincingly seem the stuff of chance
coincidence. Just how far "chance" can be strained to explain meaningful
coincidences is a statistic unlikely to be computed. To a number of people,
Ellis's examples would suggest evidence for Jung's hypothesis of synchronicity — an intricate web of meaningful coincidences clustered around an
emotional situation. The oddest thing, of course, is that Ellis seemed to be
undergoing an experience similar not only to Eisenbud's but also to the other
analyst's patient and even, in some ways, the protagonist of the novel. So,
with a deft change of word, a Jungian might classify this as a "quadruple-
threat *synchronistic* phenomenon."

In the late 1940s, though, the word synchronicity had not yet been coined
by Jung. Otherwise it might have been used to describe the unusual coincidences that began to spread among a small group of psychiatrists who were
interested in the paranormal elements occurring in their patients' dreams. It
seemed that no sooner did an interest in the possibility of telepathic dreams
develop than patients began to supply these telepathic dreams. At the urging
of the then vice-president of the American Society for Psychical Research
(ASPR), Dr. Gardner Murphy, a special medical section of the ASPR was
organized in 1948 to look into these phenomena. The medical section met
once a month to report on paranormal phenomena in the psychoanalytic
situation and discuss their findings in the light of psychiatry. The New York–
based group, which met until 1954, included Dr. Jan Ehrenwald, Dr. Jule
Eisenbud, Dr. Montague Ullman, Dr. Robert Laidlaw, Dr. Geraldine
Pederson-Krag, Dr. Joost Meerloo, Dr. Gothard Booth, and others.

Dreams, being one of the main tools of the psychoanalyst, took first place in the discussions. Jan Ehrenwald's book *Telepathy and Medical Psychology* (1947) illustrated the ways in which telepathy was subject to the same psychological laws as are found in dreams and neurotic symptoms. Ehrenwald drew upon a rich background of experience in neurology and psychiatry to describe in convincing detail many carefully observed telepathic exchanges between patient and therapist via the patient's dreams. Ehrenwald observed that the occurrence of telepathy was sometimes conditioned by a patient's "minus function," that is, a certain lack or deficiency, such as blindness or deafness. He noted too the curious "emotional contagion" of telepathic effects in which ESP interchanges spread infectiously in an ever-widening circle of emotionally related events and individuals.

In his book *New Dimensions of Deep Analysis* (1954), Ehrenwald offered illuminating comments about schools of dream interpretation and telepathy. He states,

> If a patient treated by a Freudian or Adlerian or Jungian analyst dreams that his motor-car has been stolen the manifest content of his dream is obviously culturally determined.... The interpretation of such a dream in terms of castration fears, inferiority feelings, or the like, is largely a matter of the individual therapist's personal bias. In the last analysis general agreement as to the "real" meaning of such a dream is perhaps impossible to reach.
>
> True telepathic leakage [between therapist and patient] goes, however, beyond cultural conditioning. For instance, Jung's patients, at certain periods of his work, seemed to furnish ample evidence of uncommon abilities and hyperfunctions of the unconscious. Sometimes they contained grandiose allusions to ancient Egyptian or Assyrian or Hindu texts. At other times they seemed to bear out some of the fanciful beliefs of medieval astrologers and alchemists. No Freudian or Adlerian analyst seems to have ever recorded material of this kind. Yet I, for myself, have noticed peculiar changes in the dream imagery used by my patients at various periods of my analytic work. The changes seemed to be largely conditioned by my own preoccupation with the dream material encountered in the records of various analytic schools. The frankly telepathic repercussions of my later preoccupation with the problem of telepathy are amply demonstrated [earlier in the book].[17]

Before we examine Dr. Ehrenwald's cases, let us note one very important point. If the analyst is a Freudian, the patient tends to dream in Freudian symbols; if the analyst is a Jungian, the patient dreams in Jungian archetypal symbols; and, as Ehrenwald suggests, if the analyst is interested in telepathy, the patient may comply with telepathic dreams. Thus the openness of the therapist to telepathy seems to be an important conditioning factor in the production of telepathic dreams in his patients. This may explain why Dr. Ellis's patients refrain from telepathic dreaming. Ellis might object that Ehrenwald verbally encourages his patients to dream about his own personal life, but on the contrary, Ehrenwald is very circumspect in bringing up the subject of telepathy to his patients.

The following is a dream visit to a strange apartment reported by "Ruth" to Ehrenwald on March 10, 1948.

> ...It consisted of a beautiful long, well-shaped living room, spacious, with high ceiling. It opened out to a nice open terrace where the sun shone. It was long; it stretched along the whole building across the front ... some 50 feet or so. It had a brick wall and the floor was made of planks with cracks in between. There was not much furniture in the room, not so much as you would have if you would furnish it yourself. There was quite a lot of space left between the things. It was not a cluttered room. There was no carpet, only oriental rugs, a big one in the middle with figures like the one you have here in the office. There were smaller rugs at either end. But they covered only part of the floor, much of it was showing. There were also a few mahogany chairs and an open fireplace. A french door and two french windows opened to the terrace. A dingy little hall led into the bedroom and into a bathroom. I thought this would be the apartment I would like to live in, except that it did not have a maid's room and no extra bathroom.... [18]

Ruth didn't say how much the rent was, but that is about all she missed in describing the apartment into which, only a week before, Ehrenwald had moved. On the night of Ruth's dream Ehrenwald was proudly showing some relatives around his new apartment, a fact which Ruth had no ordinary means of knowing. Ehrenwald lists thirteen points of correspondence between Ruth's dream apartment and his own from the spacious, high living room with french doors and windows on a large terrace to the unfortunate lack of a maid's room and a second bathroom.

Just why Ruth was unconsciously prompted to such a telepathic tour de force might be glimpsed in one of Ruth's earlier dreams: "You were annoyed with me because I don't try hard enough. I was afraid you would drop me and say I have to stop and that further coming would be just a waste of time and money."

To a psychiatrist fascinated with the idea of telepathy, Ruth proved she could outdo them all — and there was little chance of Ehrenwald dropping a star dream telepath. In his analysis of the dream, Ehrenwald noted that if the telepathic origin were not taken into account, "a large portion of the dream remains unintelligible." Yet Ehrenwald, with characteristic caution, did not tell Ruth that her dream was about his own apartment.

When a similar type of dream was reported by another patient later, Ehrenwald set up an experimental condition to see if the patient could recognize his dream location. The patient was a middle-aged man in his second week of therapy. His dream one Monday morning was:

> I walked along a canal; it was quite straight and there were dams on both sides. It resembled a lake. Along with me walked two women and a boy

about five years old. Then I tried to phone somebody, I don't know whom, but the connection was cut. But then I found the wires, put them together and could establish the connection. Then I walked around a square several city blocks large. I thought I saw something like the Eiffel Tower and the Champs Élysées at a distance. The earth of the dam was like sea dunes or sand in the desert and the whole terrain went up and down and up and down.[19]

There was no Eiffel Tower in Ehrenwald's life on the Sunday morning preceding the dream, but there was, oddly enough, a "Champs Élysées" in the wilds of Queens. Ehrenwald records,

As it happens, on the Sunday morning preceding the dream I had taken a walk with my wife and my daughter in our neighborhood. We wanted to have a close look at what we used to call our private Champs Élysées, that is, an area of wooded wasteland off the outlying parts of Queens Boulevard through which a new connecting highway to Idlewild Airport was to be built. Huge mounds of earth cut through the hill terrain. . . . Looking down to the levelled ground in which rainwater had accumulated indeed gave the impression of a dam being built. The mounds of earth dug up by the bulldozers had a sandy color. Proceeding from our "dam," we continued on our walk by skirting the adjacent Maplegrove Cemetery which occupies several city blocks and returned home. Charting our walk on a street map would amount to a rectangle of about a mile square. I may also mention the structure of a big water tower which dominated the view from the far side of the "dam."[20]

In identifying the "tracer elements," or the manifest elements of the dream that are telepathically derived, Ehrenwald suggests that in the dream the five-year-old boy was the dreamer himself since he had associations with boyhood walks with his family. And of course we know who the adult man and the two women were. The identification of the water tower with the Eiffel Tower seems reasonable enough once we have recovered from the stunning correspondence of the two "Champs Élysées." Ehrenwald did not tell his patient about that Sunday walk, but sometime later showed him ten photographs of outdoor scenes, including the "dam." When he asked the patient if any of the pictures reminded him of one of his recent dreams, the patient pointed to the photo of the "dam," without realizing that it was evidence for telepathy.

There remains to puzzle us only the dream image of trying to telephone, finding that the wires were cut, and putting them together "to establish connection." To the members of the medical section of the ASPR, however, this dream symbol was no mystery. Specifically, Jule Eisenbud had pointed out that telephoning, as well as other images of indirect or exotic communication, often symbolized telepathic communication. And there could be little doubt in this case that the dreamer had "established connection."

The ways in which the dreamer engages in telepathic communication vary not only with the dreamer but also with the psychiatrist. Each man seems to have his own individual pattern of telepathic interaction, not only, as Ehrenwald notes, according to his analytic school, but more specifically according to his own individual interests.

Jule Eisenbud, who has used Freudian techniques of dream interpretation, has contributed probably more cases of paranormal dreaming to parapsychological literature than any other psychiatrist. The dreams, frequently having to do with sexual themes, get complicated, but the reader of Eisenbud's book *Psi and Psychoanalysis* is not likely to be bored.

Eisenbud has demonstrated that the dream telepathy hypothesis can actually be applied in the psychoanalytic situation to hasten a patient's recovery. In one case a woman patient reported a dream that seemed to be connected with what another woman patient was telling Eisenbud the day before. The two women had never met. But when Eisenbud told the second patient the first patient's dream — which included the odd association of inedible stolen corn with a husband's impotence — the second patient was able to break through a long-standing block by remembering a repressed episode that involved inedible stolen corn and her first husband's impotence.

How do patients react to such psi*-derived material? In Eisenbud's words,

> They tend to respond with the well-known confirmatory signs of an effective interpretation — laughter, pleasant excitement, astonishment, the disappearance of a symptom or resistance and the release of further material — which are characteristically seen in the case of ordinary interpretations that hit the mark. There may be a slightly greater sense of awe at the omnipotence and omnipresence of the unconscious but I have never known a patient to exhibit signs of anxiety referable to the use in interpretation of the psi hypothesis itself or to the analyst's readiness to think in such terms.[21]

The characteristic sense of awe experienced when a person is confronted with extraordinary and meaningful coincidences has been termed by Jung as "numinousity" (from the Latin *numen,* meaning divine will). It is this sense of numinousity, then, that impresses the patient who is confronted with the meaningful coincidence of his dream with an outer reality. The emotional impact of this "divine will" burns the experience in his consciousness — and the patient takes the dream message profoundly to heart. He probably does not dwell too long on the perplexing thought of just *how* it happened.

In many of the cases reported by Eisenbud, the conventional telepathic hypothesis becomes strained. When patients who have never met have intermeshing dreams on different nights and these dreams become meaningful only when discussed with their common point of contact, the psychiatrist, one begins to wonder just who might be sending telepathic messages to whom.

*A Greek letter used generically for all types of psychic phenomena, i.e., anomalous interactions between organisms and their environment (including other organisms) that appear to be inconsistent with conventional scientific understanding of the sensory and motor systems.

Such experiences may indicate that psi is extraordinarily more complex than commonly realized, since there is no easy classification of psi events into "cause" and "effect." One might speculate that human relationships may be guided and influenced by some fundamental underlying force that occasionally surfaces into consciousness as psi events, particularly during emotion-laden situations. Perhaps, during these times, a collective consciousness is formed between the individuals involved.

Since each dream analyst tends to have his own individual style of telepathic interaction with his patients, it is not surprising that each one tends to have different theories about what is happening and why.

Most of these analysts, though, would probably agree with the views of a prominent Italian psychoanalyst and parapsychologist, Dr. Emilio Servadio. Since the mid-1930s, he has been known for his work in relating telepathic dream elements to unresolved components in "transference," or the relationship between the patient and the therapist that springs from the patient's earlier behavior patterns in situations where there was a father figure. Dr. Servadio cites conditions occurring during analysis that are conducive to telepathy.

> These conditions are related to a particular situation of transference and counter-transference, in which the patient feels frustrated by a lack of attention on the part of his analyst, who is engrossed in problems of his own, whose direction and content closely resemble the problems worrying the patient. Other forms of expression and communication being blocked, the frustrated patient has recourse to a more direct and primitive means, such as telepathy or even precognition (in a dream or otherwise). He is thus able to penetrate the analyst's "secrets," to show him he is acquainted with them, to divert the analyst's libido to his own advantage, to reproach him for his lack of love or his aggressiveness. The analyst, in turn, appears to find himself in the conditions most favorable to such manifestations when he is unconsciously "withdrawing" too much from his patient's "infantile" desires, and when he has worries and interests which are complementary to his patient's, but which divert his attention, or even where there is an element of hostile counter-transference.[22]

Put more simply, if a patient becomes aggravated by an analyst's attention to other affairs he may resort to telepathy in order to get the analyst's attention back and also to show that he knew all along what was really going on.

CHAPTER 4

The Alcoholic Cat

The paranormal ability of psychoanalytic patients to dream telepathically about their analysts' private lives first became apparent to Dr. Ullman in 1947 during his own period of analysis — for each psychoanalyst must himself be psychoanalyzed. Just after a two-month summer vacation, Ullman had the following dream about his analyst and related the dream to him during their next analytic session on September 4:

> I entered the waiting room and was immediately aware of the fact that the arrangement of the furniture was quite different than formerly. I was struck by the brightness of the coloring, the absence of the large upholstered couch, and the prominence of several small chairs of modern design. I then entered the analyst's office and again noted a difference which also centered about the furniture. The flat, leather-covered studio couch to which I had been accustomed was missing; there was another piece in its place.... But I was struck by the fact that I did not lie down on this piece, but rather reclined, almost in a sitting position, facing the analyst instead of looking away from him. At this point there was an interruption and several men entered. These men seemed to be important and wealthy.... While the analyst conferred with them, I wandered off to another part of the room and spoke to a young chap who had come in with the three men. Upon resuming the analysis after this interruption there was some feeling of anxiety in relation to the analyst, and annoyance, perhaps, because he had allowed himself to become too much involved with these people during my session.

The dream was not discussed any further during that session and was all but forgotten until their meeting on September 18 when Ullman walked into the waiting room to find that the large upholstered couch was gone. The absence of the couch made the small, brightly colored chairs seem more outstanding. Entering the analyst's office, Ullman noticed that the flat studio couch usually present was gone, and the upholstered couch from the waiting room was in its place. When he commented on this, the analyst said that he had sent out his studio couch for reupholstering.

When they were about half way through the hour, the telephone rang. It was the manager of the hotel in which the analyst lived and there ensued a long, involved conversation about the analyst's attempt to get a larger apartment in the hotel. In contrast to previous telephone calls under these circumstances, which the analyst would ordinarily cut short, this conversation became more involved, with the analyst becoming more and more annoyed. Meanwhile, Ullman jotted down in his notebook that his uncle owned a large interest in a hotel. He handed the notebook to the analyst suggesting that his uncle might be of help. The analyst asked Ullman if his uncle was a certain tycoon, and he replied that he was only a friend of that person, which led them to a few remarks on the psychology of tycoons.

During the conversation the analyst kept fingering Ullman's notebook, and Ullman became anxious lest his doctor see some notes he had been making on psychical research and psychotherapy, which he feared the doctor would misunderstand.

It was at this point that Ullman suddenly remembered his dream of two weeks before. The changes in the office furniture seemed very like the dream. Even the substituted waiting room couch, on which it was not possible to recline, checked out with the dream. The "important and wealthy" men who entered the dream corresponded to the tycoons who had been discussed during the hour. And, of course, there was his own suppressed annoyance because the analyst "had allowed himself to become too much involved with these people during my session."

When he reminded the analyst of the dream, they discussed its parapsychological possibilities. The analyst revealed that he had decided to have his couch recovered before the dream occurred, which could be interpreted as telepathy, though the wealthy men interrupting the hour could be interpreted as precognition. Thereafter they devoted much time to discussions of Ullman's interest in psychical research. Ullman felt that the dream may have been triggered, in part, by his need to convince his analyst of the reality of psychic phenomena in order to feel more secure in his own convictions.

This sort of inner need, coupled with a mild anxiety, continued to set the stage for paranormal dreams when Ullman became active in the medical section of the American Society for Psychical Research. He had never been able to get over a feeling of being "on the spot" when it came to giving oral presentations, and it was this mild anxiety that was in the back of his mind on Sunday, April 25, 1948, as he was reviewing a patient's dreams for possible use as examples of telepathic dreaming in a talk scheduled for the ASPR on May 6. That was to be Ullman's first presentation on the subject. Somehow, as he reviewed the dreams, they didn't seem as striking and convincing of telepathy as they had when they first occurred. Ullman had neglected to record his activities and introspections, which might have had important corroborative value. The difficulties in convincingly eliminating chance and other counter-hypotheses to telepathy seemed more formidable than ever. Somewhat disappointed with this material, Ullman desperately hoped that, somehow, his patient would come up with fresh telepathic dreams before the deadline of the scheduled talk two weeks later. (What follows is from a personal account of psi experiences with this and other patients written by Ullman at the time of their occurrence.)

I was able to put off work on my presentation by remembering that I had promised someone to find some material I had on the early days of the New York Society for Medical History. I had this material in a closet, one part of which was locked. I didn't have the key for the locked section with me, so I looked for the papers in the open part of the closet. I didn't find them, but my eye caught sight of a large wooden box in which I kept microfilm. I hadn't looked in the closet for many months, and this sight triggered a memory of my having had the box made while I was stationed in France during the war, and having it mailed home.

The next day, Monday, my telepathic patient came for her analytic session. An art historian and a twenty-nine-year-old mother of one, she had been in analysis for six months. She reported a series of dreams in this session that seemed inspired by my desperate hope. Several hours before my explorations in the closet, she had had this dream:

"Mr. E., who was some kind of an instructor, came to the house to demonstrate a new gadget. His gestures were very clear. There were people in our living room. It was a meeting or a social group. He went to the hall closet and took out a large wooden box. He lifted up the cover and took out a camera very slowly and deliberately.... I said this was a box my husband had sent back from Germany. Then Mr. E. made the point of his demonstration. He looked through what seemed to be a stereopticon lens (a very special kind of lens) onto the street below.... The picture was black and white and unusual because it was three-dimensional. The lens could make you see things miles away that couldn't be seen with the naked eye.... Mr. E. demonstrated this great device...."

The patient identified "Mr. E." as me. She related the idea of "seeing more than meets the eye" to the analysis, though she could give no associations with the rest of the dream. Associations to my own life, however, were more marked:

The instructor demonstrating a "new gadget" to a group in a living room corresponded to my presentation on telepathy for a group in a waiting room of one of the members of the ASPR Medical Section.

The large wooden box in a closet was like the large wooden box in my closet. Hers was sent home by her husband from Germany; mine was sent home from France. Hers contained a camera; mine contained microfilm. The special lens that took three-dimensional pictures from miles away suggests symbolically the unique quality of telepathy that can penetrate miles to see things that cannot be seen with the naked eye. Her dream, in fact, made possible my demonstration of "this great device."

The patient's compliance with my inner wishes may be related to her compulsion to yield uncritically to the needs of others. Unknowingly on both our parts, she yielded to my compelling need for better telepathic material. It turned out, of course, to be also partially precognitive.

The theme of extrasensory perception was also in the air on February 28, 1950, when a forty-year-old woman patient came for her analytic session. "Perhaps there is something to ESP," she remarked quite spontaneously at the opening of the session. We had not discussed this topic before, and I inquired what prompted her remark. She stated that on Friday, February 24, she had been thinking of a doctor she hadn't seen for two years, when she received a telephone call from him. She thought it was probably just a coincidence, but still...

She then related two dreams she had recalled on awakening the next morning:

"...There was a bottle on the table containing part alcohol and part cream. It was sort of a white, foamy stuff.... I looked at the label. It read 'appealing nausea.' I meant to drink it when we went to bed...."

"I had a small leopard. It was very dangerous...."

The patient's associations with the first dream was that the alcohol-cream mixture reminded her of crème de menthe, a drink which makes her slightly sick. The label "appealing nausea" reminded her of her own revulsion in connection with sexual activity. "When I get very excited, I get sick."

I could scarcely refrain from making a few associations myself with her dreams. On the evening of Friday, February 24, the night of her dream, my wife and I attended a meeting at the New York Academy of Medicine to hear a presentation by Dr. Jules Masserman on animal neuroses. He showed a film on the induction of neuroses in cats. One memorable sequence showed how to make cats alcoholic. When an alcoholic cat was presented with a choice between a glass full of milk or a glass half filled with milk and half with alcohol, the alcoholic cat made straight for the milk-alcohol mixture.

One might speculate that after a few of those drinks the alcoholic cat might feel like a "small leopard," or perhaps, like its human counterparts after a few "grasshoppers" (crème de menthe and cream), it might find that the appealing mixture becomes nauseating.

It may be that this direct correspondence of her dreams with my activities was conditioned in part by her speculations that day about ESP. Another fact may have been her withdrawal from communication with me, an attitude derived from a previously unsuccessful attempt at analysis and her contempt for her former husband, who had been an analyst. The "alcoholic cat" episode was the first in a series of telepathic correspondences with my life, and seemed to open up a new avenue of communication with me.

On Monday, December 4, 1950, the patient reported this dream: "Everyone was congratulating me because I had written an article about the beauties of Michigan. I knew I hadn't but it seemed as if I had. People were quoting the critics. I asked what they said about the writing. Then I said, 'As a matter of fact I didn't write anything.'"

The patient had no associations with the article because she had not, in fact, written anything. Michigan was the patient's native state, remindful of her early family life which she abhorred because of its coldness and detached lack of feeling, which she retained, however, as a sense of "splendid isolation."

On the Saturday preceding her dream report I had been to a party which was attended also by a group of distinguished faculty of a medical college to which I had applied to become a teaching analyst. Several of this group had been judges of a paper I had presented a few days before on the topic of detachment. As tactfully as I could I inquired of the "critics" what they thought of my paper. To my relief, they congratulated me on my "article" about isolation.

The patient seemed to be telepathically aware of how the topic of my paper dovetailed with her own associations with Michigan, her own "splendid isolation."

How the patient was finally able to relate to me can be glimpsed in yet another seemingly telepathic dream, reported on Wednesday, January 24, 1951: "I was eating.... You were with me and also a younger married couple, Joe and Jean, of whom I am very fond. In the dream both Joe and Jean were patients of yours. We are eating out of a casserole dish containing chicken and rice. There was a discussion between you and Joe about Joe taking some of the food. He said, 'There is nothing to discuss about it.' You said, 'There is.' I felt happy and secure as a patient of yours, knowing that these friends were also your patients...."

The patient's associations were straightforwardly centered on the previous Sunday, when she cooked a casserole of chicken and rice for a married couple named Joe and Jean. However, Joe and Jean had never been psychoanalytic patients.

Oddly enough, though, there was a strong parallel with my own life. On the night of her dream I had gone with a young friend to a Chinese restaurant. Being more familiar with Chinese cooking, I ordered for both of us, a pork dish for him and a chicken dish for me, with the usual bowls of rice. In Chinese style, both dishes were served in casseroles. As an habitué of Chinese cooking, I had less compunction about sharing the dishes than did my friend, whom I had to persuade to invade my dish as I was invading his. The conversation then turned to his wife. My friend asked me if I could arrange psychotherapy for her, continuing a start made with another analyst. Then, to my surprise, he raised the question of himself undergoing therapy with me.

So, with the setting of eating chicken and rice in a casserole, two young friends want also to become patients. The dovetailing of our experiences is utilized by the patient's dream to strengthen a constructive relationship with me; a relationship in which a patient can also be a friend.

My telepathic experiences with this patient illustrate how psi in the therapeutic situation can have both negative and positive connotations. From the negative standpoint, it is seen in those patients who have a need to hide and withdraw. On the positive side, it represents a way of communicating with the real world.

In my own experience, psi in patients operates either sporadically or consistently: sporadically when other channels of communication are temporarily blocked by a critical situation in the analysis; and consistently when there is a pre-established block to normal communication, such as that experienced by this patient, where distrust and coldness prevent normal means of communication with the environment.

In those patients in whom one finds a consistent kind of psi functioning, the analytic problems are extraordinarily difficult. The patient has at his disposal a means of knowing reality — haphazard, inadequate, and uncontrollable as it may be — which is capable of operating outside of awareness and therefore incapable of threatening that which is most precious to him — namely, his detachment.

Freud pointed out the analyst's responsibility for the mastery of his own repressed conflicts. The facts of telepathy add dramatic power to his words of caution. The analyst cannot hide any of his own failings that the patient chooses to exploit.

Withdrawal, belligerence, distrust, evasiveness are not uncommon attitudes toward an analyst that a patient may show if he is constantly on the defensive toward the world. Analysts are used to dealing with such persons. But with ESP the situation becomes more like dealing with a superspy. The telepathic patient has a way of honing in on a perfectly "innocent" event in one's life that, actually, took a fair amount of rationalizing to make innocent. The psychiatrist, in his presumably "well-analyzed" state, will hopefully show an attitude akin to that expressed by Mae West in an old movie:

MAE: For a long time I was ashamed of the way I lived.

HE: You mean you reformed?

MAE: No, I got over being ashamed.

And so, without a trace of shame, I will relate the "Chromium Soap Dish Caper." My "superspy" patient, a forty-year-old salesman for children's clothes, related a dream to me on Monday, December 24, 1951, which he recalled on the previous Saturday morning: ". . . I was wrapping up a few of the samples that had been on exhibit and was preparing to leave. Someone gave me, or I took, a chromium soap dish. I held it in my hand and I offered it to him. He took it. I was surprised. I asked him, are you a collector, too?

Then I sort of smirked and said knowingly, well, you're building a house. He blushed. He smirked and kept on smoking his cigar."

The patient had no associations of his own with the chromium soap dish, though he did recall that he had "swiped a few towels" from a hotel where he once attended an exhibit, and had once got a thrashing for "swiping fifteen cents from my aunt for the movies."

My own associations with the chromium soap dish were not so indirect. On the day of my patient's dream I had gotten a lift from a neighbor, who drove me to my office in New York City. I mentioned to him some difficulty I was having with a picture window in my new home, built at the same time as his, a year and a half before. There passed through my mind an incident I didn't mention to him. The week before, some of the workmen who originally contracted the building of the house had come to see what was to be done with my picture window, which had gotten out of line as the foundations of the house settled. We went into the basement, and there one of them spotted a chromium soap dish lying about unused. It had been shipped to me by mistake at the time of the original building of the house, but in a spirit of belligerent dishonesty inspired by rising costs on the house, I had no intentions of returning it. The workman made a wisecrack about my having gotten away with it. Having long since rationalized it out of the realm of "larcency," I found myself somewhat embarrassed, and managed a sheepish smirk, though not with a cigar in my mouth.

It seemed my "collecting tendencies" were exposed as the butt of a joke by a patient who found a vulnerable area with which to ward off the inroads of therapy. The chromium soap dish lying about unused and unconnected with the rest of the house is a borrowed experience which serves admirably for the purpose. The dish is a potential container for a cleansing or healing substance. In its isolation and lack of appropriate setting, as well as being "stolen goods," the symbol expresses the patient's profound distrust of the therapist and his unwillingness to be considered a useless fixture in a collector's (analyst's) house.

The "Chromium Soap Dish" patient shared many similarities with the "Alcoholic Cat" patient. They were both at critical points in their efforts to maintain their relatedness to people—to me. They were characterized by a lack of emotional responsiveness and profound feelings of withdrawal, resignation, cynicism, and futility. These are characteristics of the schizoid stage, or state bordering on schizophrenia, which seems to encourage telepathic manifestations as ordinary communication is cut off.

When a person passes through this borderline state into actual schizophrenia, then he seems to lose his telepathic ability. This lack has been shown by experimental testing of schizophrenics for ESP.[1] Frequently, the schizophrenics will often make claims of having ESP, of being able to influence others by their mental activity, or in turn, of being influenced by others. This often takes the form of persecutory delusions, in which the schizophrenic feels he is under attack.

It may be that the schizophrenic's claim to ESP powers is conditioned by a recollection of true ESP experiences which occurred during the borderline period — when he was losing contact with reality and had to use a secondary communication system (telepathy).

One should not infer, of course, that all telepathic dreamers are on their way to schizophrenia. On the contrary, ESP tests have shown that those who do best at ESP tend to have healthy, integrated, and open personalities. The schizoid personality is able to manifest telepathic ability only under conditions of anxiety and withdrawal, as a last-ditch attempt at communication.

The telepathic process, as Jule Eisenbud first noted, is often symbolized in dreams by telephoning or other acts of communicating. One woman patient of mine would consistently pick up in her dreams my mild anxieties about giving a lecture on parapsychology. In her dreams I was always symbolized by her brother. He would be performing some strange communicative activity, such as writing Chinese on a blackboard. And sometimes, at the meetings of the ASPR's medical section, I would utilize a blackboard to write the symbols of that strange new science — parapsychology.

With the gradual phasing out of the medical section in 1954, my colleagues and I noted the odd phenomenon that there was a corresponding decrease in the yield of telepathic dreams from our patients. This was in marked contrast to the early days in 1948 when the excitement and novelty of sharing these experiences served to dramatically sharpen our interest. There was no dearth of telepathic dreams then. We even began to note the interweaving of some of our joint experiences into our individual experience with patients, suggestive of what Jan Ehrenwald called "telepathic contagion."

To set the stage for telepathic dreaming in the analytic situation, the most important factors are: *interest* on the part of the psychiatrist; *need* on the psychiatrist's part that dovetails with the patient's need; and *anxiety* on the psychiatrist's part that dovetails with the patient's anxieties.

The very special situation of the patient-doctor relationship provides a strong potential bond conducive to telepathy if the above conditions are met.

The unique advantage of the psychoanalytic situation for discovering telepathic dreams resides mainly in the fact that dreams are regularly reported by the patient to the analyst. Nowhere else in our culture do dreams attain such prominence. Ordinarily they are not discussed; people are not encouraged to remember them; nor are they encouraged to look for any inner meanings much less any paranormal correspondences with outer events.

What would happen if one were to regularly record his dreams and compare them with the realities of another person's life? Of another person's dreams? Would keen scientific interest be sufficient motivation for telepathic dreaming? What kind of correspondences might you get?

PART TWO

EXPERIMENTAL STUDIES

CHAPTER 5

Early Explorations:
From "Raf" to Ralph

The possibility that telepathic dreaming might be experimentally induced was a fascinating idea not only to Dr. Ullman but also to Laura A.
Dale, research associate of the American Society for Psychical Research and
later the editor of the ASPR *Journal.* Dale, who was familiar with the cases
of dream telepathy reported by psychiatrists, had also noted paranormal
elements occasionally in her own dreams.

Probably the most startling of these dream experiences occurred on
December 19, 1942, on the night of a disappointing—if not humiliating—
experiment at the ASPR. Under the direction of Dr. Gardner Murphy, Dale
was a subject for an experiment with a drug that induced mental dissociation.
The experimenters hoped that some ESP phenomena might come through as
Dale entered the drugged state. As the drug took effect, Dale drowsily stated
that now she knew more about psychical research than Mrs. Sidgwick, a
pioneer of the English Society for Psychical Research whom Dale held in
great esteem.

"What is it that you know?" asked the experimenters.

For several minutes Dale babbled incoherent nonsense, much to the
amusement of the experimenters. When told what happened, after she had
recovered from the drug, Dale was mortified. But apparently her subconscious decided that some extraordinary paranormal feat must be achieved
to save the day. That night Dale had a long, vivid dream that was so unusual
that she called the ASPR's executive secretary the next morning to report it
to her:

> I found myself in a large room on the ground floor of a house which I took
> to be in Florida.... My little dog Myra was lying on a chair toward the side
> of the room, and there were people present.... I was pushing a vacuum
> cleaner along a rug. Then occurred something that filled me with the utmost
> horror—the vacuum cleaner became *alive* and possessed of a malignant will of

its own. It began to heave in and out, or bulge and deflate . . . and I realized I was in great danger, for it was going to explode. I dropped the handle and ran for the door. As I ran I knew I was doing an unspeakable thing — I was leaving Myra to be killed in the explosion. I did not stop to rescue her, however, and just as I reached the door there was a terrible concussion (no sound) and I found myself safe on the lawn. Then followed a somewhat less vivid sequence, the gist of which was this: a man who had been present had attempted to rescue Myra. He had been killed — someone told me this. Then I had Myra in my arms; she was moving, burned, suffering, but at the same time she was dead. . . ."[1]

Two days later, when Dale's mother was visiting her in New York, they decided to go to the movies at the Embassy Theater on Forty-second Street, which specialized in newsreels. As they walked into the theater a cartoon entitled *The Raven* was being shown: A mongrel dog and a raven called upon a Scottish terrier (as opposed to Myra being a Boston terrier) to demonstrate a vacuum cleaner. While the raven was pushing the cleaner along the rug in a large ground floor room, the mongrel dog went upstairs and attempted to break into the Scottie's safe. Suddenly the vacuum cleaner "came alive" and began to suck up some liquor from bottles under a grill-work in the floor. Then it began to bulge, heave in and out, and finally with an explosive movement it sent the Scottie dog spinning to one side of the room. While the vacuum cleaner was going through its contortions, the mongrel dog upstairs set off a dynamite explosion that shook the room.

Thus the highly unlikely dream scene of a vacuum cleaner coming alive to attack a dog was repeated in the reality of Dale's experience two days later, allaying her anxiety of failing at an ESP experiment.

In discussing their paranormal dream experiences in early 1953, Ullman and Dale conceived the idea of a long-term experiment in which they would record their dreams daily to check for paranormal correspondences with events in each other's lives. Faced with the problem of how to link their dreams with some common bond, they seized upon a theory put forward by the British researcher Whately Carington in his book *Telepathy*. (American edition entitled *Thought Transference*, 1946.)[2] Basically, Carington postulated that telepathic interchanges were facilitated by common associations between the two minds. His "association theory" held that if an idea or word (so-called "K-object") were presented to a person who was in telepathic rapport with another person (that is, having a shared consciousness), then the second person would have mental associations with the "K-object." Tell the first person the word "dog" and the second person might think of "bark, bite, or bone" as if the two persons were of a single mind.

What would happen, wondered Ullman and Dale, if both persons were presented simultaneously with the same stimulus word? They obviously couldn't use conventional words as stimuli, since if they both heard the word "dog," they would both think of "bark, bite, or bone." No, the shared stimulus word would have to be new to them, a nonsense syllable like "Raf."

In the hope that such common associations would give rise to shared telepathic experience, Ullman developed a plan whereby two tape-recording devices with timers (so-called Memory Trainers or Dormiphones) would play simultaneously for each of them some nonsense syllable stimulus word while they were sleeping. Obtaining identical Dormiphones, they set their timers to go off at the same time, so that the recorded message would be played through speakers placed under their pillows. This, they hoped, would telepathically beam them across the twenty miles separating their homes. To see if the Dormiphone made any appreciable difference, they also planned a control series without it.

The first few days, beginning in December 1953, were mostly spent in getting used to the apparatus awakening them in the middle of the night. The first stimulus word was "Raf," accompanied with the command, "On awakening in the morning, you will remember your dream."

Ullman's dream at 3:00 A.M., December 1, was:

> Heard the tape, but there was French dialogue on it, mostly a female voice, but occasionally a male voice.... I heard it all with dismay, feeling that a mistake had been made, that the tape had not been erased or that the wrong tape had been used.... Great sense of disappointment at the "failure" of the experiment. Janet [Ullman's wife] asked what the stimulus was. I humorously replied that it was in French and there was a translator in the machine. She felt frustrated by my answer....

Dale's dreams that night had little to do with the experiment, but a dream she had on December 3 seemed more on target:

> It seemed Janet was talking to me and telling me how Monte was reacting to his stimulus tape, which was different from mine — with much more on it. She played this tape for me. It was very noisy, with a lot of shouting on it. This disturbed me as I feared I would not hear my own tape which I believed was about to go off. It seemed that both Janet and Monte felt there was something of great interest on his tape, but all I could get of it was noise and shouting.

An intriguing start, though out of time by two days. To Ullman, the "French" he dreamed he heard on the tape suggested the foreign language symbol for psi communication, much as his patient dreamed of writing in Chinese. When he told this interpretation to Jule Eisenbud a few days later, Eisenbud countered with the suggestion that French was the language of love.

In the two-year period of the experiment, Ullman and Dale would meet once a week on Fridays to compare notes of their dreams and other events in their notebooks, which Dale would then type up. A meeting date that was an exception was Monday, December 14, and the dream that night of Dale was also exceptional (if trivial): "I was on a friend's lawn and a man came to plant some evergreen trees. He had a wooden board and bored holes in it to represent where the trees should go — their spacing. . . ."

The Sunday before, Ullman was having a reverie in which he was wondering how to build a drinking fountain for the birds. He thought of drilling three holes in the house and putting plastic screws in them. Dale's holes were for the trees; Ullman's for the birds, but their sketches of what they saw were remarkably similar.

The stimulus word that night had been "Zivid." As the experiment continued, using both stimulus words and control periods without any stimulus, it seemed that the stimulus word in fact made little difference.

On a control night, January 13, 1954, Dale had an exceptionally vivid and unpleasant dream: "Had terribly vivid impression that upper left molar was loose. I wiggled it as a child does with thumb and forefinger and finally it came out. Could feel the hole with my tongue and taste the blood. Very real."

Although considerably overdramatized, Dale's dream is suggestive of a real life event. That night Janet Ullman had inadvertently left a dental bridge — a left lower tooth — in the bathroom. Dr. Ullman discovered it and returned it to her. She may have been feeling the hole with her tongue, but there was, of course, no blood.

Such seemingly trivial events seemed at first to dominate the apparent telepathic interchange. On a night when Dale was at a car show, admiring a Rolls-Royce attended by a liveried chauffeur and footman, Ullman dreamed of ". . . two men in liveried uniform in the foreground and the vague picture of a woman in the background."

On February 11, however, Dr. Ullman had a dream that was closer to the "crisis" dreams more often reported to parapsychologists: ". . . I was in my car. A child named Jane Morey jumped from the top of the car and injured her head. She suffered a depressed fracture of the skull. . . ."

Jane Morey was the name of the child of a physician living near Ullman. On February 27, sixteen days later, the real Jane was seriously injured when she tried to jump out of the path of an oncoming car. The car hit her left leg and fractured some bones.

This type of apparent precognition was also experienced by Dale. In her dream of March 1, "There was a question as to whether or not I was pregnant. I went into labor. . . . Then several physicians present said . . . if there was a baby, it would be very tiny. I hoped there was no baby as I did not want one and hated the idea of having one. I could not imagine how I had gotten pregnant."

After she had recorded the dream, Dale went out to buy the *New York Herald-Tribune*. The first item that caught her eye was:

ARRIVAL OF 2ND BABY SURPRISES MOTHER

John L., 40, a painter, was out for a drive last night with his wife, Caroline, 25, and their daughter, Marianne, 18 months old, when Mrs. L. complained of feeling pains.

They were on Bell Blvd. in Queens and Mr. L. ran to the nearest house. The occupant turned out to be patrolman Christian S., 40. He delivered Mrs. L. of an 11-pound 6-ounce girl . . . Mrs. L. told nurses she hadn't suspected she was pregnant.

Mrs. L's surprise at being pregnant with an eleven-and-a-half-pound baby almost overshadows the oddness of Dale's dream about it.

It was soon Ullman's turn for a dream about an unusual newspaper article. His dream of March 22: "Someone discovered a snake on the golf course. There was a discussion of the use of a forked stick in catching it. Then someone had bashed the snake's head into the ground and all one could see were the two holes where the teeth had disappeared."

In the next day's *New York Post*, a story datelined March 22 told of a snake expert being fatally bitten by a rattlesnake. "As Johnson started to slip a loop over its head, the snake sprang free and bit Johnson on the back of his hand. He jerked away with such force the fangs stuck in the flesh. As Sparks killed the snake with a rock, Johnson pulled the fangs out. . . ." The corresponding details of the snake's head being bashed and the "two holes where the teeth had disappeared" give this experience more than a touch of veridicality.

A dream that fits into the classic pattern of crisis telepathy was seemingly evoked in Dale by a bizarre incident that happened to Ullman. A neighbor's wife had developed functional paralysis of her legs — apparently an hysterical symptom. On Sunday evening, June 13, the woman became hysterical and her husband asked Ullman to see if he could help her. When Ullman arrived, the woman begged him to amputate her useless limbs with an ax. She confidentially confessed that she was disturbed by thoughts of violence toward her children.

Compare that incident with Dale's dream of June 14: "Horrible nightmare: A baby's arm had been amputated. It was dried and in a leather case. My arm was to be amputated and grafted on to the baby and the baby's dried arm was to be grafted on to me. I was assured that this arm would grow normally and so I was willing to permit the operation. But the physician started to cut my arm without giving me an anesthetic. I screamed and fought and yelled for an anesthetic and woke up in a sweat of fright."

The neighbor's wife's psychotic episode seems to have made good nightmare material for Dale twenty miles away. It makes one wonder just how often nightmares might actually reflect someone else's psychotic thoughts. More often reflected in Dale's dreams were less unpleasant, but still painful, visits to the dentist by Janet Ullman. Fortunately for Dale, her dreams were usually symbolic, having to do with a dental inlay rather than the actual pain experienced at the dentist.

In attempting to assess the correspondences between dream and event, it is, of course, difficult to be certain that the correspondence is not due to chance. Common topics and daily activities would be expected to correlate occasionally. But how often does the philosophical topic of "time" come up? On June 2, 1954, Ullman was discussing the work of Dr. Joost Meerloo with an associate. One of Meerloo's chief interests is a philosophic conception of the nature of time. His essay "The Time Sense in Psychiatry" closes with the words: "Only man hopes and only man has a notion of time, and death. Though time remains for him a *memento mori* [remember to die], creative man builds his own time."[3]

Dale's dream that same night seemed a rejoinder to Meerloo: "Stimulus woke me, but it sounded like a rolling of drums and blare of music which worked up to a deafening crescendo, with a man's voice repeating the words, 'Time and space may not endure, but personality is deathless.'"

Important sounding statements accompanied by drumrolls seem to be fairly rare in dreams, though dreams of one's colleagues happen more frequently. In a short dream of June 25, 1954, Dale "was looking at a copy of Gertrude Schmeidler's book. It was rather skinny with red covers and had a lot of stuff written in the margins in pencil." Dr. Schmeidler, a psychologist and parapsychologist at City College of New York, had not written such a book, but on that day Ullman was ill and stayed in bed where he read a borrowed book with red covers. He recalled wishing that he owned it, for he had the urge to annotate it in the margins. His wish seemed to be fulfilled by Dale.

A series of dreams and events with a common theme began on July 6, 1954, when the Ullman's cat had four kittens. Two days later Dale, who is a dog fancier and has several boxers, had this dream: "Tina had four beautiful puppies, all females. However, there was a possibility that one had a congenital eye defect — if so, I would have had to have her put to sleep."

Many months later, in the spring of 1955, Dale's prize-winning dog Tina developed a serious eye condition that made necessary constant visits to a veterinarian and caused Dale great anxiety. Her dream diary entry for April 19, 1955, in association with a dream of blindness, reads: "Blindness has been on my mind because of Tina's eye condition." The same day's diary entry for Ullman reads: "The kitten with the leg injury was disposed of yesterday."

These correspondences fit well into Carington's association theory. Four kittens being born in the Ullman home triggers the associative dream of Dale in which four puppies are born. The associations seem also to extend to the future, anticipating Tina's eye condition and having to put to sleep one of the newborn kittens. This possibility is underscored by the fact that Dale's worry about her dog's eye condition comes through in a dream on the same day that the kitten is put to sleep because of an injury. Dale's anxiety about her dog may have served as a sort of psychodynamic bridge to anxiety in the Ullman home over the kitten.

The theme of pets seemed to be activated again on April 9, 1955, when Ullman unexpectedly met Dale on the street and startled her; Ullman was on his way to counsel a young man about his phobia centering around dogs.

That night, Dale had this dream: "Was in my office at old ASPR headquarters. Gertrude Schmeidler came in. . . . . She said Gardner Murphy had told her: 'Laura [Dale] psychically cured the medium Margery's *delphinium plant.*' I was incensed and said I knew nothing about this — I had never cured anything psychically, least of all Margery's plant. As proof of this, I cited the fact I had never seen the woman."

At first glance it seems most unlikely that this absurd and amusing dream might have any correspondence with reality. Margery was the most celebrated medium of her time. In the 1920s and 1930s the ASPR had published several volumes of *Proceedings* on her mediumship — though later evidence discredited at least some of her phenomena as fraudulent. However, Margery's repertoire, large as it was, did not include psychic healing. The topic of Margery had come up a few days before, when Dale answered a query about the date of Margery's death (1941).

It was quite true that Dale had never met Margery, but she did know another celebrated medium, Eileen Garrett, President of the Parapsychology Foundation. A month after her dream about psychically curing the delphinium plant, Dale chanced to meet Garrett on the street, and told her about the difficulty her dog Tina was experiencing with her eye trouble, which the veterinarian said was making little progress. Garrett then offered to send her trance control "Abduhl Latif" to give the animal a psychic healing treatment, since healing *was* in her repertoire. (The attempted treatment was apparently not successful.)

This incident suggests a possible meaning for the dream: A psychic treatment for a medium's plant becomes a psychic treatment by a medium for a pet. Dale's disavowal in her dream of being unable to cure anything psychically might be related to her frustration of being unable to cure the dog's eye. The skeptic may well object that delphinium plants are not easily equated with pet dogs, and certainly one would expect the devotion lavished on a plant to be less than that felt for a pet. Yet one woman's plant may be another woman's pet. That Dale's dream symbols should be taken from the future poses an embarrassment for conventional psychoanalytic thinking, but no more so than most of the other material in this book.

Psychoanalysts might feel more at home with the following dreams of May 1, 1955, in which sexual symbolism seemed to be shared.

Dale dreamed that "A strange woman had Tina with her in a car. Tina wore a collar and leash made of cellophane. The woman had a pocketbook that opened and closed electrically. I tried to close this purse, but it wouldn't work. The woman said she couldn't get at her car keys, so I took Tina and we walked to our destination."

In Ullman's dream: "There was a parked car. I had to connect a long fire hose to a hydrant. I was unsure how to do it. I got the top of the hydrant off. I was surprised at the delicate and intricate machinery underneath. It was like a motor that had to start. I finally started it but it stopped. There were two older men who pointed out the trouble. There were rubber springs which had stuck together. I was trying to fix it."

In both dreams, a car was not moving (not functional). In Dale's dream, a female sex symbol (a pocketbook that opened and closed electrically) was not functioning; in Ullman's dream a male sex symbol (a hydrant with a long fire hose) was not functioning. There were three females in Dale's dream; three males in Ullman's dream. The overall symbolism is of attempts to activate sexuality ("delicate and intricate machinery"), and in both dreams, the attempt failed ("she couldn't get at her car keys"; "I finally started it but it stopped."). The only clue we have as to why the dreams should have taken a sudden psychoanalytic turn is that the evening before, Ullman went to a dinner dance attended by psychoanalysts and their wives. Discretion prevents us from further developing this line of thought. . . .

Dream-dream correspondences turned up several times in the Ullman-Dale experiment. Sometimes these were just a word or idea in common, but often an underlying emotion connected the two dreamers. In her dream of April 2, 1955, Dale "went to see a doctor. He turned out to be a seedy little man with a shabby office. . . . I waited a long time for my turn, then the doctor saw me. I was shocked at his ungrammatical English. I don't recall my complaint, but he said nothing was wrong with me and called the next patient." Dale's association with the dream was of being examined by a doctor a month before, and being told her hearing was normal. The doctor, however, had been quite respectable and showed none of the negative qualities of her "dream" doctor.

On the same night, Ullman dreamed "I seemed to be trying to recall the name of a doctor I interned with who went into the Navy and then into psychiatry." Ullman recalled that he did not like that doctor, and it may be that Dale's dream doctor was downgraded by Ullman's negative feelings toward his doctor acquaintance. However, chance coincidence could possibly account for such brief correspondences.

A similar correspondence appeared in their dreams of June 15, 1954. Dale dreamed "something about being in a summer resort — small hotel or boarding house — Atlantic City?" while Ullman was dreaming "something about being on a beach." In his dream the next night, "I was walking on a boardwalk." Atlantic City, of course, is famous for its hotels, beach, and boardwalk. Curiously, a more direct correspondence to Dale's dream had appeared in Ullman's dream of more than a month before, May 4, 1955:

> There was a tattered slip of paper. Something about an interview with the FBI in Atlantic City. The words on it said, "He will talk." I was going there on the subway and going into a hotel in Atlantic City. They would be surprised when they saw that I put up a stand.

If the two dreams mentioning hotels in Atlantic City had occurred the same night, they would have been impressive evidence for telepathy. But, more than a month apart, they remain enigmatic.

Just how the dreamer's subconscious reacts to such frustrating misses may be seen in Dale's dream of May 20, 1955:

> Was talking to Mrs. A [a psychical researcher]. I told her that in our experiment *all* our dreams were telepathic and highly significant. If Monte Ullman dreamed about sex, then I dreamed about sex. If I dreamed about money, then M.U. dreamed about money. I bragged quite a lot, and Mrs. A. seemed much impressed.

Such moments of triumph were to remain wish-fulfillment dreams, for such neat correspondences were seldom achieved. Yet, when they did happen, they were most impressive. Here, for example, are dreams one night apart, both concerned with vocal music, piano pupils, and people whose initials are B.R. Dale's dream was about a girl to whom she had given piano lessons years before:

> A girl named Betsy Richards gave me a written analysis of a certain popular piece of music. This song was apparently quite unusual in form. She gave analyses of several typical forms, then the analysis of the song in question. . . .

Ullman's dream of the next night was:

> I was on an outing with Bernie Robbins. I was then in a theater attending a concert. My former piano teacher, Shaffer, whom I thought of as [Leonard] Bernstein in the dream, was giving a concert. It was a vocal concert instead of playing the piano. . . .

The odd twist in both dreams was of piano players concerning themselves with vocal music. In Dale's dream, her piano pupil is featured; in Ullman's dream, his piano teacher appears. Both dreams evoked memories of years before when music lessons had been respectively taught and learned. As in many of these examples, time is out of joint. Just why both dreamers should have tuned into such an odd shared experience remains a mystery.

A tidier example of apparent dream telepathy was afforded on June 6, 1955, when Ullman met with another doctor to discuss ways of preventing suicide in schizophrenic patients. This may have telepathically stimulated a painful memory of Dale's, whose sister had committed suicide some years before by jumping out of a window. In her dream that night, she was with a woman who reminded her of her sister:

> I was on the roof of a tall building. Someone said D.B. was in a room a couple of floors below and was planning to jump out the window. Although deathly scared of heights, I crawled off the roof and down to her room, where I argued her out of her suicidal idea.

As in many of these examples, an experience of Ullman's seemed to be reflected in the dreams of Dale. Ullman seemed to be a natural "agent" or telepathic sender; and Dale seemed to be best as the percipient or receiver. They decided to undertake an experimental series in which Dale would try to dream about specific events in Ullman's life. Starting on June 15, 1955, Ullman would note an interesting event in his life each day and record on his tape machine a target word centering around this event. Meanwhile, Dale was told only that she must try to dream about Ullman's target word, which, of course, she knew nothing about. Since this short series of sixteen nights somewhat resembles the later experimental series, let us examine it in more detail.

On the first day, June 15, Ullman resolved to give up smoking. So his target word that night was *smoking*. That night Dale had two dreams: In one, she took her dog home from the hospital without the vet's permission. In the other dream, she and her brother (often a symbol of Ullman, whom he physically resembled) were staying in someone else's apartment. No correspondence.

On June 16, Ullman went with a friend to pick up his dog, which had strayed — a similar situation to Dale's dream of picking up her dog. Ullman's target word that night was *lost dog*. He was still trying to give up smoking.

Dale's dream the next morning was: "I was going to a lecture hall where I was supposed to give a presentation. But the chairman didn't call on me — he called on a man who gave a long speech, illustrating it at the blackboard. I felt resentful at not being called up, but also relieved at not having to get up in front of the crowd.... Groups were standing on a flight of stairs *smoking*...."

The incidental reference to smoking was a day late, but it was interesting since none of her other dreams had ever referred to smoking. But what about being passed over for a presentation at a lecture hall? That might have reflected Ullman's mild anxiety about a talk he was scheduled to give a few days later, but it might also be related to a letter Dale received a few days later from England. She had been scheduled to chair a meeting on "haunts" at a conference there, but learned that a European parapsychologist was to do it instead. As in her dream, Dale noted in her diary, "Great relief to me."

On June 18, Dale recalled no dreams. A sure miss.

But on the next night, Ullman's target word was *successful party*—reflecting the success of a party that he and his wife had attended that night. The Ullmans, incidentally, had been unable to attend two other parties that night to which they had been invited. The next morning, Dale dreamed: "I was a guest in a very swell house. I was sitting in the kitchen with my brother. A gay *party* was going on upstairs.... My brother had not been invited to this party and I said he had better leave...." A direct hit on the target word.

On June 20, Ullman's target word was *Ralph,* the name of the son of acquaintances. Ullman had visited them and was shocked to find that their boy was confined to his room. He was mentally retarded and his actions were erratic and unpredictable, especially in the presence of strangers. His thin frame was tense with embarrassment and dread.

That night Dale dreamed "I went to a prison and was taken to a cell where a young man lay in agony on a cot. I could see his face very clearly ... thin, tense ... in a waiting mood ... and his slight body. He was a dope addict awaiting the horrors of withdrawal symptoms. He was not yet at the height of them, but was in a state of profound dread."

This close correspondence with the target was one of the most interesting correspondences in this series. Out of all the events experienced during the day by Ullman, the target event, a young man being confined, came through in Dale's dream with only minimal elaboration.

The next night showed no great correspondence with the target, the name of one of Ullman's patients, and the next few days were also barren of correspondences.

On June 27, however, Ullman's target word was *Alfresco*—referring to an alfresco or lawn party at which a large painted canvas had been displayed as a "fake fresco" in a spirit of punning fun. In Dale's dream that night, she "was visiting a beautiful chateau in France. I admired the lawn and said so to someone who was with me. Then I examined the lawn more closely and found it was a fake, it was actually a huge green carpet...." Dale's preoccupation with a fake lawn seems to correlate well with a lawn party featuring a "fake fresco."

On the next two nights Dale had no recall of dreams, but on June 30, she dreamed, "I was in England, in the home of a family that had a crippled child in a wheelchair. It had been born without legs...."

Nothing quite so drastic was occurring at the Ullman home, but there did seem to be a relation to the target word *surgery,* which referred to surgery undergone the day before by Ullman's sister-in-law who was to convalesce at the Ullman home.

On the final night of the series, July 1, Dale's dream seemed to have nothing to do with the target word (a friend whom Ullman visited that day) but it was an odd dream for Dale:

> My brother and I were attending a medical convention in Atlantic City. We got there and found only a very few people were attending. . . . The stimulus went off and woke me. I heard Monte's voice, very clear, saying "Give me my badge" instead of the words actually on the tape.

It seemed almost as if Dale were dreaming Ullman's dream; she had never been to a medical convention in Atlantic City, but Ullman had. In fact, this dream seems almost like a continuation of Ullman's earlier dream of May 4, 1955, in which he was confronting the FBI in Atlantic City. "Give me my badge," becomes clearer when an association is made with the FBI, and Ullman is awarded his "badge" for standing up to them.

Such tentative musings on the possible interrelatedness of two people's lives and dreams must remain as subjective impressions; there is no apparent way to consider them in any objective or statistical relationship. In attempting to assess correspondences between dreams and events, Ullman concentrated on the non-inferential manifest content rather than symbolic correspondences.

Out of their combined total of 501 dreams (283 for Dale, 218 for Ullman), they noted about 10 percent (58) as being probably paranormal. In the last series, when target words were used for sixteen nights, there was a good correlation on four nights, a mild correspondence on two nights, and none on the remaining ten — on six of those nights Dale didn't record any dreams. So, out of ten nights on which Dale had dreams, six seemed to show some paranormal correspondence — a very high proportion as compared with the earlier tests.

Did the tape-recorded stimulus word with accompanying instructions to recall a dream make any difference? Apparently so, though it may well be that the command to remember the dream was more significant than the stimulus word itself. Out of the 58 significant dreams, 45 had been recorded on "stimulus" mornings.

A significant feature in the differences between Dale's and Ullman's dreams was that Dale dreamed more often of Ullman (or his symbol, her brother) than Ullman dreamed of Dale. This seemed to correlate with Dale's greater success in incorporating events of Ullman's life into her dreams — as if she were more talented at "reaching out"; or conversely, that Ullman was more talented at "sending."

Dale's frequent dreams about events in the life of Janet Ullman might, in psychoanalytic thought, be connected to the triangularity involved in an exchange between a man and a woman in which the man's wife is not involved. Other areas of special sensitivity related to anxiety-producing events or events which carry a strong emotional impact.

While valuable in probing the possibilities of telepathic dreaming, this exploratory experiment had several drawbacks. There was no way of knowing when a dream would occur. On many nights no dreams were recalled at all. There seemed to be no way to properly evaluate the material in statistical form. Cicero's complaint was as valid as ever. Yet, there were correspondences that *seemed* to be unlikely by chance alone.

Time was also a problem. Although paranormal correspondences between dreams and events clustered around a simultaneous time axis (to be interpreted as telepathy), a number of these correspondences spread out in time, both before and after. This finding was similar to that of Whately Carington, who noted such displacement effects in his telepathy experiments with drawings. If dream telepathy were to be experimentally demonstrated, however, it would be necessary to narrow the focus to same-time dream and event. Therefore it would be necessary to know *exactly* when a person was dreaming so that a target could be simultaneously "transmitted."

Parapsychologists have devised tests to determine whether persons can acquire information that is shielded from their sense perception (ESP), and have sought to differentiate such forms of ESP as telepathy (ESP of another person's thoughts), clairvoyance (ESP of external objects and events), and precognition (ESP of a future event). What we are calling "dream telepathy" *could* be interpreted as clairvoyance (the dreamer's knowledge of the written target word rather than the target word in the agent's mind), or precognition (the dreamer's foreknowledge of the revealed target). Some parapsychologists use the term "general ESP" or GESP when it is impossible for a clear differentiation to be made between, say, telepathy and clairvoyance. For simplicity, however, we will continue to use the term "dream telepathy" as we describe further experiments.

CHAPTER 6

Moving Eye Witnesses

The study of sleep and dreams took an enormous step forward during the 1950s when scientists at the University of Chicago discovered that the state of sleep we call dreaming has fairly reliable physiological correlates. In 1952 Eugene Aserinsky, a young physiologist working with Dr. Nathaniel Kleitman, the distinguished authority on sleep, noted that when a subject's brain waves were recorded by an electroencephalograph (EEG) continuously throughout the night, rapid movements of the eyes periodically occurred. This was associated with electrical activity of the brain resembling the waking state. If the subject were awakened at this point, he was apt to report a dream.

In September 1953, Aserinsky and Kleitman published in the journal *Science*[1] their first experimental report on the topic. It was titled "Regularly Occurring Periods of Eye Motility and Concomitant Phenomena During Sleep." The "Regularly Occurring Periods of Eye Motility" are now called Rapid Eye Movements (REMs), while the "Concomitant Phenomena During Sleep" have the age-old name of dreams.

In the years since this discovery enormous progress has been made in elucidating the physiological nature of sleep and dreaming. Importantly, for research on dreams themselves, the former hit-and-miss method of collecting dreams then gave way to sophisticated techniques utilizing the EEG to indicate the best time to awaken a subject for a dream report.

As an interesting footnote, it might be added that Hans Berger devised the electroencephalograph in Germany in 1929 to amplify and record minute electrical pulses in the brain and that Berger by employing this tool hoped to reveal the energy responsible for telepathy. It is now known, of course, that these extremely minute electrical currents of the brain could not account for the great distances traversed by ESP, and, as Soviet parapsychologist Leonid Vasiliev has demonstrated,[2] ESP does not appear to be affected by conventional electrical shielding.

Although not as mysterious as ESP, the phenomenon of rapid eye movements that accompany dreaming still provokes controversy. Some researchers, basing their opinions on controlled experiments, link the back-and-forth movement of the eye to action being watched in the dream. If a person dreams about watching a tennis match, with its side-to-side action, her eyes move back and forth. If a person dreams about someone walking up and down a flight of stairs, his eyes move up and down.

Still other researchers link REMs with scanning activity. When we walk into a strange room our eyes dart back and forth to take in as much as possible. Perhaps this scanning activity — shared with other mammals — is part of our instinctual apparatus for self-preservation, a vigilance that persists periodically even through sleep.

Another hypothesis put forward by researchers investigating the differences between amphibians, with eyes on opposite sides of the head, and mammals is that rapid eye movements serve to train the mammal's eyes to work together. Amphibians, whose eyes do not have to work together, show little rapid eye movement.

Another puzzling physiological concomitant of dreaming is penile erections in men and sexual arousal in women. This is not linked with erotic content of the dream but seems to be a merely physiological response, which suggests a common area in the brain that influences both dreaming and sexual arousal.

As an indicator of dreaming, rapid eye movements alone are not sufficient. The sleeper must also be in what is referred to as emergent Stage I sleep. (Sleep is commonly divided into four stages, each with its characteristic EEG brainwave pattern. The subject does not dream during the initial, or descending Stage I. Dreaming occurs in subsequent or emergent Stage I periods.) For the sleep researchers watching the EEG's pens recording a graph of a person's brainwaves, this means that they must wait until the brain channels show the emergent Stage I phase and the eye channels indicate the occurrence of REMs. Then they can be fairly certain that the subject is dreaming.

Virtually everybody has at least four dream periods a night. They occur at the approximate rate of one every ninety minutes. The dream periods start out as short, about ten minutes or less, and end up in the morning considerably longer and sometimes lasting half an hour or more. This last dream is generally the one we tend to remember in the morning and is liable to be more elaborate than the earlier dreams.

Of the many variables affecting dreaming, age has perhaps the strongest effect. Studies of newborn children have shown that they spend about fifty percent of their sleeping time in REM sleep, while adults dream only about twenty percent of their sleeping time. As old age approaches, this percent diminishes even further.

As might be expected, the physiological study of sleep and dreaming has had an enormous impact on theorizing about why we dream. The question is still far from being settled, but we can at least draw the distinction between variables that *influence* dreaming and the actual *cause* of dreaming. Emotional conflicts, events of the day, anticipated stress and dangers certainly influence the content of dreams, but we still go through the regular, cyclic process of dreaming no matter what combination of variables may have been acting on us.

Individual styles of dreaming vary as much as our psychological patterns. In studies by Herman A. Witkin and his associates, people were divided by psychological tests into categories of "more-differentiated" and "less-differentiated." The "more-differentiated" persons tend to be more inner directed and rely less on outside influences than the "less-differentiated" persons who rely more on the outside world for their sense of identity. Characteristically, more-differentiated persons tend to use isolation and intellectualization as psychological defenses, whereas the less-differentiated rely more on denial and repression.

The tendency among the less-differentiated to repress conflicts correlated with their inability to recall dreams, while the more-differentiated tended to report dreams more often. Comparison of the content of the dreams showed that the more-differentiated were also more imaginative in their dreaming.

Some people, apparently the less-differentiated, claim that they never dream at all. One such person was a young psychiatrist undergoing his own analysis. His lack of dream recall was an embarrassment for one who was to become a specialist in dream interpretation. He went to the University of Chicago dream laboratory with a request that he spend the night there to see if they could help him. About an hour and a half after the psychiatrist fell asleep, the EEG showed the beginnings of Stage I sleep and the rapid eye movements. The lab assistant waited a few minutes before awakening the alleged "non-dreamer." "At first," the assistant said, "he said he wasn't dreaming, just thinking. Then he said, 'Wait a minute. I remember a conversation. Somebody called me a sad son-of-a-bitch.'"[3] This was his first dream. If they were all like that, one can understand why he repressed them.

So it seems that virtually *everyone* dreams, whether they remember the dreams or not. Indeed, if a person is prevented from dreaming over a sufficiently long period of time the consequences can be dire—he or she may start to hallucinate in the waking state.

Some of the blind (depending on whether or not the eye muscles have atrophied) also have REM periods and accompanying dreams, although these dreams are not visual unless some degree of vision was present before blindness set in. Helen Keller, who as an infant lost her senses of sight, hearing, and smell, described a moving dream experience in her autobiography:

> Once in a dream I held in my hand a pearl. I have no memory-vision of a
> real pearl. The one I saw in my dream must, therefore, have been a creation

of my imagination. It was a smooth, exquisitely molded crystal. As I gazed into its shimmering deeps, my soul was flooded with an ecstasy of tenderness, I was filled with wonder, as one who should for the first time look into the cool, sweet heart of a rose. My pearl was dew and fire, the velvety green of moss, the soft whiteness of lilies, and the distilled hues and sweetness of a thousand roses. It seemed to me the soul of beauty was dissolved in its crystal bosom.....[4]

Helen Keller's experience of seeing color in her dreams would come as no surprise to the modern dream researchers who have found that people dream in color far more than is realized. Often the dreamer takes color for granted. He or she may report, for instance, walking on a grassy path. When the experimenter asks if any color was in the dream, the sleeper is likely to reply indignantly that the grass was green — of course. Some people always dream in color, while most others dream occasionally in color or have elements of color in their dreams, though these may be forgotten when recalling the dream in the morning.

People can in some degree train themselves to remember dreams by giving themselves the suggestion to remember the dream before they go to sleep. Then in the morning, they should lie quietly in bed and allow their mind to dwell on the first thing that comes up. The first waking thoughts may remind them of their last dream and allow them to remember more and more details of the dream, working backward from the last remembered fragment. Trying this several mornings in a row, and writing down the dreams, often proves successful.

Infrequent dream recall may be partially conditioned by our cultural bias against discussing dreams. If children tell their parents their dreams the parents are likely to remark that it is "nonsense" and that they should not pay any attention to it. "It is only a dream." If, on the other hand, a culture should regard dreams as meaningful and worthy of discussion, the children may be far more apt to have good dream recall.

A commonly-held notion about dreams is that they last for only a few seconds while portraying events of a much longer duration. This idea stems from a book written by a nineteenth-century Frenchman, Alfred Maury, who cited a dream in which he found himself being tried during the French Revolution and sent to the guillotine. He felt the blade fall, but awoke to find that the bedrail had fallen on his neck. He reasoned that the physical stimulus of the bedrail falling on his neck had triggered the dream, compressing events of days into seconds.

It is not yet known whether some individuals might be able to accelerate "time" in their dreams, akin to hypnotic time distortion in which hypnotized subjects are able to compress events of days into minutes, or if the time-rate of dreaming is always constant. Perhaps it is speeded up at the beginning or ending of the dream, while in the middle it progresses more slowly. These are questions that must be investigated by further research. Most modern researchers using the EEG-REM technique have found that the dream time matches fairly well with the duration of the events, though the dream often uses the cinematic technique of cutting from one scene to another.

For instance, a boat trip from America to Europe in a dream would not require a week but would only need to show the boarding, a few minutes on the boat, and the disembarking, much as a movie shows the essential elements. The mind of the viewer makes the necessary connections.

Maury's theory that dreams are caused by external stimulation has now been modified to show that dreams can be *influenced* by such stimulation. When someone held a burning match under the nose of the sleeping Maury, he had a dream that he was at sea and that the powder magazine of the ship had blown up. Holding cologne under his nose produced a dream of a perfume factory in Cairo. Twanging a pair of tweezers in his ear led to a dream of bells ringing during the Paris revolution, and so on.

During the experiment described in the previous chapter, in which a tape-recorded stimulus awoke Ullman, a similar effect was found. The waking sound recorded on the tape was that of a Chinese gong. The first time Ullman tried the experiment on himself, he had the following dream. "I dreamed that bells were sounding in a nearby church. It occurred to me that since this was the case [that the bells had already awakened him] the stimulus record would be unnecessary.... I was somewhat puzzled in the dream as I did not think there were any churches that close to my home."

How many of us have had similar dreams when we hear the alarm clock go off in the morning. We may dream that church bells are ringing — that it is Sunday — and we don't have to get up to go to work.

Experimental explorations aimed at influencing dream content by presleep stimulation have included showing emotion-laden films and using hypnotic suggestion. In an experiment by Dr. Johann Stoyva[5] at the University of Chicago, subjects were hypnotized before bed time, were told to dream about a certain theme (but that they would forget the hypnotic suggestion), and then were allowed to go to sleep. When the EEG indicated a dreaming state, the subjects were awakened for their dream reports.

When the subjects were given the hypnotic suggestion, "You will dream in every dream tonight of climbing a tree," they had the following dreams.

Subject 1

We made a,... an outing trip, and I don't know where we went; we went through the *woods*. We marched and marched. Oh, it was very colorful, very much so....

Mmmmmhh, I'm walking, I don't know, with people. I'm going places in *woods* and then we climbed on an apple tree to pick some ripe beautiful apples.

I was dreaming about ... Egypt, my beloved Egypt! And I was taking people to a tomb in Upper Egypt. And we were looking for some shadow, people to a tomb in Upper Egypt. And we were looking for some shadow, shade — couldn't find any. And I took them inside to some of the king's tombs so that we could escape the strong heat.

It was a long trip along the Nile and we were thirsty and were looking for some shade — couldn't find it. *Trees* were very scarce there. So we visited some tombs in the meantime to escape the strong heat and I showed them all some beautiful paintings in the king's tombs. . .

Subject 2

There's this old *maple* in front of our house in Philadelphia. It used to scratch against the window and, ahhh, sometimes we had to cut off the *branches*. So, I don't know, usually we just go out on the roof but we were *all going up the tree* by the base to do it. All of us. The whole family and my grandmother — and she's been dead for about five years now. We couldn't get up it and just scratching (sic) against the windows and making scraping noises.

Note how each dreamer supplies his or her own content for the tree-climbing task, based on his or her past experiences. Apparently Subject 1, after he had successfully climbed an apple tree, felt relieved that he could now dream about more interesting memories of Egypt — where tree-climbing is an unlikely activity. Since climbing trees is an activity associated with childhood, it is not surprising that Subject 2 dreamed about a childhood scene.

Not all the subjects were so successful in incorporating the hypnotist's suggestion into their dreams. Sometimes the subject's dream would have only a slight thematic relationship with the suggestion. For example, when the suggestion was, "You will dream in every dream tonight that you are rowing a boat," the subject dreamed: "I was standing by our *pool* at home. Then I decided to call up my girl-friend for a date. That's all I can remember."

Sometimes the hypnotic suggestion drew a complete blank. When a subject was told to dream about swimming a river, he dreamed instead that "I was taking a test. It was very much like filling out the form here tonight. You were in it, too. My EEG wires were all tangled up."

It is well to keep in mind that the artificial situation of the dream laboratory can have a great influence on the content of dreaming.

A somewhat similar study was done by Dr. Charles Tart at the University of California at Davis in which ten subjects were given posthypnotic suggestions, narrated and played on a tape recorder, by which they were to dream about a threatening situation. In their natural sleep later, the subjects reported their dreams. Five of the ten subjects showed not a single element of the stimulus in their dreams. The dreams of the five successful subjects ranged from a very low to a quite high incorporation. As Tart remarks,

> The reported dreams, even those showing the greatest effects of the post-hypnotic suggestions, were not straightforward reproductions of the stimulus narrative. Rather, there was considerable embellishment. The best subject, e.g., constantly added a happy ending to the dreamed about stimulus narrative rather than being left stranded in a fearful situation![6]

A closer model to dream telepathy would be speaking something to the subject while he or she is asleep and dreaming. The closest experimental approach to this was carried out by the sleep researcher Dr. Ralph Berger. When subjects were having REM periods, Berger would repeatedly speak out personal names to them. The dream reports were then transcribed and both the subjects and independent judges tried to match the dream reports with the stimulus names. They did almost equally well in the matching, getting 32 right out of 78, with a success level of 40 percent. The actual name turned up in the dreams only rarely. Sometimes a person with the actual name appeared in the dream or there were common associations between the name of a dream representation. In most of the successes, though, the target name was changed to a similar sounding word (so-called "klang" associations).

Berger concluded that

> perception of the external world, be it impaired, does occur in the REM periods associated with dreaming. However, the external origin of such perception is not normally recognized and external stimuli are perceived as belonging to the events of the dreams. Furthermore, it seems that perceptual awareness is coincident with cortical analysis (processing by the brain) of the stimulus, but is not dependent upon the significance of the stimulus to the sleeper . . . although the manner in which the stimulus is perceived sometimes appears to depend upon its meaning to the sleeper.[7]

Berger's findings constitute strong evidence that the dreamer is scanning his or her environment for information, responding to stimuli, and incorporating these stimuli into his or her dreams in a disguised and personal manner. Of course someone speaking names into his or her ear is scarcely a sufficient threat to the dreamer to test his or her vigilance. What would happen if the experimenter said, "I'm going to cut your throat!" We would not be surprised if the subject woke up at that moment. It should make an interesting experiment some day — if not an unnerving one for the subject.

Nearly every mother can testify to great selectivity in responding to outside stimuli while asleep. A truck rumbles by an open window. She turns, still soundly asleep. Her infant child in the next room begins to cry, and instantly she is awake.

Although REM sleep is a time when the sleeping brain most closely resembles the waking brain in its degree of excitation, mental activity occurs also in other stages of sleep. Sleepers awakened during non–REM periods report more conceptual thinking, less perceptual material, and, in general, content that is less vivid, emotional, or distorted. These non–REM "dreams" seem to be populated by fewer people but bear a greater correspondence to the sleeper's daily life than the REM dreams.

A few rare individuals, who have trained themselves to control their bodily and mental processes, have an unusual degree of awareness of their external environment while asleep. This was dramatically demonstrated by

Swami Rama at the Menninger Foundation laboratory in experiments conducted by Elmer Green[8] and his associates. When the Swami was emitting very slow brain waves (which characterize a "deep" stage of sleep not associated with dreams) Dr. Green's wife walked across the room and became engaged in some activity. After the Swami was awakened, he reported in detail what had been happening in the room while he was theoretically "dead to the world." Characteristically, in that stage of sleep, we are not responsive to nor aware of what is going on around us.

The question of how individuals vary in their special abilities, especially during sleep, brings us back to our prime question about the occurrence of ESP in dreams. Is dream-mediated ESP a rare occurrence that happens only to a few specially talented people? Or is it an experience that any of us might have under optimum conditions?

The EEG-REM technique of monitoring dreams has answered Cicero's questions, "Can dreams be experimented on?" and "By what method can this infinite variety be either fixed in memory or analyzed by reason?"

Now, finally we can tackle the question of whether it is possible to experimentally induce telepathic dreams.

CHAPTER 7

A Dream Comes to Life

With the advent of the REM-EEG technique for monitoring dreams, Montague Ullman thought it had become feasible to attempt experimental explorations of dream telepathy. In 1960 he began its planning: One would need an electroencephalograph, a sleep laboratory, a staff, and some experimental subjects. The last might volunteer, but the rest would involve a great deal of money. Ullman proposed his idea to Eileen Garrett, then president of the Parapsychology Foundation, and, until her death in 1970, one of history's most renowned mediums. Garrett had funded many parapsychological experiments through her foundation and had participated as a subject in countless ESP experiments. She believed that Ullman's plan would be a suitable project for her foundation and that it might shed light on some of her own dream experiences, such as one she related in her book *Telepathy.*

In London, one night, I had gone to bed with a strange feeling that all was not well with my daughter, who was then away at school. It was a Sunday evening, and so I discounted the experience when I recalled that she was probably writing her usual weekly letter, believing that I had "caught" her thoughts. I awoke, however, at two o'clock in the morning with the impression that she was in the house, and had just been at my side talking to me. In the dream she had said, "I have not written you, dear, as my chest hurt. Tonight I am coughing, and have a fever. When the principal found that I hadn't written, she was very cross, and called me neglectful and undutiful; but now she has been in my room, and understands that I am not well."

Although I was still uncertain of the validity of this communication, I decided to write down what she had said. The next morning I again felt disturbed, since no letter had arrived. Remembering my dream, I telegraphed the head-mistress to inquire if all was well. In her reply she stated that my daughter was in bed with a heavy chest cold, and then continued, half-apologetically, to blame what she termed the child's "sullen behavior," in refusing to write to me, on the illness.

A subsequent letter from my daughter suggested that she had felt confused, "not well, hurt, and misunderstood in the evening." These were the "feelings" that I had "caught" in the waking state, before retiring, while the ensuing dream had revealed her illness and the cause of her emotional disturbance, at a time when we were both sleeping...[1]

Garrett was eager to see such dream experiences validated in a scientific way and put at Ullman's disposal her research personnel, Karlis Osis and E. Douglas Dean, both prominent parapsychologists. Two rooms at the foundation were outfitted for an EEG room and a sleep room. A four-channel EEG was installed in the EEG room along with a two-way intercom system connected to the sleep room so that the sleeping subject could be awakened to report his or her dream and have it recorded on tape.

Garrett agreed to serve as subject for the first experiment, which was to take place on June 6, 1960, and was to deal with long-distance telepathy. Dr. Osis selected a target pool of three pictures from *Life* magazine, sealed them in envelopes, and gave them to Garrett's secretary to take to her home many miles away. She was to wait for a phone call from the foundation to tell her when Garrett was beginning to dream so that she could choose a target and concentrate on it in an attempt to transmit it telepathically.

Garrett arrived at the foundation about 8 P.M., was wired to the EEG with electrodes, and went to bed in the sleep room. For this initial attempt, she planned to stay only to midnight. She explained that she tended to sleep in intermittent catnaps, and this was borne out by the EEG record. Dean and Ullman watched the EEG tracing looking in vain for indications of dreaming. Disappointed that the procedure did not seem to be working, they did not telephone Garrett's secretary. However, at 11:00, Ullman was surprised to hear from Garrett that she recalled a dream: She was watching horses furiously running uphill, and they reminded her of the chariot race in *Ben Hur,* which she had seen two weeks before.

Not until two weeks later did Ullman learn that the target pictures from *Life* included a color photo of the chariot race in *Ben Hur.* This stunning correspondence seemed encouraging, even though Garrett's dream seemed to have picked up the target by direct clairvoyance rather than by telepathy, as her secretary had never opened the sealed envelope.

Roman epics turned up again in her next experiment on the night of October 19, 1960, some four months later. On that occasion Garrett spent the night at the laboratory and reported a total of six dreams. Ullman, stationed in the EEG room, was to act as "agent" and was to concentrate on a picture chosen at random from a target pool made up by Osis. About midnight, still waiting for Garrett's first dream, Ullman was musing about the book *Spartacus,* by Howard Fast, which describes a Roman slave revolt that ended in crucifixion for Spartacus and his followers by Roman soldiers. Ullman doodled, drawing some crucifix-like figures, and continued to think about Spartacus.

Garrett's first dream, at 1:45 A.M., involved the following. "I went to see a Roman picture . . . I think that *Spartacus* was the thing that I was going to see. But I never went inside; I was standing on the outside looking at pictures of Roman soldiers—Roman invasion. . . ."[2] (In the morning, Garrett added that she had not seen the currently advertised film *Spartacus* but would like to now.)

After Garrett related her dream and was going back to sleep, Ullman opened the target picture: a black-and-white photo of a doctor examining a patient seated on an examining table. Intrigued by his apparent success of transmitting Spartacus, Ullman decided to combine his own associations with the picture. He drew freehand sketches of a sword for Spartacus and a stethoscope for the doctor.

About two hours later, at 4:30, Garrett's fifth dream seemed to combine Ullman's images. "I saw my doctor yesterday and he was at the Olympic Games; we talked about the Olympic Games and Rome. . . . Then I saw a picture of two men and they were swordsmen but that again may be something to do with him because he is a fencer. . . ."

Somehow, a dream that combines Rome, swordsmen (two men), and a doctor seems highly unlikely, by chance alone, to have corresponded with the targets.

In the next experimental session with Garrett, Ullman was again the agent. The target picture was a photo of a metallic gold South American Indian mask—a somewhat grotesque face having closed eyes and surmounted by three circles. Ullman was surprised to see the circles because before he opened the target envelope he had drawn four sketches with variations of three circles.

Garrett dreamed not of three circles but of three pictures.

> There are several abstracts, and one of them is fascinating because it is a kind of three-dimensional picture . . . It has a Mexican look to it . . . there are several pictures and there is one that looks as though it were a sunburst. There is a lot of yellow in it . . . I was very struck by the three pictures. One Mexican-looking, one sunburst, and then there was one which seemed to have two figures and their faces were slightly distorted as though they had just fallen down tired and were kind of sleeping. . . .

Garrett seemed to have divided the face into three pictures, for "Mexican-looking," "sunburst-yellow," and "two faces" being "slightly distorted as though they had just fallen down tired" accurately described the mask. The other tired face may have belonged to Ullman, for the time was 4:17 in the morning.

Another dream of Garrett's that night seemed to relate to a situation three thousand miles away. Appearing in her dream was the psychical researcher Whately Carington, who had died in 1947. Carington urged Garrett to write to his widow in England. He seemed to be concerned with some unpublished papers. This dream was reinforced by two more dreams in the following days, prompting Garrett to write Carington's widow. In this way, Garrett learned that the widow was ill and in difficult financial circumstances. Garrett was able to arrange for her to be hospitalized and for his papers to be sent to the foundation. Although Garrett had never met Carington personally, she had published the American edition of his book *Telepathy*.

Garrett's success at dream telepathy seemed to show that her ESP ability, as demonstrated in waking states and in the trance state, carried over to the dream state. Her trance personalities have been the subject of a great deal of study by psychical researchers and psychiatrists, though the true nature of the "controls" continues to remain elusive. When Hereward Carrington (no relation to Whately) asked her trance personality "Uvani" what happens to her mind when she goes to sleep, the reply was:

> Very much what happens to it when I come in, only more so in her case than in those who are less psychic ... At the time when I take control, the soul goes out to gain experience and refreshment. Very much the same thing happens in sleep. Not in the spirit state, as generally supposed. It is not possible to get the full expression of those who have passed over. The soul can project itself into all kinds of experiences, and return to impress these memories upon the mind at the moment of waking.[3]

It should be added that Garrett herself felt ambiguous toward her controls, sometimes suspecting them to be fragments of her unconscious mind but still retaining respect for what they said. And certainly, as we shall see, it was demonstrated that Garrett's dreams tended to show more ESP than the dreams of those who are less psychic.

When a psychiatrist was a dream telepathy subject, the target concentrated on by Ullman was a picture of a colored mosaic. The color violet, prominent in the picture, came through a couple of references. However, a more startling reference seemed to describe a situation that had disturbed Ullman's wife the night before. She was rehearsing in a chorus for a Christmas concert and, along with the others, was dismayed when the conductor expressed great dissatisfaction with their performance and threatened to storm out.

The psychiatrist's dream references (his fourth dream in one night) to this included the following: "I was dreaming of a conference, like instead of a conference it was like chamber music. Someone had a baton." When questioned further about this image, the doctor added: "Yes, it was like a chorus, but not a formal chorus. But the leader was kind of angry ... he was going to leave...."

The theme was repeated in the sixth dream: "There was a group of singers. The director was to leave the group..."

This correspondence seemed reminiscent of Dale's dreams (see Chapter 5) about Ullman's wife, especially when she was experiencing an anxiety-provoking situation.

A similar relationship arose in the next dream study, in which Ullman acted as the sleeping subject. Acting as agent was Douglas Dean, who was assisting in the experiment. The target did not seem to be incorporated in Ullman's dreams, but the following dream was interesting for other reasons. "I was listening to the Kentucky Derby being broadcast on the radio. I could hear all the excitement. And there was so much excitement I couldn't hear who the winner was. Somewhere in the room on a shelf in a container was a check. It was blank. I recall wondering what it was doing there."

Dean's association with the Kentucky Derby referred to the day before when he had received a note from friends who wanted to take him to the Kentucky Derby. The "blank check" in Ullman's dream seemed to relate to their son who had recently been convicted of passing bad checks. Ullman's own associations to the dream were of his father, a devotee of horse racing who often attended the Kentucky Derby. As Ullman noted before going to sleep, Dean strikingly resembled his father in body build — and it may be that this incidental fact operated as a facilitating link for the Kentucky Derby associations, which is in line with the Carington association theory.

An experimental night with a dentist as subject, with Ullman as agent, produced effects similar to those in Garrett's dream in which two targets were combined. The first part of the night a model of a yellow Citroen automobile was used, and then later a photograph was used of a monk meditating at the corner of an oriental garden that was bordered with a walk of large diamond-shaped stones. After a dream including references to a yellow road and a tractor-like vehicle, the dentist dreamed the following. "Approaching a masonry wall, with the stones put together very, very neatly. And someone else and I are seated in the cab of some large vehicle. There seemed to be a tractor coming up through this wall. . . . The wall is gray in color, and there are mortar clean stones."

The next dream described the wall as having a "small diamond-shaped hole." Yellow, vehicle, mortar clean stones, wall, diamond-shaped holes — the descriptors seemed right on.

Throughout the experimental nights so far recorded, Ullman's main concern was in exploring the possibilities of transferring target images directly into the manifest content of the sleeping subject's dream. A number of striking correspondences between the targets and the dreams indicated that this was possible, although by no means possible in every attempt. Yet, as a number of psychoanalytically oriented researchers had shown, the dream's latent content, or symbolic significance, often revealed strong correlations with sexual conflicts and other matters of deep concern to the individual.

As a psychoanalytic practitioner, Ullman speculated on the possibilities of using telepathy as a means for influencing the symbolism of dreams. When

Ullman drew a circle and concentrated on its symbolic female character, the sleeper (a psychiatrist) dreamed of going through the Holland Tunnel. Additional geometric figures were used as targets that night, and, somewhat confused, the psychiatrist wondered "why so many geometrical figures seemed to appear in my dreams."

A more extensive opportunity for experimentation with dream symbols arose when a forty-two-year-old theatrical publicity agent — we will call him Joe — volunteered as a subject.

Joe, a stranger to Ullman, had been in analysis with another psychiatrist for one year. He had not told his analyst that he had come for the experiment, which took place on July 11, 1960. When asked whether he had had any personal ESP experiences, he replied: "I feel that uncanny things have happened many times. I feel as if I lead a charmed life. I firmly think there is something to it."

Joe then reviewed a dream involving a conflict between jobs; his analyst had interpreted it as relating to the duality of his sex life, which was actively bisexual.

After Joe was wired with electrodes and put to bed, Ullman also slept for an hour. On waking, Ullman's thoughts went back to a psychoanalytic session earlier that day with a patient who was very much like Joe and who was also "bisexual with profound homosexual conflicts." Joe could not recall his dream on being waked from a REM period, but he mentioned that before falling asleep he had been thinking about music. His association to this was: "My analyst thought I had substituted an interest in music for 'cruising'!"

Half an hour later, Joe had this dream: "I went to bed with a female producer; also with a Negro actress. I saw a play. It was called *The Legend of Lizzie*. It was about Lizzie Borden."

The dream strengthened Ullman's association with his patient, who that day had spoken about physical acts of violence in his family, particularly of his mother toward his father, and also of himself toward his wife. This assumed some significance when Ullman learned from the EEG technician of the limerick, "Lizzie Borden took an axe, gave her mother forty whacks." Joe's dream seemed to express hostility toward women, since in life he disliked the woman producer and disdained blacks.

At 3:35, Joe reported the following dream. "I was in Provincetown with my friends Mary and Jack. It was very pleasant."

By a very striking coincidence, Mary and Jack were also the names of an actor and his wife that Ullman had been trying to recall that afternoon; like Joe, the actor was bisexual.

When Joe started his fifth REM period, Ullman drew a small circle and concentrated on it. Joe's dream "involved my sister and a banjo. She wouldn't teach me how to play. She and her husband were standing like in a Grant Wood painting, only they were using banjos instead of pitchforks. She's

divorced now." In the morning, he added: "I like the banjo. I have been playing banjo records lately. My sister does not know how to play. In the dream
they were suddenly standing stiff and rigid, with severe expressions on their
faces. . . ."

Ullman's reaction to the dream's symbolism was that a banjo represented
a sexualization of the circle (female) with the addition of a phallic symbol. (A
similar traditional symbolization of the male and female genitalia is the ancient Egyptian *ankh,* which looks something like an upside-down banjo. This
same symbol is found in the place of genitalia on an ancient Indian god
represented as being bisexual.) Joe's difficulty in uniting his male and female
aspects (banjo) in response to women is shown by his sister's reaction: "She
wouldn't teach me how to play." Ullman noted, "The dream seemed to be expressing once again the superiority of the female and her ability to refuse him
that which he desires. If this line of interpretation is correct, he appears to
have shifted from an instrument of crude aggression to a music or sexual instrument."

Joe's next dream shifted to a male figure: "I was thinking of Murray, a
client, a comedian." His association was: "Murray was just fun. He's about
twenty-eight, but he's really a child—he's really only about twelve."

Joe's shift to a male figure with a positive affective tone led Ullman to
sketch a phallic symbol and concentrate on its sexuality.

Joe's dream a few minutes later was this: "I was with Al. He is the principal dancer in a current show. He was dancing with me. He said, 'This is
for you.' We were sitting at a bar. We were drinking. I went home with him,
but I couldn't face his wife. I felt embarrassed for his wife." Joe later stated
that he had had a homosexual liaison with Al, who had been married for ten
years. The dream's distinct homosexual overtones seemed to be in response
to the sexualized target.

While it is not possible to make any definite conclusions from this brief
study, it was nonetheless suggestive of symbol transformation and psychodynamic interplay mediated by psi. Such a technique of capturing dream sequences as they occur could offer a unique opportunity for the study of inter-
relations between personality, symbol formation, and the role played by psi
in psychodynamic interactions.

During the year and a half that the pilot experiments at the Parapsychology Foundation ran, there was an enormous range in the sensitivity
of the subjects to incorporate telepathic elements in their dreams. At one end
of the spectrum was a known psychic sensitive, Garrett, who demonstrated
great ability; at the other end were three subjects whose dreams showed
no apparent paranormal sensitivity. Two of the three subjects were chosen
because of their negative attitude toward ESP, which would test the nocturnal aspects of the "Sheep-Goat" hypothesis of Gertrude Schmeidler that
believers in ESP score above chance while disbelievers score at or below

chance in ESP tests.[4] The third subject had no particular interest in ESP but merely wanted to record his dreams. Since at this stage there was no system of evaluation against chance, we would say that at face value the disbelievers in ESP either had no ability or succeeded in blocking it. Since such all-night experiments are expensive — upwards of one hundred dollars a night — this hypothesis for null effects did not seem to warrant further exploration.

An encouraging aspect that did emerge, though, was that some subjects with no previously known psi experiences were able to dream paranormally. A positive attitude toward ESP and the dream experiment, coupled with a good ability at dream recall, seemed to be sufficient requirements for successful subjects, even though individual sensitivity would be expected to vary considerably.

While the experimental controls of these experiments might seem adequate to many psychologists for a purely psychological experiment (if, for instance, the agent were trying to influence the subject's dreams by speaking aloud to him), the traditions of parapsychology require far stricter controls. All possibilities of sensory cues to the subject must be tightly excluded. And, importantly, Cicero's bugaboo of the last two thousand years — chance — must be reckoned with.

There is an old saying that you can prove anything with statistics. The key to that trick, however, is that the one who quotes the statistics must also be the one who computes or selects them. We have probably all encountered the proverbial man who "uses statistics as a drunken man uses lamp-posts — for support rather than illumination" Yet, when a body of independent statisticians comes up with the same statistical answer time and time again, we have reason to respect their findings. Packs of American cigarettes now include such warnings as: "The Surgeon General Has Determined That Cigarette Smoking Is Dangerous to Your Health." That is because reliable statisticians time and time again showed a statistical correlation of smoking to lung cancer. The cigarette companies were "disbelievers" in such a correlation, but the statistical facts, backed by government order, were overwhelming.

In the scientific world, chance is the measure of all things; and the more unlikely a thing, the more it must be measured, which puts ESP at the top of the list in its need for statistical proof.

To pile up the wealth of data needed and to arrange for its impartial statistical evaluation require: a) a repeatable experiment to collect the data; b) outside judges to evaluate the dream transcripts against possible targets; and c) the application by a statistician of appropriate statistical techniques to evaluate the work of the judges.

CHAPTER 8

A Dream Grows in Brooklyn

The experimental dream nurtured in the laboratory of the Parapsychology Foundation showed healthy signs of viability. Now it was time to transplant the dream to the fertile soil of the Maimonides Medical Center in Brooklyn, New York, where Ullman was director of the Community Mental Health Center. In 1962, with the aid of Gardner Murphy, then Director of Research for the Menninger Foundation, Ullman was able to obtain funding to establish a dream laboratory.

The Dream Laboratory of the Maimonides Mental Health Center became the only sleep laboratory devoted exclusively to parapsychological research. The director of the laboratory, Stanley Krippner, joined the staff in 1964 when the first formal dream studies were beginning.

The design of the first experiment had already been worked out by Ullman and Sol Feldstein, then a doctoral student at City College of the City University of New York. Feldstein and another staff member, Joyce Plosky, were to alternate as experimenter and agent for a series of twelve nights of experiments using seven male and five female subjects. The subject (Plate 1) was to sleep in a sound-isolated room while his or her EEG tracings were monitored by the experimenter in a nearby room (Plate 2). The agent was to spend the night in a third room, also acoustically isolated, thirty-two feet from the sleeping room (Plate 3). (In later experiments the agent's room was across the building from the sleep room, ninety-eight feet away or in a different building entirely.)

After the subject was asleep, the agent would randomly select an art-print target from a group of twelve by closing his eyes and pointing to a random-number table,* then counting down the envelopes until he or she reached that number. Using the same target all night, the agent would concentrate on it and write down any associations. The agent would renew his

---

*A published table of randomly generated numbers useful in insuring randomness when arbitrary selections have to be made as part of an experimental procedure.

or her efforts throughout the night whenever the experimenter signaled that the subject had begun a REM period as indicated by the EEG. As the REM period came to an end, the experimenter would wake the subject for a dream report which was tape recorded and then let him or her go back to sleep until the next REM period. In the morning the experimenter would use his or her notes of the dreams to refresh the subject's memory for a review of the dreams, adding the subject's associations.

The subjects, all young adults, were selected on the basis of their ability to recall dreams and their positive attitude toward ESP and this experiment. The dream lab staff hoped that this screening study would yield a particularly good telepathic dreamer who might be the subject for more intensive study. They also hoped to test the difference in the abilities of the two agents, Feldstein and Plosky, at "telepathic transmission."

The targets were chosen from a large pool of art prints on the basis of emotional intensity, vividness, color, and simplicity. Also, the targets had to be sufficiently different from one another to minimize possible confusion and to make the judging task easier.

After each night's dreams were transcribed, the transcripts along with the target pool of the twelve prints were sent to three independent judges. The judges, selected for their familiarity with psychological and parapsychological processes, were asked to rank the transcripts for correspondence against all of the twelve targets from number 1 for most correspondence down to number 12 for least correspondence. Each of the subjects also ranked the targets against their dreams in the same way, hoping that "their" target was in the upper half from 1 through 6 — a "hit." A more sophisticated statistical analysis was performed later by a professional statistician.

The study began in the summer of 1964. Let us follow each night according to which experimenter was serving as agent. Feldstein's first subject was a woman teacher. The randomly selected target that night was *Animals,* by Tamayo, which depicts two fierce dogs flashing their teeth and eating pieces of meat. A large black rock is prominent in the background.

The teacher found Freudian symbolism in her third dream.

> I was at this banquet . . . and I was eating something like rib steak. And this friend of mine was there . . . and people were talking about how she wasn't very good to invite for dinner because she was very conscious of other people getting more to eat than she got . . . That was the most important part of the dream, that dinner . . . It was probably Freudian like all my other dreams — you know, eating, and all that stuff, and a banquet. Well, there was another friend of mine, also in this dream. Somebody that I teach with, and she was eyeing everybody to make sure that everybody wasn't getting more than she was too. And I was chewing a piece of . . . rib steak. And I was sitting at the table, and other people were talking about this girl . . . and they were saying that she's not very nice to invite to eat because she's greedy, or something like that.

Despite the transformation of the dogs' savage mealtime manners into an exchange at a human level, the similarity of emotional tone is suggestive of a telepathic triggering of the dream. Even the black rock of the painting came through in the teacher's associations in her second dream. "And the second one . . . was about Vermont. Black Rock, Vermont . . . Yesterday, I was at the beach, and I was sitting on one of the rocks . . . and I felt like that mermaid from Black Rock . . ." The judges assigned *Animals* a mean rank of 3.0, a "hit."*

It is interesting to note that the beverage company featuring a wood nymph is "White Rock," and that the name of the Vermont town is "Black Hills." One could make a case for the subject's attempt to match the black rock of the target by combining two of her memories and distorting the pertinent proper nouns.

Feldstein's second subject was a young New York psychologist, William Erwin. Erwin had been interested in parapsychology for some time and, as a practicing analyst, was familiar with dream processes. Feldstein's target that night was *Zapatistas,* by Orozco (Plate 4). The painting depicts Mexican-Indian followers of the Mexican revolutionary Zapata. The traveling revolutionaries, a few mounted, most on foot, are followed by women and are shown against a stark background of massive mountains and clouds.

To get a better idea of the judges' task, let us go through Erwin's dreams one-by-one to see what correspondences there might be with the target. Although it is always much easier to see the correspondences after one knows what the target is, our remarks alongside each dream may give some insight into the judging process.

First Dream Report	*Possible Correspondence*
A storm. Rainstorm. It reminds me of traveling — a trip — traveling one time in Oklahoma, approaching a rainstorm, thunder cloud, rainy; sort of a distance . . . it was on a much greater scale than this rainstorm; a very distant scene . . . It had an aspect of grandeur about it . . . My associations go to almost a Biblical scene of some sort . . . almost as though you were dealing with an early element of creation . . . it was to the left of me, in a way . . . direction was important, and distance was important.	The painting shows clouds, suggestive of rain. The people are traveling. The scene is shown in perspective of a great distance. The scene has aspects of grandeur.

The revolutionaries are traveling to the left. |
| For some reason I got a feeling of memory, now, of New Mexico when I lived there. There are a lot of mountains | Mexico is similar to New Mexico. The scene shows mountains and Mexican |

*As there were three judges, a mean of the ranks was taken. Therefore, ranks of 1, 2, and 6 would produce a mean of 3.0; ranks of 1, 2, and 2 would produce a mean of 1.7.

around New Mexico, Indians, Pueblos; now my thoughts go to almost as though I were thinking of another civilization. The association to New Mexico, I think, has to do partly with a feeling I had in living in New Mexico ... You're surrounded by mountains ... the name of one of the mountain ranges in New Mexico, Sundre Christo....

Indians. They are suggestive of another civilization.

They are surrounded by mountains. Sangre de Cristo is a Spanish name.

Second Dream Report

... I was thinking about ... the experiment. I was thinking about this room ... a visitor to the [New York World's] Fair might find it nice to find a room — some place to sleep ... I was thinking ... about other people that had been in the experiment....

Possible Correspondence

No correspondence. This is a typical dream on a first night in the dream laboratory.

Third Dream Report

... the action of two people. It was either a man ... it was a woman, I think ... Something had happened to time for a few minutes.

Possible Correspondence

No apparent correspondence.

Fourth Dream Report

I was dreaming that I was dreaming ... I was attempting to tell what I dreamed the first time, and I couldn't get it out ... There were a number of people in the room. In fact, there were two of them. They were either on television or they were two old-time movies, and I was going through an old part of town ... the old street cars, watching a car turn into a street that was very narrow. There were two little kids in this dream, meeting this car ... they were running along beside it.

The movie in the dream was strange ... I seemed to recognize Wallace Beery ... There was a woman ... they were trying to convince this woman that she should go in a particular direction to see something that was going on. I think this particular part makes me think more of Los Angeles, like the early period of motion pictures ... I recall now, seeing a Harold Lloyd picture ... it was a silent film, yet you knew what was going on.

Possible Correspondence

No correspondence. Again, the dream is preoccupied with the experimental situation.

The theme of traveling.

Most of the revolutionaries are marching beside men riding on horseback.

A film version of Zapata's life, *Viva Zapata!* starred Marlon Brando. The women are going in the direction led by the men.

Zapata was active during the early period of silent films (1914–1915).

For some reason I recall now ... a trip when I was younger. I was in the Scouts, and I went to camp one summer ... It was out in the country, by a river; a lot of activities went on there ... There was a great deal of noise in the dream. The noise was made by the activity.

Again, the theme is traveling. As in the painting, it is out in the country.

Revolutionary activity — firing of guns, and so on — is noisy.

Fifth Dream Report
Lucky Strikes ... I remember about the time during the war when they changed the color of their pack ... and their slogan was "Lucky Strike green has gone to war ..."

Possible Correspondence
The theme of going to war.

Associations
... my first dream impressed me very much ... I spent a few summers in Santa Fe ... and during the Fiesta a great many of the Indians came in with their wares ... it seems there were heavy clouds behind this ... Perhaps the coloring in New Mexico fits it, the mesa as it runs up the mountains ... Here it gets into this epic type of thing ... a De Mille super-type colossal production. I would carry along with it such ideas of the Pueblo going down to the Mayan-Aztec type of civilization.

Possible Correspondence
A large number of Mexican Indians are shown traveling. Heavy clouds are behind. The coloring is similar to that in Mexico, with mesas and mountains.

The painting has epic qualities.

Zapata's followers traced their Indian ancestry back to the Mayans and Aztecs.

Guess about the target
The first dream which impressed me so — the feeling of mountains — it doesn't sound quite right ... I kept thinking of an automobile, driving ... it's just sort of association, but it had something to do with force or power, and that leads me back once again to my thunderhead and certain elements of nature.

Apparent Correspondence
The first dream shows greatest correspondence to the target, with its mountains. Driving is thematically related to traveling. The painting has great force. The thunderhead is prominent.

The brief excerpts quoted above are taken from a transcript that runs 29 pages — and it was this that the judges had to compare against each of the twelve targets. They assigned *Zapatistas* a mean rank of 1.7, a highly rated "hit." (A full transcript of one night's dream will be found in the appendix so that the reader may understand more fully the complexities of the judging process and "get the feel" of what happens during a night at the dream laboratory.)

Feldstein's third subject was a female artist. Her target was *The Sacred*

Fish, by de Chirico, which depicts two dead fish lying on a wooden slab in front of a candle. Some correspondences in her dreams related to the themes of death, going swimming, lighting a candle, and perhaps even a punning correspondence, since several dreams about France contained pointed references to the word "poise," similar to the French word for fish, *poisson.* The judges gave her target a rating of 2.7, another "hit."

A chemical engineer was Feldstein's fourth subject, and the target was Gauguin's *Still Life with Three Puppies.* The puppies are depicted lapping water from a pan behind three blue goblets.

Some of the engineer's dream correspondences to this were water, "dark blue bottles," and "a couple of dogs making a noise." The judges declared a mean rank of 5.3, a low "hit."

Another Gauguin painting was randomly selected for Feldstein's next subject, a female secretary. *The Moon and the Earth* shows a nude, dark-skinned native girl by a stream of water. In her second REM period, the secretary dreamed that "I was in a bathing suit . . . doing the dream experiment in the bathtub full of water, and we were finishing, and we had to get up and out of the wet bathtub, out of the water . . . and we were dripping wet. . . ."

And in her fifth dream, ". . . somebody introduces a girl who is a dancing girl . . . and she comes over and she says, 'Oh, I want to get a tan.' She's very fair. And I'm yelling to her to stay in the sun instead of running in and out all the time." The subject added later, "Look, your shoulders are tan. If you take your time, you can get the rest of your body tan."

The native girl, of course, did not have to worry about that since she had been born tan. The judges gave this target a mean rank of 5.0, still a "hit."

Feldstein's sixth and final subject was a female model. The target was Rousseau's *The Sleeping Gypsy,* which shows a lion hovering over a gypsy sleeping in the desert, a rather fearsome painting. The model preferred to dream that she was home "and there was a little cat in the room . . . and my mother . . . was sleeping." In a way this transformation is similar to the one reported by Dr. Tart about his subject who always dreamed a happy ending to a hypnotically suggested fearful situation. The judges, however, gave this target a mean rank of 8.3, a "miss." This was the only "miss" for one of Feldstein's subjects. What had happened?

A possible source of confusion might be some homework Feldstein was doing that night in preparation for a psychology class. He was studying a book that contained the "double alternation problem," a psychological test of simple reasoning; an animal must make a series of turns in the sequence, "right, right—left, left." Body cues are eliminated, since on one turn a "right" precedes a "right," whereas on the next turn a "right" precedes a "left," and so on. Feldstein was reading the last paragraph of this problem at 3:07 A.M. when the model reported a dream.

For some reason I was thinking about [what] the words *right* and *left side* mean when people use it in reference to the human body. Like what, exactly, is a right side or a left side? This sort of sounds strange, but when we say east or west — you know — we're talking about a direction that's sort of pre-determined, that has all kinds of things to do with very carefully worked out things. But when you talk about right and left sides of people or things, what the hell does the word *right* and *left* mean? I don't know. I got sort of involved with that. I don't know what the dream means.

Since at this stage of experimentation the agent's room was wired so that he could hear the subject's dream report, Feldstein was able to hear the model's self-puzzling dream about his psychology problem. This was particularly frustrating since he was not permitted to tell anyone at the time the (non-target) source of her dream.

Feldstein's preoccupations with reading matter may have turned up again during an experiment when Joyce Plosky was the agent and he the EEG monitor. On July 7, 1964, after the sleeping subject, a male graduate student in French literature, had finished a dream period, Feldstein thought he would have time to read a copy of *Life* magazine before the next REM period began. An article on topless swimsuits caught his undivided attention. The photo article traced the historical precedents for the topless look. A photo of a bare-breasted Minoan goddess and one of a Greek priestess, "who felt that the bare bosom gave them added grace and did not detract at all from their modesty," seemed uncannily similar to the dream reported less than an hour later by the subject. "In a park, and we were talking about two busts — women's busts — of ancient times. And we were arguing about that."

The student's dream also referred to "Gulliver" traveling to the "Island of Lilliput" in the South Pacific. Also in Feldstein's issue of *Life* was a story about General MacArthur, with a photo of him wading ashore to an island in the Philippines, towering over his much smaller oriental companions. Feldstein's apparent "bootleg" telepathy resulted in a ban on reading during experiments.

As for the target that night, the student's dreams contained not a single reference to the picture being concentrated on by Plosky, Van Gogh's *Starry Night*. The judges gave it a "miss" with a mean rank of 10.7, the worst night in the whole series.

In general, Plosky fared less well than Feldstein in attempts at programming the subject's dreams. Her first subject, a male psychologist, dreamed of a "revolving something . . . this lone object . . . and it's spinning like a top" when the target was *Football Players,* by Rousseau, which depicts a turn-of-the-century football game, with the ball indeed whirling. The judges gave this target a mean rank of 8.0, a "miss."

Her second subject, also a male psychologist, had as his target Schlemmer's *Bauhaus Stairway,* in which some school boys are climbing up a staircase.

He dreamed about "something ascending . . . moving upward . . . going upward toward a hill. . . ." but this was insufficient, for the judges assigned the target only a 9.0, another "miss."

After the frustrating miss with the *Starry Night* (her third) subject, she began to make a comeback with her fourth subject, a male medical student. The target was *Departure,* by Beckmann, which portrays a family making a voyage in a small boat. The medical student dreamed of a highway, going back to school, and driving through the rain. The theme of departure was echoed in his dream — that he and his wife "were moving from our apartment." This target squeaked through as a "hit" with a mean rank of 6.0.

Plosky's fifth subject, a female graduate student in sociology, had as her target Chagall's *Green Violinist* (Plate 5), which depicts a man playing a violin with a dog in the background. The student dreamed of a dog barking in a field and later mused, "I wonder if the target could have to do with a tune or something to do with music?" This was sufficient description for the judges to assign a 4.7 rank, a "hit."

A male photographer was her last subject. The target, Picasso's *Sleeping Peasants,* depicts a man and woman with exaggerated hands and feet sleeping in a field. The photographer's dreams included references to "rolling country," early American and primitive tools, "winding something . . . with my right hand," and "a foot kicking or moving about." This target, too, was a hit, with a mean rank of 5.3.

Overall, the judges' rankings produced eight "hits" and four "misses," consistent with the telepathy hypothesis, but not "demonstrating" it statistically. However, when the subjects' own rankings, analyzed on the same basis the independent judges used, were considered, the score was ten "hits" and two "misses," which did provide statistically significant evidence that the dreamers had incorporated elements of the targets into their dreams.

Comparing this experiment with Tart's experiment cited in Chapter 6, in which subjects attempted to dream about narratives they had listened to earlier under hypnosis, an interesting fact emerges. Half of Tart's ten subjects showed not a single correspondence in their dreams to the stimulus tape, even when Tart looked for disguised or distorted versions. Yet the Maimonides study's subjects showed a far greater number of dream correspondences to telepathic targets, and even three out of the four "missing" subjects showed at least a modest correspondence.

A difference between the Maimonides study and Tart's study was that the Maimonides experimenters elicited the subjects' associations for inclusion in transcripts sent to the judges, whereas Tart did not. Tart commented that

> the dreams may have been so thoroughly disguised that I couldn't see the connection. But, if this was the case, it is atypical compared to the earlier psychoanalytic reports, in which the sophisticated reader could see a connection

between the "disguised" dreams and the stimulus narratives even without benefit of the free associations.[1]

In this initial Maimonides study, separate judgings of the associations showed no differences in target correspondences from the dreams.

This initial experimental study of dream telepathy suggested that telepathy could be a powerful force in influencing dream content, even more powerful than post-hypnotic suggestion. The study suggested that the average person might be expected to have at least modest success in incorporating telepathic elements in his dreams provided he was positively oriented toward this goal. To their knowledge, few of the successful subjects had previously experienced any striking psychic phenomena. Yet now it seemed that in the dream state it was possible for a person to become "psychic."

An important part of the subjects' orientation may have been that they were consciously trying to dream about the target. If they had not known that someone was trying to "send" thoughts to them, they might well have been far less successful.

However, the primary goal of the experiment had been to optimize factors that might contribute to a scientific demonstration that dream telepathy was in fact possible to control (and for the skeptics, to convince them that dream telepathy was in fact *possible*). The secondary goal was to find a specially talented subject for further experiments. Here the choice was clear cut: Dr. Erwin's striking success in dreaming about *Zapatistas* singled him out as the subject for the next experimental series.

Probably the most striking finding of the first series was the difference between the two agents: Feldstein's subjects got five "hits" out of six tries in comparison with Plosky's six subjects getting three "hits." This statistically significant difference* in apparent ability to telepathically "transmit" became even more pronounced when Feldstein's "bootleg" telepathic correspondences were considered. His only subject who had "missed" had incorporated into her dreams his reading of a psychology text, whereas Plosky's worst subject had also incorporated some of Feldstein's reading material. Whatever it took to excel at "transmitting," Feldstein seemed to have it.

It would be premature at this stage to attempt to identify any particular psychological traits as being directly conducive to being a good telepathic agent. But it should be noted that Sol Feldstein had a lively interest in psychological theory and in psychotherapeutic practice. Considering himself somewhat of an iconoclast in psychology, Feldstein vehemently rejected therapies based on tranquilizers, and other somatic approaches. Later he

---

*Statistical tests use the known mathematical properties of numbers to enable one to decide when a difference is probably due to chance and when a difference is so large that chance seems unlikely. If the outcome of a particular test could have happened by chance only five or fewer times in a hundred trials, we begin to doubt that this is a chance variation. In this book, the term "statistically significant" is used whenever the outcome of an experiment could not be easily attributed to coincidence as determined by mathematical techniques.

devoted himself full-time to doctoral study in psychology, eventually becoming a psychotherapist.

It seemed natural to pair the better agent, Feldstein, with the best subject, Erwin, for more intensive study (this study is fully described in the next chapter).

But for the purpose of comparison with the initial screening study, let us briefly look at a second screening study made in the spring and the summer of 1965. The procedure was identical to the initial study: Krippner selected a target pool of twelve art prints; twelve subjects (six men, six women) were chosen; Feldstein was to alternate with another research assistant, Sally Van Steenburgh, as agent and experimenter. Outside judges as well as the subjects were to rank the twelve targets from number 1 for most correspondence with their dreams to number 12 for least correspondence. The best subject was to go on for a more intensive study.

As in the first screening study, some interesting dream correspondences with the targets emerged. Feldstein's first subject was a woman writer. The target that night was *Rock Crystal Easter Egg,* by Fabergé, a black and white photograph of a crystal Easter egg in which there are two panels of a diptych, one showing a large mansion surrounded by shrubbery and the other showing a large house at a closer perspective. In her third dream the writer dreamed of a beautiful house, "an enormous estate-kind of modern mansion," and in her fourth she dreamed of two huge heads, a Polynesian head and an Egyptian-Negroid head with a gold face and a bald head. "The whole thing was grayish." She added in the morning, "At the outset there were two huge heads. They were very eggish because the men were bald. . . ."

Fabergé, had he been alive, might have objected to his elegant diptych Easter egg being compared with two "eggish" bald heads, but at least the heads were somewhat exotic. The writer ranked the Fabergé egg number 1, although the judges ranked it further down, 3.7, but still a "hit."

When Van Steenburgh was concentrating on a painting of a boxing match at Madison Square Garden, *Dempsey and Firpo,* by Bellows, her subject, a male artist, dreamed "something about Madison Square Garden and a boxing fight." This too was a "hit."

Another of Van Steenburgh's subjects was a psychologist, Dr. Robyn Posin. Her target was *Mystic Night,* by Sheets (Plate 6), which depicts five women performing a night-time ritual in a wooded area surrounded by mountains. The greenish-blue color of the foliage and grass pervades the entire picture.

In her first dream, Dr. Posin seemed to join the group: "Being with a group of people . . . participating in something. . . . There were three people and there's a woman in it." In her second dream she was "driving in the country" looking at "a lot of mountains and trees." In her third dream, "I kept seeing blue." In her fourth dream, she saw "huge crowds of these students out in this kind of grassy . . . parking place, trees. What strikes me most about the whole thing was the trees, again, and the greenery and the country." And in the morning, she added: "I remember the greens and blue being terribly bright." She had the feeling that "there's some sort of primitive aspect . . . I can almost see it as some sort of tribal ritual in a jungle."

Four people, with Posin making the fifth, performing a tribal ritual amidst blue-green mountains and trees seemed to be an uncannily accurate description of *Mystic Night*. Her associations to her dreams and her guesses about the target in the morning were particularly apt. Without associations, the three judges ranked this 4, 9, and 6, but with associations, 1, 2, and 2. Posin also ranked it number 2, a "hit." Posin's success led her to be a subject for a formal study, which we will examine in Chapter 10.

As in the initial study, the subjects proved to be better judges of the targets than the independent judges. But here, the difference was more striking. The independent judges ranked the targets at mean chance level, six "hits," and six "misses," whereas the subjects scored nine "hits" and three "misses." The difference in judging ability may be related to non-verbalized dream imagery and feelings. "Something — I don't know exactly what — about this target reminds me of my dreams" is a comment we have heard often from subjects who give a higher rank for the target picture than do the judges. This may indicate that ESP impressions for those subjects did not rise above the subliminal level even though the impressions were retained as a sort of "intuition" about the target.

As in the first study, the subjects' rankings showed that Feldstein had greater success as agent (five "hits") than the other alternating agent (four "hits"). The second screening study lacked one hit of being statistically significant but was still consistent with the telepathy hypothesis.

Overall, the two screening studies produced nineteen "hits" and five "misses" out of twenty-four subjects' rankings. Cicero's ghost, while perhaps startled by these results, was not yet laid to rest. Skeptics might object that almost *any* dream would have *some* correspondence to almost *any* target picture — and perhaps the Maimonides staff had had an incredible run of good luck. However, the experimenters' minds turned to more sophisticated judging techniques and eventually to more emotionally involving targets. After all, the emotional impact of an art print, while considerably greater than the impact of an abstract symbol such as a cross or square, was still only a small-scale imitation of the emotion-provoking episodes found in spontaneous dream telepathy.

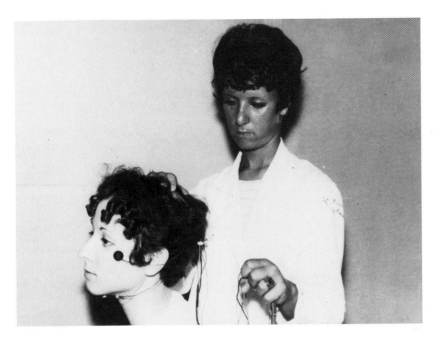

Plate 1: Electroencephalographic (EEG) electrodes are placed on a subject prior to the night's dream study (courtesy of Harold Friedman).

Plate 2: Charles Honorton and Stanley Krippner monitor the electroencephalographic (EEG) machine during an experiment (courtesy of Harold Friedman).

Plate 3: To intensify the images, the agent sketches the target picture (courtesy of Harold Friedman).

Plate 4: *Zapatistas* (José Clemente Orozco, 1931), used as a target picture in the first screening study (courtesy of the Museum of Modern Art, New York; oil on canvas, 45 × 55″; given anonymously).

Plate 5: *Green Violinist* (Marc Chagall, 1924–1925), used as a target picture in the first screening study and in a pilot study (courtesy of the Solomon R. Guggenheim Museum, New York; oil on canvas, 78 × 42¾"; photographed by Robert E. Mates).

Plate 6: *Mystic Night* (Millard Sheets, 1937), used as a target picture in the second screening study (courtesy of the Art Institute of Chicago; Watson F. Blair Purchase Prize, 1938.226; watercolor, 38 × 58cm;

Plate 19: *Aquamanile Horseman,* a bronze water vessel from early 15th century France or Germany, used as a target photograph in the study with Alan Vaughan and others (courtesy of the Metropolitan Museum of Art, New York; the Cloisters Collection, purchase, 1947).

Plate 20: *Painting* (Francis Bacon, 1946), used as a target picture in the study with Alan Vaughan and others (courtesy of the Museum of Modern Art, New York; oil and tempera on canvas, 6′ 5⅞″ × 52″; purchase).

CHAPTER 9

"Color His Wounds Red"

After the initial screening study had established a basic experimental design and discovered a particularly good telepathic subject—Dr. William Erwin—the Maimonides experimenters hoped that their dream-telepathy technique would be sufficiently effective for Feldstein to be able to influence Erwin's dreams each night of a series. Beginning in the fall of 1964, the "First Erwin Study" was scheduled to run for twelve nonconsecutive nights, with a different art-print target for each night. However, Erwin became seriously ill after the seventh night, and Ullman, who had no knowledge of how things had been going, decided to halt the experiment after those seven nights.

As in the initial study, an experimenter (Krippner) operated the EEG and sound equipment while Feldstein concentrated on a target picture in another room. The transcripts of Erwin's dreams for the seven nights were sent to three judges along with the seven art prints that had been used so that they could rank them from number 1 for most correspondence to number 7 for least correspondence. Any rank from 1 to 3.5 would be a "hit."

On the first night, the randomly selected target was *Bedtime,* by Walter Keane, which portrays a girl with long, dark hair holding three puppies. The girl's eyes and those of the dogs have exaggerated pupils that seem to stare out at the viewer.

Erwin's dreams centered around "looking for something" and a "woman that had long hair, long black hair." This mild correspondence was given a mean rank of 3.7 by the judges, barely a "miss."

The next experimental night's target was *The Yellow Rabbi,* by Chagall. It depicts an elderly rabbi sitting at a table with a book in front of him. Here was a target that Feldstein, because of his orthodox Jewish background, could easily relate to. But how would Erwin, whose religious background was Protestant (Disciples of Christ) react?

In Erwin's second dream, a man was riding in a car with a woman. "He was a foreigner . . . She was . . . in her forties. He was older—in his fifties . . . He could have been in his sixties."

In his third dream, "someone asked me if he was actually a national figure . . . it has to do with, well, a feeling of older people. The name of Saint Paul came into my mind."

And in Erwin's fifth dream, "This doctor, Dr. Heimsdorf, is a professor in humanities and philosophy. He was sitting . . . and he was reading from a book. . . ."

Elaborating on his dreams in the morning, Erwin said, "So far, all I can say is that there is the feeling of older people. . . . The professor is an older man. He smoked a pipe, taught humanities as well as philosophy. He was an Anglican minister or priest."

These dreams seemed a direct hit. "A foreigner," "in his sixties," a professor sitting and reading from a book. Interestingly, the Jewish religious figure is transformed into a Christian religious figure, "Saint Paul" and "an Anglican minister or priest."

It should be added that in his dream report of the professor, Erwin mentioned the word "Maimonides," ostensibly referring to the hospital where the experiment was being conducted. The hospital, of course, is named after the Jewish sage and philosopher, Maimonides. This correspondence may well have been a coincidence, but, provocatively, this was the only night the word "Maimonides" had been referred to, during either of the first two studies. The judges gave the *Yellow Rabbi* the rank of 1, a direct "hit."

On the third night, chance provided a contrast of religion in the target *The Sacrament of the Last Supper,* by Dalí. The painting shows Christ at the center of a table surrounded by his twelve disciples. A glass of wine and a loaf of bread are on the table. In the background is the sea, and a fishing boat can be seen in the distance. While Feldstein was trying to associate to the target, Erwin began to dream.

His first dream was of "an ocean . . . It had a strange beauty about it. . . ." In his second dream "boats come to mind. Fishing boats. Small-size fishing boats . . . There was a picture in the Sea Fare Restaurant that came to mind . . . It shows, oh, I'd say about a dozen or so men pulling a fishing boat ashore right after having returned from a catch."

In his third dream he was looking at a "Christmas catalog," and in his fourth dream he was talking to someone about why "a doctor becomes a doctor." His fifth dream reiterated the theme of doctors, reminding him of a painting, *The Physician,* and in his sixth dream he was in a doctor's office.

In his seventh dream he was in "a kitchen" and thinking about going to a restaurant, while in the eighth dream he was sampling spices and herbs in a grocery store. "Place to eat, food of different types."

In the morning, Erwin seemed to zero in on the target: "The fisherman dream makes me think of the Mediterranean area, perhaps even some sort of Biblical time. Right now my associations are of the fish and the loaf, or even the feeding of the multitudes. . . . Once again I think of Christmas . . .

Having to do with the ocean — water, fishermen, something in this area. . . ."

Erwin obliquely refers to "Christmas" and Christ's action of feeding the multitudes but seems to settle on the "doctor" or the "physician" as a symbol of Christ, who was often referred to as a physician or healer. This obliqueness may be due in part to Feldstein's difficulty in relating to the Christ figure. Erwin's other dream images contain direct references to the setting, "an ocean," "small-size fishing boats," "a dozen or so men," references to food and eating, the Mediterranean area in Biblical times, and even the loaf. The judges ranked this 1.3, a high "hit."

The same painting had once before been used in a pilot experiment with Feldstein as the agent and Erwin as the subject (although Erwin did not see the picture until the formal series was completed). At that time, too, Christ was symbolized as "a small-town doctor." Erwin dreamed of the ocean that time too. Another repeated theme was going into a store that had unusual things to eat (the Eucharist?). Complementing "the loaf" of the second night, he dreamed about "a kitchen," "food," and "preparing the meal." The same stimulus seems to have triggered the same responses.

A darker theme may have arisen from the association of Judas about to betray Christ: "People began to come into the room . . . I had the feeling that . . . somebody or someone . . . was trying to do something that wasn't good. Destructive, perhaps. Or that one of them was not good. . . ."

Let us digress for a moment from the Erwin study to take up the question of the effect of religious background in telepathic dream correspondences to prints of religious nature. It would seem reasonable that a person from a different religious culture would have very different associations, which stem from his own background. A chance to test this hypothesis arose in 1968 when two young men from India, identical twins who had come to the United States for graduate work in electrical engineering, volunteered as subjects for a dream experiment. Their religious background was Zoroastrianism, a religion founded by the Persian prophet Zoroaster (or Zarathustra) in the sixth century B.C.

Cyrus, the more dominant of the twins, was to act as telepathic agent, while Darius acted as sleeping subject. The randomly chosen target that night was an impressionistic painting of a New England church. That night Darius dreamed of a rectangular plaque of marble and a friend lighting candles. In his last dream Darius was viewing a television program. "There was some kind of scientific experiment going on, something like taking a head for someone else's body. There was a plaster cast with a head sticking out. I also got the definite impression of eating rock candy. Almost continuously."

When Krippner queried Darius about his associations, he replied that his *only* association was with a Zoroastrian religious ceremony in which participants eat rock candy. Other associations to this ceremony included marble statues and lighting candles in the temple.

From a transcript of this night, an independent judge ranked the New England church print number 1 out of a pool of six pictures. The associations with the Zoroastrian temple rites had been strongest, of course.

Returning to the Erwin study, the target for the fourth night was Degas' *School of the Dance,* which depicts girls in white ballet costumes practicing in a dance studio. Some of the girls are putting on their costumes.

Erwin dreamed about being "in a class. . . . Now, at different times, different people would get up for some sort of recitation or some sort of con- tribution. . . . The woman — the instructor — was young. She was attractive." In a later dream in which Erwin was trying to get dressed, he complained that "there was one little girl that was trying to dance with me." This enabled the judges to rank the target 1.3, a high "hit."

A surrealistic painting was the target on the fifth night. The print was Chagall's *Paris Through a Window* (Plate 7), in which a man is observing the Paris skyline from a window. This colorful painting has such unusual elements as a cat with a human face, flowers sprouting from a chair, and small figures of men flying through the air. (The full transcript of this night may be found in Appendix B.)

In Erwin's second dream the little men seemed to become bees. "Sort of bees flying around flowers."

In his third dream he was walking through

the French Quarter. And I was walking through different departments in a department store . . . , talking with a group of Shriners that were having a con- vention. They had on a hat that looked more like a French policeman's hat. . . . I said French Quarter earlier, but I was using that to get a feel . . . of an early village of some sort . . . It would be some sort of a blend of this romantic type of architecture — buildings, village, quaint.

In his fifth dream, Erwin saw "a man, once again walking through one of these villages, these towns . . . French attire." Even the painting's perspec- tive seemed to come through in this walk "up the side of a hill above other layers of the town."

Putting it together in the morning, Erwin said, "The thing that stands out is the dream where I described the village . . . It's a festive thing . . . Early nineteenth century . . . either the Italian or French or Spanish area . . . Houses very close together covering the hills." The judges agreed that *Paris Through a Window* should be ranked 1, a direct "hit."

The sixth night's target was also surrealistic: the famous *Persistence of Memory,* by Dalí, which portrays several limp, distorted watches in a desert. In the background are rocky cliffs and a blue sea.

Erwin dreamed that "All the impressions are distorted . . . A picture looking down into the water . . . Rather jagged mountains," and later, "I was out in the desert." In the morning, he noted that continuous distortions char- acterized his dreams. The judges ranked the Dalí target 2.3 — a "hit."

The target for the seventh and final night was the toughest. The print was the still life by Cézanne entitled *Apples and Oranges,* which depicts a bowl containing fruit.

Erwin dreamed of "ancient pottery" and "a student eating something from a tree." This correspondence was mild, with the judges assigning the target a rank of 4.0 — the lowest rank of the series and a "miss" by half a point.

The "First Erwin Study" was overall a remarkable success. The rankings of the transcripts by the three judges supported the telepathy hypothesis against odds on the order of a thousand to one that it could have happened by chance. (Cicero, are you listening?) Erwin's associations and guesses about the targets in the morning proved particularly accurate, suggesting that his own psychoanalytic work gave him significant clues in understanding the transformation of pictorial material into personalized and symbolic events within the framework of his dreams.

The target art-prints that came through into his dreams most clearly tended to possess emotional and vivid qualities to which he and Feldstein could relate. The theme of religion, for instance *The Yellow Rabbi* and *The Sacrament of the Last Supper,* conveyed strong telepathic impact. In general, paintings of human figures involved in activity seemed to be more successful in engaging the dreams of Erwin (*School of the Dance, Paris Through a Window*); whereas purely abstract paintings lacking a human element fared less well (*Persistence of Memory, Apples and Oranges*).

Although all seven dream transcripts had striking correspondences with the target pictures, some were far more striking and detailed than others. The ranking system of judging, while adequate for rough comparisons, was insensitive to the large range of target-dream correspondences that were possible. Skeptics critical of ESP in general were still maintaining that the judges were very *lucky* (a prescientific but still pervasive explanation for unknown factors favoring chance), while skeptics more knowledgeable about ESP suggested that the ESP was to be found in the judging process rather than in the dreams. It would indeed be a marvelous stroke of "luck" to find several judges who consistently maintained the same high level of psi in their judgings. But the point had been made. A more sophisticated and sensitive judging process would not only answer the skeptic's objections but would also demonstrate dramatically more meaningful degrees of correspondence between dream and target.

Such a judging form was finally constructed (Plate 8). The dreams alone, the associations, and the entire transcript were to be rated separately on a 100-point scale that runs:

1–20	Little correspondence
21–40	Some correspondence
41–60	Moderate correspondence
61–80	Great correspondence
81–100	Very great correspondence

Individual judges might be expected to vary considerably in how they would fill in these forms, but averaging together the ratings from several judges would give a meaningful result. With these forms one would also be able to compare the results of any one judge's ratings; if a judge tended to rate the correspondences very low or very high, comparison with non-target ratings would give the proper perspective. If the ratings for the targets were at the same level as the non-targets, then it would be obvious that there was no striking ESP effect.

This procedure would allow each rating to be made independently of each other. Certain types of statistical analysis are only valid if the data analyzed are independent from each other. The introduction of this rating scale would allow these types of statistics to be used.

This procedure would also take longer. For an eight-night series (which the next series was) each judge had to read each of the eight transcripts eight times when making comparisons with the eight targets, which makes 64 readings. In addition, the judge had to fill out three forms for each of the transcript-target pairs (one for dreams, one for associations, and one for the entire transcript), which totals 192 forms for each judge to fill out. Using three judges, that made 576 judging forms to appear on the desk of our statistical consultant, Dr. Michael Capobianco.

By late 1966 Dr. Erwin's health had improved sufficiently so that he was able to volunteer for a second dream study in an attempt to duplicate the excellent results he had had with Feldstein as agent in the first study. For two years he had gone to bed without electrodes on his head, but now an eight-night series over a four-month period would give him a chance to get used to them again.

An innovation for this new series was suggested by Feldstein, who thought that some of the more dramatic successes in dream telepathy in the earlier studies may have been due to his active involvement with the target picture. He would attempt to draw the picture or act out any part of it he could in order to immerse himself in the theme and the mood of the target. Perhaps such emotional involvement would be aided by props designed to reinforce the impact of the painting in a more life-like way? Ullman and Krippner agreed and set their staff in search of "multisensory" materials. Props ranging from a boxing glove to toy soldiers were found to accompany a pool of ten art-print targets already selected by staff psychologists for emotional content and vivid color. Each target had its own multisensory accompaniment in a separate box coded with the target picture. Erwin, however, was not told of this new development; his dreams, the experimenters gambled, would speak for themselves. Would life imitating art in the laboratory result in a high yield of dream telepathy? We shall see.

On the first night, November 30, 1966, Erwin arrived at the laboratory before bedtime, chatted with Feldstein while he was wired with electrodes, was plugged into the electrode box in his sleep room and fell asleep while Krippner monitored his EEG pattern in the adjoining experimenter's room. Meanwhile Feldstein had gone to the agent's room (now moved to a location 98 feet away) where he was opening an envelope and a box that had been randomly selected.

The envelope contained a print of *The Barrel Organ,* by Daumier, which shows a group of French men and women singing hymns around a portable organ. The box contained a Protestant hymnal. This was the first time Feldstein had ever held one.

Erwin's dreams did not feature any hymn singing, but music was definitely in the air that night. In his second dream, a "little girl was banging on the planking, in some way playing. . . . I don't know where the guitar came in. That might have been what the little girl had — a guitar. . . . Someone was playing a guitar."

In his fourth dream, "I was dancing with . . . four women . . . The dancing was movement, really, but it was together. It wasn't a dance, it was a movement . . . There was one girl on the end who didn't move in rhythm because she was a little too self-conscious . . . just movement in unison to rhythm . . ."

And in the morning, "Guitar music . . . There was a statue called *The Kneeling Nun* . . . a rock formation and it looked like a nun kneeling down . . . I'd say I was talking with a French woman. . . . It might have been an earlier period . . . There were supppposed to be four women and one of them was supposed to be very sensitive to this movement. . . ."

Erwin's guess for the night was for a musical instrument: ". . . the guitar was unusual . . . Someone playing a guitar. . . ."

Using the new rating system, the judges gave this a mean of 26.3 points in the Some Correspondence range (two others of the eight target pictures were rated slightly higher, 27.7 and 28.7). But in view of Feldstein's inexperience at singing Protestant hymns, the correspondence with a French group moving in unison seemed encouraging.

On the second night, December 7, the target print was *Downpour at Shono,* by Hiroshige, which portrays a Japanese man with an umbrella trying to escape a driving rain. The accompanying box revealed a toy Japanese umbrella and instructions to Feldstein: "Take a shower." Feldstein popped into the shower adjoining his agent's room several times that night, glad that there was no one around to see him with his toy umbrella.

That night Erwin dreamed "Something about an Oriental man who was ill . . ." His fifth dream was about "A fountain . . . a water spray that would shoot up . . . ," and in his seventh dream he was "Walking with someone on the street . . . Raining . . ." In the morning he remembered fountains in Rome and "I was walking on the street. It seemed it was raining . . . and the street was blocked. So we had to walk out into the street and around."

His guess was "Something to do with . . . fountains. Maybe water. . ." Erwin's "Oriental man" and images of walking in the street in the rain earned a judges' rating of 44.3 in the Moderate Correspondence range — the highest rating for that night's transcript with any of the eight targets. (In case you're wondering how often people's dreams refer to rain, the answer is slightly more than one dream out of one hundred.[1])

On the third night a week later, an Indian painting, *Portrait of Jahangir as a Young Prince,* by Bichitr, was randomly chosen. Bordered by a green foliage design, it depicts an elegantly dressed young Indian prince in a flowing robe looking at himself in a mirror. He is wearing a string of green glass beads. In the box was a string of green beads for Feldstein to wear.

In his first dream, Erwin "was looking at these movie cameras. . . ," and in his second dream he was thinking of "a festival in . . . costume." In his third dream, he seemed to see the border design: "willowy trees hanging around the edges. . ."

In his seventh dream the prince's flowing attire may have suggested the fairer sex. "There were a lot of women around and they were . . . showing off . . . They would go through these skits . . . and in the dream their costumes would change . . . They would go through all sorts of colorful movements and all colorful actions . . . They might have had flowing dresses. . ." And he added later, "This last dream I was talking about was sort of unusual . . . The scene was of the fifteenth century. It was a court scene, like the French Court. Like the DuBarry, Madame Pompadour period. High headdresses, the stockings, and buckled shoes. . ."

A court scene it was, but not French. The Indian print got a rating of 26.3 from the judges — a ranking of second best.

On January 4, the fourth target was *Both Members of This Club* by Bellows (Plate 9), which shows a crowd watching two boxers fighting. Feldstein's surprise package that night contained a genuine dark-brown leather boxing glove (Plate 10).

Erwin's first dream seemed to pick up the crowd. "There were a lot of people . . . There was a lot of activity going on. . ."

And in his third dream, things started getting violent: "I was watching some cars parked on the beach being pounded in. One of them was pounded in and hit another car and completely broke it to pieces . . . and the ocean began to pound in and knock the car back and the wave pounded and hit the car. And I thought it was really going to hit the other car hard. . ."

Feldstein's leather glove seemed to get off to the wrong start in Erwin's fourth dream. "The only thing I can remember is cleaning a shoe . . . And there was a tiger coming out of the drain . . . It was just a black leather shoe. . ."

In the morning Erwin reviewed his associations.

There were a number of people ... It would be ... competition ... Ships
were being pounded and driven into the beach ... The water would pound
in a great distance ... It picked up a car and slammed into another car ...
The waves were pounding us in and we were being pushed toward another car
... Maybe I enjoyed the violence in the dream ... The violence ... was
exciting. . . .

Where in the devil did the tiger come from?

In his guess about the target, Erwin dwelled on the underlying feelings
of the dreams. "I think I was portraying a great deal of violence, destructiveness, aggressiveness ... Something to do within nature because the tiger is
an independent, powerful creature to be respected ... I have the feeling of
nature in its broadest sense. You might say the raw aspects of nature more
than the more refined aspects of a human being."

Erwin's dream transformation of a boxing fight into scenes of aggression
and violence (the two cars being pounded back and forth) was easily recognized by the judges who gave it a rating of 78.7, high in the Great Correspondence range — a first rank.

On the fifth night the target was a photograph of a Civil War centennial
display that depicted four wax Confederate soldiers loading a cannon. The
box contained some toy rubber soldiers with which Feldstein could play.

Erwin's third dream seemed to focus on the texture of the soldiers' skin.
"It's like it's all immersed in a very soft texture ... Skin. Soft skin..."

His fourth dream was "Something about a military band ... Marine
band ... It seemed the uniform would be the Marine blue pants with the
khaki shirt ... My feeling is they were outside on a parade area rather than
inside. It seemed to me they were standing ... There was no movement..."
His guess for the night had to do with

the band. I don't know how that got there. But it was just there...

The fact that there was the military campaign involved would be the only
association with softness. Of course, I think the comparison of such a thing as
the soft-hard concept is the women being taken by these — captured by these
soldiers, the invaders.

I had the feeling of dreaming on two levels...

The theme of soldiers in uniform seemed very apt, particularly when
coupled with "soft skin" and "no movement." The judges ranked the photo of
the wax soldiers at 59.0, high in the Moderate Correspondence range — and
with a "direct hit" ranking.

The sixth night's target was *Descent from the Cross,* by Beckmann (Plate
11). The painting shows a brown, emaciated Christ being taken down from
the cross. The box of multisensory materials contained a crucifix, a small
wooden cross, a picture of Jesus, some thumb tacks, and a red felt-tipped pen
(Plate 12). Feldstein's instructions were: *"Nail Christ to the cross and color his
wounds red."*

Erwin's fourth dream started off with a birthday party, and then

> We passed by an area where Winston Churchill was making a talk . . . and then we drove on home, and went back in the house, back in the kitchen, and there was a lot of wine that I tasted, and I think I got a piece of cake . . . Churchill was . . . old, emaciated . . . sort of drying up. I had remembered him as being a fat, chubby guy, and here he was old and getting thinner and drawn . . . He was speaking with his usual biting, clever, dynamic way . . .

His fifth dream was of a ceremonial sacrifice.

> It started out in some sort of a native community . . . We were going to be put in the stewpot . . . We were going to be sacrificed, or something, and there were political overtones. It seemed like there was a speech by President Johnson being played to them. I was trying to figure out how we could change their minds . . . There was one loud-speaker there and we decided that what we would do is pretend we were the gods . . . by forbidding this by speaking in the loud-speaker and also . . . we could use fireworks . . . Red . . ., I think red. Another thing, I think in looking at the so-called king, chief, or whatever the native was . . ., his skin was a very rich chocolate color . . . His head was very strange looking. It would almost be like you were looking at him, looking at one of these totem-pole gods . . . They, too, were going through a whole ceremony to the gods. And the idea was to scare them by speaking through the speaker as though we were the gods forbidding them to kill us . . .

Elaborating on this in the morning, he added: "There was just an awareness that they were going to kill us in some way, that it was part of their ceremony . . . It began to have ritualistic feeling." He tied together the common elements of the dreams in his guess for the night.

> In the Churchill thing there was a ceremonial thing going on, and in the native dream there was a type of ceremony going on . . . leading to whatever the ceremonial would be to sacrificing two victims . . . I would say the sacrifice feeling in the native dream . . . would be more like the primitive trying to destroy the civilized . . . It believed in the god-authority . . . no god was speaking. It was the use of the fear of this, or the awe of god idea, that was to bring about the control. Not that [the] god spoke.

Particularly striking in its symbolism was the ancient theme of the god who must be sacrificed and then reborn (hence the birthday party). The body and blood of Christ seemed to be transformed into the Eucharistic cake and wine of the birthday party. Churchill, a leader of his people, becomes mysteriously emaciated as is the figure in the painting.

In the fifth dream President Johnson might be equated with Pilate, who as a political figure, tried to convince the Jews to release Jesus, "whom ye call the King of the Jews." However, they chose to release Barabbas, leaving the victims to be crucified (as in the dream). The "awe of god" was certainly present, and also "no god was speaking" might be equated with Christ's lament, "My God, my God, why has thou forsaken me?" More literal transformations of the painting were the dark skin of the "king" and the equating of Christ on the cross to a "totem-pole god."

The strong symbolic and ritualistic elements of the dreams drew the high rating of 80.7 (very great correspondence) from the judges—the highest rating given to any target in the whole series.

"Color his wounds red" seemed a potent way of heightening the telepathic impact of the Crucifixion.

The randomly chosen target for the next night, by contrast, was far easier to Feldstein to relate to since it evoked childhood memories: Katz's *Interior of the Synagogue*. The multisensory box contained candles similar to those in the painting as well as a candleholder, matches, and a button with Hebrew script.

Erwin's first dream was "something about school" and in his second dream there was a little town and himself as a small boy. Summing up his dreams in the morning, he said:

> Some kind of impression of school . . . going to school. . .
>
> The building that I was speaking of—I spent a little time with the boy in it . . . It could have been an experience that Sol [Feldstein] had, because it was sort of . . . exploring . . . During one of the studies . . . he talked something about a synagogue . . . maybe it was the one where he was dealing with the *Yellow Rabbi*. . .

It was, of course. References to a "synagogue" and "rabbi" enabled the judges to give this target a rating of 62.7 (Great Correspondence)—again, the highest rank for this transcript.

The target for the last experimental night was a creative challenge for Feldstein. The print, *Advice to a Young Artist,* by Daumier, portrays a bearded man giving advice to a young protégé about his painting. The colors brown, gray, and white predominate. The multisensory materials that night were an artist's kit: water colors, a brush, a canvas, and instructions to reproduce the target picture on the canvas (Plate 13).

In Erwin's first dream, he saw the colors "brown, white, chalky, grayish" and thought of a novel he had recently read, *The Mask of Apollo,* by Mary Renault. His fourth was "a dream within a dream," and his fifth was about Dick Powell, the movie actor. Erwin's associations in the morning were about actors, artists, and a portrait.

> The story was about a young Greek actor from Athens . . . He met a man who was very close to Plato. . .
>
> For some reason, Klee comes to mind, the artist . . . It seems to me that I recall . . . that in Van Gogh's earlier period he did paint peasants and . . . he did use a lot of browns. . .
>
> I referred back to having met Dick Powell earlier. It was in some room, some meeting place . . . And it seemed as though I saw his portrait. And then I met him, but they didn't look alike, exactly . . . Why a portrait of him as well as

alive? Why, I introduced him first as a portrait and then brought him in as an individual . . . as chairman of the board. Which would mean the portrait of someone who is some sort of an authority . . . Prestige. A position of some respect, some accomplishment.

The thematic correspondences of a young man coming under the influence of a prestigious older man (Plato, who was bearded) and the portrait of someone in authority (as well as direct references to articles and painting) gave this target a rating of 47.3 (Moderate Correspondence) — again, the highest ranking for this night's transcript.

In general, the "Second Erwin Study" with its "multisensory" technique produced extraordinary results: six nights out of eight were "direct hits" by ranking and the remaining two nights were very high "hits." As before, the rating system showed that the degree of correspondence was greatest in his associations and guess for the night. A statistical analysis of the ratings demonstrated that dream telepathy was indeed occurring — again as in Erwin's first study — with odds on the order of one thousand to one against chance.

Cicero's ghost seemed to be fading away.

CHAPTER 10
Women's Night

Critics of parapsychology often say that only successful ESP experiments are published—that the ones that fail are stuffed into dusty filing cabinets to be forgotten. At the Maimonides Dream Laboratory, however, every single experiment ever attempted has been published in journals or made available in public reports. And sometimes we find that we can learn as much from our failures as our successes, especially about the psychology of telepathic dreaming.

Two women served as subjects in two formal studies that "failed," that is, the number of nights when they dreamed telepathically was not significantly greater than the number of nights when they did not. Our telepathy hypothesis, you recall, requires the subjects to dream telepathically *consistently* over a long series of experiment nights.

A dreamer who had done well in the first screening study was a young Maimonides secretary, Theresa Grayeb. Her target had been Gauguin's *Moon and the Earth,* with a nude dark-skinned girl by a stream of water. Grayeb had dreamed of being wet in a bathing suit and of a girl trying to get a tan.

Two additional pilot nights were also successful. When Don Smoot, a research associate, had concentrated on a photograph, *Oriental Warrior,* which shows a carving on a temple wall of a man holding a three-pronged whip, Grayeb dreamed about "a ritual," three plastic knives and forks ("prongs down"), "a hunter," and looking at something "on the wall."

When Sol Feldstein had as a target *Merry Jesters,* by Rousseau, which shows several monkeys and a white bird in the jungle, Grayeb dreamed about "a large fur rug or an animal skin" and "a white bird."

In the light of her previously successful dream telepathy nights, Grayeb was chosen as the subject for the fourth formal study, which was to investigate the dream telepathy hypothesis by including control nights when there was no target. There were to be eight target nights and eight control nights in this series, which ran from March through June 1966. The order of target and control nights was to be determined randomly. If the agent, Don Smoot, was handed an envelope that was empty this meant it was a control night, and he would leave the building. If it contained a target picture, then he would stay in his agent's room and concentrate on it. As far as Theresa Grayeb knew, however, this was to be a sixteen-night series for dream telepathy with a different target each night. She was not told of the experiment's design because she might have tried to guess which night was for telepathy and which night was a control.

At the end of the series transcripts of all sixteen nights were judged against the eight targets actually used. Both Grayeb and three outside judges ranked the targets from number 1 to number 8 for correspondence to the transcript, and they also rated them on a 100-point scale. For both the subject and the judges the ratings and the rankings between target nights and control nights showed only chance differences. The telepathy hypothesis was not confirmed.

In the light of later experience, however, we think that a possible factor operating in this experiment was the fact that Grayeb had not been told of the experiment's design. Was she sensing something amiss by ESP? We didn't know.

The first night was a control night. Smoot left the building, and there was no target. Yet Grayeb was expecting the agent in his room to be looking at a target. She had been "tricked." Her comments became defensive, and the length of her verbal reports grew shorter until the twelfth night of the series, the fifth target night, when she began to recover her equanimity. By the last night, she bounced back with an excellent "hit."

This possible ESP-mediated resentment is further suggested by Grayeb's rankings of the target nights. For the first four target nights, she ranked three "misses" (8, 8, 7) and one "hit" (4); for the second four nights, she ranked four "hits" (1, 1, 4, 1), including three "direct hits."

The first night of the experimental series, March 20, 1966, was, as we saw, a non-target night. On the second night, March 24, the target was *Apple Thiefs*, by Goya, which shows four children stealing apples from a tree. Grayeb's brief dream correspondence to this target might also apply if she used psi to learn of "being tricked": "I think there were one or two of us talking, and I think we were talking about moral values. . . ." She ranked that barely a "hit" (4).

A target night three days later produced only two dream reports, so it was discarded as previously arranged. Again, her presumed ESP-mediated resentment seemed to shorten the number of dream reports. (Presumably, the number of her actual REM periods would be physiologically regular; it is her recall of the dreams that seemed to be adversely affected.)

On experimental night four, April 6, the target was *Love Song*, by de Chirico, which shows a sculptured head, a sphere, and a bright red glove. Only one dream seemed to have some mild correspondence to this: a wedding and the color red. She ranked this at the bottom of the eight as a "miss," although the judges gave it a low "hit."

Experimental night five was the next night when the target was *Hanukkah Candelabrum,* by Boller, which depicts a menorah, a metal dog, and a pink stone at the base. Although she dreamed about "a dog" and pink and green stones, she entirely missed the picture's main theme and ranked it a "miss" at the bottom of the eight.

Nights six through nine were control nights with no targets. And her dreams on night ten, April 27, had no correspondences with the target. She ranked it a "miss" with a 7. Night eleven, May 11, was another control night. But by night twelve, the fifth target night, she began to improve. The target was *Uncertainty of the Poet,* by de Chirico, which portrays a bunch of yellow bananas on a street beside the nude statue of a headless woman. She dreamed that "I was comparing two writers or authors and their style," which was thematically related to the picture's title; she also dreamed of the color yellow and a song from "Funny Girl." She picked this as number 1 (a "direct hit").

On the fourteenth experimental night, May 23, the target was a picture of a black and white striped zebra. She dreamed "Something to do with horses. Maybe a horse show or a horse race" and "a dark suit with a striped tie and a white shirt." She ranked the target as number 1, although the judges didn't catch the close correspondence and gave it a "miss."

On the fifteenth night, May 26, the target picture showed a bullfight scene with a female bullfighter holding a peach-colored piece of cloth and wearing a peach scarf.

The bull seemed to turn into a pig. "And I think the pig is alive when you start with it"; she also dreamed of "a soft peach color." She ranked the target as a "hit" (4), although, again, the judges did not catch the correspondence and gave it a "miss."

On the sixteenth and last night, the target was a postcard showing a fifth-century B.C. Attic amphora or vase and five naked men in black racing from left to right around the amphora (Plate 14). The amphora is basically black, with red-orange trimmings at the top and bottom. The racers are shown against a light orange background that is framed by black. A red line encircles the amphora at the runners' feet.

In Grayeb's third dream there were "People standing in the street and walking by. They're dressed in slacks, I think. They have jackets on; dark clothes." (It would have been unseemly for a young woman, perhaps, to tell a male experimenter about dreams of unclothed men.)

In reviewing the dream in the morning, she added:

> Wait a minute! There's something coming back . . . We were following cousin Joannie . . . we were following her down the street; I was coming out of some place . . . there were a lot of people around . . . and I was following Joannie

. . . a couple of us were. She was running, you know, to go some place . . . and we were supposed to go with her, yet she was going ahead of us . . .
Her fourth dream was

You walk through . . . like a circular driveway . . . and two mailmen pass . . . two people are coming from the left, and I'm coming from another direction . . . and the hostess or the person who owns the place is coming from another direction, and I go to meet her . . . and these other two people pass by . . . they're mailmen . . . and one of them speaks with an accent; sounds like an Italian accent . . . and they didn't have any mail . . . to deliver.

The runners, all identically black and coming from the left, also didn't have any mail to deliver but were running anyway. And their accent, presumably, was Greek instead of Italian.

In her fifth dream, the red line came through. "It was a yellow piece of paper, and he was circling them in red . . . and he showed me a picture of him — it was, you know, in glass, with a light background and a black frame." The light background being framed in black is right on.

In her seventh dream, she was looking at a photo album. "And in this little album, it listed how many people I don't know (nationality-wise) . . . I think there were twelve Syrians — just the number twelve, and it was a black page, and it had little cut-outs." A half-dozen Greeks in a little cut-out would have been more accurate, but, telepathically, telling Greeks from Syrians isn't always easy.

In the morning even her banter with the experimenter seemed to touch on the target's theme. "Do you realize that it's nine o'clock and there are other people on this floor, and I'll be running around in my pajamas?"

Grayeb seemed to have completely recovered her spirits and equanimity. As for her judging, she gave *Attic* a rank of number 1, a "direct hit." Although her series had not been a statistical success, it may offer insights into the psychology of dream telepathy.

The other formal series in which a woman was subject also provided some insights, in this case, from the subject herself, Dr. Robyn Posin, a psychologist. Posin, who had done so well with her target of *Mystic Night* in a screening study (see Chapter 8), was attempting to dream telepathically for an eight-night formal series with Sol Feldstein as her agent. When the eight transcripts were later judged against the eight target pictures, Posin did slightly better than the three outside judges. She got 6 "hits" and 2 "misses," which was not bad but not good enough.

Some months after the study, she wrote Krippner a lengthy comment analyzing the series from her own point of view. She referred to three of her best nights, the second, fourth, and seventh, and so we will give them here as examples, letting Posin speak for herself about her psychological attitudes that may have played an important role in blocking dream telepathy.

On the second night, October 28, 1965, the target randomly selected by Feldstein was *The Duelers,* by Goya, which portrays two Spaniards fighting a sword duel. One man has just made a fatal thrust into the other's abdomen.

In Posin's first dream, she was

> in the office of a man who is sort of waiting for this woman to arrive. He's actually . . . talking about her in the sense that the venom and anger that I experience in him is reserved for her . . . And he has this thing that's like a bullwhip . . . and he hits the wall with the whip and makes a crack . . . and then thinks of a woman. There was something very impotent about this man's rage . . . It wasn't a bullwhip that he had, it was really a cat-o-'nine tails . . . It had its origins . . . in Spain . . . It was a very frightening experience.

In her seventh dream, she was at a Black Muslim rally. "They were really raging, and all of a sudden some doors from an auditorium opened and out came Elijah Mohammed and a bunch of his followers . . . He had this huge flaming torch with which to set some more stuff on fire, and I got very scared." Her associations to this were "It was like a real chaos scene . . . the terrorism, that same kind of lack of control, I guess, that seemed to me to be the case of the guy with the whip too. There's such . . . wide open anger and hostility and acting out in it . . . It's some sort of conflagration, either symbolically or realistically . . . something rather violent." And so was the target.

On the fourth night, November 14, the target was *The Drinker,* by Chagall, which portrays a head, separated from its body at the neck, drinking from a bottle. The face is white with eyes and lips outlined in black. The body (from the neck down) is clothed in black.

In her first dream she managed to combine drinking with the two neck halves. "There's a commercial song that's going through my mind — it's about a beer. About Ballantine beer. The words are, 'Why is Ballantine beer like an opening night, a race that finishes neck and neck. . .'" Then she combined wearing black with drinking. "A young woman was wearing what was supposed to be a cocktail dress, and it was black. . ."

In the morning she remembered more to the song. "'There's more spirit to it,' that's why the beer is supposed to be so great. And . . . I remembered thinking about a movie . . . *Juliet of the Spirits* . . . One of the characters . . . wears this wild black outfit that's really very outlandish, and heavy make-up."

In her third dream, she saw a bartender. "There was another guy there, and . . . they sent over a drink for me . . . This girl wanted them to go or something . . . She had loads of makeup on, and lots of black eye shadow, and black eye pencil lining her eyes, and black eyebrows, and her lips were black too." Dreams combining drinking and black lips are even rarer than paintings of them.

The seventh night's target was a photograph, *The Public Gaol, Williams-*

burg, Virginia. It shows an outdoor scene at the colonial restoration in Williamsburg, Virginia. In the foreground are stocks and a pillory. A guide is about to take a group of tourists on a tour of the jail.

In Posin's first dream she was talking to someone on the telephone. "I think of Sol's hypothesis about communication dreams . . . like if the sleep subject has those dreams, like telephones and things—that it's coming through . . . the material that the agent is working on. I just feel like tonight is going to be a good night."

Her second dream was

> I was talking to Monte, looking at a subway map while I was talking to him . . . He kidded with me about the fact that I really ought to keep a carton of cigarettes down here . . . he thought it would be a good idea for the visiting people and just in general for me to keep a second carton of cigarettes out here in Brooklyn . . .
>
> I was looking at that map . . . and there was something about the connecting links in the map between Manhattan and Brooklyn . . . It wasn't quite a subway map, but there were lots of bars running through it . . . I was looking at it and tracing the lines across the waterways from Brooklyn into Manhattan . . . in some peculiar fashion, it almost became a miniature model of what I was looking at.

(In her letter Posin speculates about what meaning cigarettes might have in the dream. The visitors seem clear enough.)

Her fourth dream involved her sister and some girl friends.

> And this whole troop of kids came riding by down a hill on bicycles, going swimming, and they asked this girl if she was going to come with them . . . This whole building on the corner which had been a bank . . . was all boarded up . . . It was like the property was condemned, and they were going to be tearing all this down to build something new.
>
> Two television sets going at the same time . . . Apparently she was having a lot of difficulty with reception, and both pictures on both these sets were pretty bad . . . It's one of those communication dreams, and . . . it seems to suggest some difficulty . . .

Her fifth dream took place in the waiting room of a hospital. "There's a woman—a couple of women—kind of demanding shock treatment . . . we should have facilities to allow them to feel that way if they wanted to . . ." The Williamsburg "gaol" facilities would also take care of them.

The following is the letter written by Posin to Stanley Krippner.

> As I've reread the set of transcripts I first read for judging and then reviewed when you first sent them (how many months ago), I've had a number of thoughts which seem quite relevant. I think my reluctance to get my "subjective" report on paper has much to do with what I now "hear" in the transcripts of my dream protocols—namely, a clear sense of unwillingness to allow the ESP experience to develop and a resentment at what unconsciously I had

experienced as an intrusion (the dream reporting and even being a subject). In reading the very long dream of the first night and then again the eighth night, these feelings seem quite striking and intense. It wasn't until this weekend and this rereading that I became aware of what seems to have been going on throughout the experiment. I remember — at the time of judging — that I felt the eight nights were nothing like that first night I'd spent before I started working (with *Mystic Night* as the target) or the experience I had as an agent. With the exception of the second, fourth, and seventh nights, there was little of the intense and vivid conviction of an ESP experience that I'd felt before participating in this experimental series.

Reflecting from this distance in time and space on what was going on in my life at the time of the experiment, I can begin to see that the whole ESP involvement then was a great threat to my equilibrium. At the same time it is clear too that I couldn't have allowed myself the open awareness that was needed. I was, at that time, too much concerned with being "open" psychologically. It is obvious now that I was far from open — with myself, with you, and with Monte about the experiment and certainly in my dreaming and responding during the experiment. I suspect, too, that my tardiness in writing a subjective report has something to do with being still reluctant to acknowledge these feelings. Partly I suppose the reluctance has to do with what seems to me to be an admission that I was then engaged in "sabotaging" the experiment. Still, that's the impression I now have as I read through the dream reports. I hear my own fear of losing control (having an ESP experience or, more generally, allowing an impact from another person) and of being "exposed." Though I then laughed and kidded about being called "a witch" (I think my skepticism about ESP became very personalized), for me to have such experiences then would have been, and I guess was, very disrupting. In this new light, I really wonder what was happening on the second, fourth and seventh nights that made my control over myself either unnecessary or else ineffective. I wonder, too, what the data from me and from the judges look like for those nights. Let me give you my recollections of those nights. They were the most vivid and impelling experiences of the lot and the ones I'd remembered and intended to write about even before rereading the protocols.

The violence, anger and rage in the dreams during the second night (when *The Duelers* was the target) were unique in my dream experience — more so than anything in the dreaming of all the other nights during the experiment. I have no recollections of any such dreams in my ordinary experience. In the second REM period awakening, I stated, "It's not quite a dream again. It's like a thought theme . . . A projection of myself, I think, having to do with the influence I would have over my own behavior with the sense — as if my own behavior is in response to some external direction."

I wonder whether the impact of the pictures on Sol might have made it more difficult for me to screen out his "sending." I seem to have been concerned throughout the night with themes that seem related. Following REM period number four, I recalled ". . . sinking further and further into a drowsing state — and then my *contact* lenses started to bother me . . . I started to take them out but I didn't have a guard for them. . ." I underlined the word "contact" as it may have indicated a feeling of closeness to the agent.

I said that I was "feeling close to Sol" but also had "thoughts" about a "need to be alone." The concern about "not being forced" in "making decisions" shows my ambivalence. The intrusion in the seventh REM dream period (seemingly the most telepathic) of something about "prisms" which "could be oriented to restrict my eyes" is significant as were my interview comments after having trouble putting the lenses "in the container."

I also recall that on the morning after this night I had the kind of conviction of having had ESP that I had felt with the *Mystic Night* target.

On the fourth night, when *The Drinker* was used, I remember the very vivid feeling that something was going on vis-à-vis you, Stan. It was when I couldn't fall asleep after the second awakening. I kept turning toward the control room when usually I slept facing the opposite wall. Then, too, there was a really extreme feeling of *tension*. In telling you of these feelings I remarked about feeling "spooked." This was the night you were doing some statistics and then when you stopped I was able to go back to sleep.

I'm also struck in rereading the transcript by the double meaning of "spirit" throughout. "Spirit" means "alcohol" (in terms of the target picture) but I also talked about a "kooky psychic friend of *Juliet of the Spirits.*" Also, my many references to "craziness" and "peculiarity" seem related not only to the target but to my own sense of "craziness" in having an ESP experience. Also there were many "fleeting" parts of dreams I couldn't remember. Just as in the second night, there is throughout the protocol the indication of experiencing ESP or communication (even to my reference back to the *Mystic Night* target and experience) and the attempts to ward it off as frightening.

Having gotten this far, I begin to think about the fact that this target, like the one on the second night, is a very provocative one. It is very unusual in its content and has a violent theme. Could it be the content as well as the possibility of Sol's associations to it that overwhelmed my attempt to ward off its impact on me? Or, too, might this be more generally true about targets in your studies — that really *strong* target themes — violent, bizarre, emotionally stimulating themes — have a greater chance of getting through to a subject who's trying to ward off the agent's impact?

The seventh night in some ways was the most exciting night for me. When I finally saw the targets I was astonished. In the fourth REM period dream my picture of my sister and her friends, as well as the house and outdoors scene was *exactly* that of the Williamsburg target picture. I was standing at the corner where the "visitors" are on the right side of the picture, and looking out towards the field behind them! When I saw the target pictures I really felt *spooked* with that!

I noticed during my rereading that all my dream reports have a "near miss" quality—as though to disguise the ESP impact for me. The dream about the map of Brooklyn and Manhattan with so much emphasis on the "connecting lines" and "waterways between" could have been a reference to the *Williamsburg Bridge* connecting Brooklyn and Manhattan. Yet I never actually mentioned "Williamsburg Bridge" in the interview. The same seems true about the "*shock* treatment" as a veiled reference to *stock* treatment.

The many references to cigarettes here seems also connected to Virginia as the home of most tobacco companies. In seeing the target and recognizing the scene as the one in my dream I was struck by the many references through the night to two dimensions versus three dimensions.

Again, on this night as on the other two, my recollections now and my statements through the night and the interview all point up the vivid and intense experience. I seem on the seventh night much less guarded in reporting and much less concerned about the impact than I had been on the second and fourth nights.

I am also struck by the fact that Sol's hypothesis about the appearance of "communication symbols" as indicative of telepathy seems to hold up in each of these three nights. All three dream reports contain very clear, positive references to *good* communication.

What seems more important in reviewing all my notes in this letter is the importance of using really *potent* target material. Clearly with subjects who aren't afraid of telepathy this may be relatively unimportant. Still, with an "ordinary," or—more so—with a "defending" subject, the more unusual and potent the target material the less likely it is to be kept out.

Posin's comments were helpful to us in planning further experimental series that would incorporate more potent target material and investigate psychodynamic aspects of telepathic dreaming.

CHAPTER 11
"The Prince of the Percipients"

At a symposium on ESP at the University of California in Los Angeles in 1970, Dr. Robert Van de Castle, Director of the Sleep and Dream Laboratory at the University of Virginia, confessed his innermost motivations for becoming a dream telepathy subject.

"At one level," he said, "I was concerned with competition, achievement, and exhibitionism. Due to my ability to recall dreams in such great detail during laboratory awakenings, I was kiddingly described as 'The King of the Dreamers.' I was proud of this title and also wished to accumulate further laurels by now becoming 'The Prince of the Percipients.'"

Van de Castle's title of "King of the Dreamers" was not given lightly. In his eight-night dream telepathy study (extending from January through November 1967) at the Maimonides Dream Laboratory, Van de Castle's ability at dream recall far surpassed that of previous subjects. His transcripts of one night's dreams run from 60 to 70 pages, as compared with 20 to 35 for more ordinary mortals. When five formal studies were analyzed for "units of meaning"—the smallest basic descriptive units—it was found that he was by far the "King," with 2,439 units. His closest runner-up was Erwin, in his second study, with 1,762.

·But let us trace how the aspiring "Prince of the Percipients"—a well-known sleep and dream researcher as well as a leading parapsychologist—became involved in dream telepathy. Van de Castle tells the following part of the story in his own words.

The first series of experiments in which I was involved took place at the Institute for Dream Research when it was located in Miami, Florida. Dr. Calvin Hall, who is the director of the Institute, and I were working on a project comparing laboratory dreams obtained through REM awakening procedures with dreams that were spontaneously recalled at home.

Although Hall and I had had frequent discussions about ESP, his attitude could be characterized as falling somewhere between neutralism and slight skepticism. One day, Dr. Ullman came down and paid us a visit to encourage us to try some telepathic dream studies. Dr. Ullman was also rather openly attempting to recruit me for a position in his dream laboratory. It was probably this latter activity on Dr. Ullman's part which acted as the triggering stimulus for Dr. Hall's decision to attempt some telepathic studies.

Both Hall and I had been serving as subjects for our own study. One night I had the following dream: I was walking across some unknown university campus at night when I felt myself strongly impelled to enter a particular building. In the basement of this building there was an elevated boxing ring and there was a boxing match going on. I found myself becoming extremely engrossed with the boxing match and began to strongly root for the person who appeared to be the underdog. I remember yelling encouragements to my fighter and in my enthusiasm was throwing vigorous jabs and hooks myself to show my boxer what he should be doing. The round ended and I walked away from the building to return to my leisurely stroll across the campus.

After I had reported this dream, Dr. Hall walked around the room with a very strange look on his face. Without informing me, he had decided to liven up his dull hours of monitoring the EEG machine by attempting to send a target stimulus through telepathy. The situation he had selected was that of a boxing match which had recently taken place in Miami between Cassius Clay and Sonny Liston. After telling me what had transpired, we decided that this first attempt at telepathy had turned out so well, that we should make further efforts to see if we could achieve similar results.

On another occasion I had a dream about a large crowd of skiers being towed up the hill while others were skiing down the side of the mountain slope. Dr. Hall had been concentrating on a skiing scene as a target stimulus.

Since our study required that all subjects keep a diary of home dreams, we could note the frequency with which certain themes appear under non-ESP conditions. In my own case, I had recorded about ninety dreams at home within a few months. There were no incidents of boxing or skiing during any of the ninety home dreams or during any of the other laboratory dreams except for the two occasions when boxing and skiing were the target stimuli. We knew from our other investigations that some subjects dream of particular topics with great frequency. It would not be very impressive if someone who regularly dreams about football games in nearly one third of his dreams reported a football event when that was the target stimulus. As a consequence of having these outside norms on my dreams available, we felt greater certainty that ESP was actually functioning in those dreams.

Hall published his successful (that is, statistically significant) study of telepathic dreaming in the German journal of the Freiburg University Institute for Border Areas of Psychology.[1] Of the six male subjects in the study, the one who did best was "Osceola" — the name of a famous Seminole Indian chief taken by Van de Castle as the aspiring "Prince of the Percipients." And now he faced the challenge of big-time competition: Maimonides.

The following are Van de Castle's comments on his strong motivations in striving for telepathic success at the Dream Lab.

There was a strong feeling that every night had to yield success because so much preparation had gone into each night. I flew from North Carolina [where he was at the time the experiment was initiated] to New York for my one night stands and whatever results were going to be obtained had to be produced on that one night. There were no tomorrows as my visits were spaced about six to eight weeks apart. When you're making a round trip of over a thousand miles for the single solitary purpose of being a telepathic dream subject, you feel that the pressure is on you to dream, and to dream telepathically.

One of the advantages of the infrequent trips was that it enabled me to sustain a high interest level for each individual session. If the trips had been scheduled too closely together, I think the task would have become somewhat dull and routinized. As the time for a visit neared, my excitement began to increase. It provided a welcome change of pace to leave the quaint rural village atmosphere of Chapel Hill and come to the huge throbbing metropolitan center of New York. Such visits also provided a chance to discuss parapsychology with the Maimonides staff. The entire staff always gave me the feeling that I was a visiting sultan and the red carpet was rolled out with a royal flourish. Unquestionably, this lavish indulgence of my narcissistic needs made an important contribution to my desire to please the staff with a successful night's work.

Also, they had just finished up two telepathic dream studies with another psychologist [Erwin] who had been a very successful percipient. I was hoping to surpass his accomplishments and leave behind a performance record that would be unbeatable.

The hypothesis for the Van de Castle study was the same as the earlier ones, requiring him to have telepathic dreams consistently over the eight nights of the series. In order to investigate psychodynamic aspects of his dreaming as they related to the telepathic target, Ullman planned a psychoanalytically oriented depth interview with Van de Castle the next day after Van de Castle had judged his night's dreams on a 100-point scale against a target pool of eight art prints. In this series, each night had its own target pool of eight pictures, assembled by an outside research aide. Later, an outside judge also ranked and rated them. There were three agents for this series: Ullman served as agent on night three; the agent on the first two nights was a psychologist, Margaret Kinder; and the agent for nights four through eight was Barbara Lidsky, a Maimonides psychiatric social worker.

Van de Castle, who was given a free hand in selecting the two women agents on the basis of what rapport he felt he could achieve with them, candidly confessed that an important criterion was their sex appeal. "They were attractive, well endowed, single young women about whom it would be easy to develop sexual fantasies, and I did. It was as if I were attempting to consummate a sexual relationship telepathically — consummate in its basic meaning of 'bringing to completion or fulfillment.'" Before each night when the women were agents, Van de Castle would spend time with them in getting to know them better and attempting to establish a rapport that would facilitate telepathic dreaming.

The first experimental night was January 5, 1967. The agent was Margaret Kinder, and the randomly selected target was *Discovery of America by Christopher Columbus,* by Dalí. This large and enormously elaborate canvas depicts the young Columbus in a dream sequence about his future voyage across the Atlantic. The Virgin Mary is shown on a banner borne by Columbus as he walks forward on the beach. He wears a white transparent robe through which can be seen the nipples of his breasts. Behind him are his ship, a church, and a row of nude boys, shown from behind, holding banners aloft as they stand in the sea. There are also several young Catholic acolytes dressed in white robes, and bearing crosses.

Van de Castle's first dream seemed to catch several of the painting's elements.

> Something to do with a Polish mother . . . Something to do with motherhood . . . I came out there into the room, and . . . it seemed as if . . . that had been changed into a church . . . A big Mass was going on. It seemed now that it was a whole big church . . . crowded with people on all sides, and it was very filled and it was like church or Mass was now going to begin . . . In the church some of the people seemed to be dressed in the white robes . . . Some fairly youngish male figure . . . There was this person and another one, and they were now talking about the girl . . . in Atlantic City or Atlantic Beach. . . .

In the morning he added:

> The part that didn't seem to have any tie-in . . . with personal dynamics or with the experimental situation was the crowded church scene. . .
>
> It just seemed like it had been sort of a shrine or it had been something of national importance, something of historical significance. The Mass, I think I associated with the Catholic Church only because as a youngster I had been raised for a few years as a Catholic before I gave it up, so most of my associations seem to be that this was a very elaborate affair. It seems as if the people were wearing the kind of little white frocks that altar boys wear, and it seems that there was a white row of these across the front . . . It was solemn and dignified and mysterious in a way. . .

His third dream was "It seemed like I was standing out in the hallway and then . . . Angela went by. And it seemed Angela had pajamas on and they were sort of silky and they were semi-transparent. She still had a bra and pants on underneath, but you could still somewhat see through the pajamas . . . and it looked as if her breasts weren't quite as large. . ." He added later, "you could sort of see the nipples underneath the bra, and I remember looking with interest at this. . ."

Angela was an attractive girl he had seen the day before. She turned up again in his guess for the night. "Her breasts were not as large in the pajamas as they had appeared in the sweater yesterday . . . There was a great crowd of people . . . Something to do with the church, perhaps. Something to do with crowded conditions . . . Those were the things that seemed to have impressed me as having the most intrusive quality."

When Van de Castle looked at the eight pictures in the target pool in the morning, he was relieved to find that Angela's breasts had not really shrunk at all; they belonged to the young Columbus. He gave the Dalí painting a rating of 100 percent as his first choice. He was well on his way to princeship.

Psychodynamically, his preference for seeing female nipples through the transparent robe instead of a male's seemed not very mysterious.

The second night was February 2; Kinder was again the agent. The target was *The Wine Taster,* by Van Delft, which shows a Dutch couple in old-fashioned dress at a table. The man wearing a black hat stands holding a bottle of wine and looking at his wife, who is seated and drinking from a glass. On the left wall of the room is a stained glass window; the floor is composed of black and white tiles in a checkerboard pattern. An embroidered cloth with a colorful flower design covers the table.

Van de Castle's first dream had to do with dancing. "It seemed as if one of the figures had on sort of a checked coat, black and white checked coat . . . A dancing or night club cabaret scene." He added in the morning: "I had the impression like one of the Toulouse-Lautrec posters where . . . there is this fellow with a long, thin jaw . . . dressed in the clothing of that era . . . As I think of this guy, I see him sort of wearing a black derby hat. . ."

He summed up his second dream in the morning.

> I was over visiting some friends . . . and it seemed if we stayed around there for a couple of weeks we could help her . . . with her household chores . . . We were going in this jeep and having to force . . . through . . . this shrubbery and very brilliantly colored flowers . . . reds and yellows and purples and just about the whole color spectrum . . . and this one black flower . . . I was taking pills in the dream for a headache . . . I think they were in a green bottle . . . It seems like I was taking a glass of water to take this last pill that the girl was offering me . . . The dream scene was set in the home of the Foxes . . . We're close friends . . . and get together and socialize for a drink and so on. . .
>
> I like *Girl Before the Mirror* very much. I like the colors in it. They're vivid reds and blues and purples and yellows and so on. I used to have a copy of it on my wall. . .

His guess for the night was

> There would be people in the picture. The people, I think, would be predominantly female. There may be males involved but their's would not be so much in the doing role. They would be more as directing or watching. It's the women

who are doing whatever it is that's getting done. I think that it would involve movement on the part of the women...

Some of these correspondences, imbedded in the long detailed dreams he recalled, seemed thematically very apt. The "black and white checked coat" seemed to correspond with the floor; the Toulouse-Lautrec poster man with old-fashioned clothes and a black hat were on target; the many colored flowers were suggestive of the tablecloth; drinking from a glass and the bottle were directly on target; and the *Girl Before the Mirror* with the vivid colors seemed to correspond with the stained glass window in the wall, and so on.

But these transformations were also somewhat descriptive of some other targets in the pool, and Van de Castle chose *The Wine Tasters* as number 4 with a rating of 28. Still a "hit," but he would have to do better if he were to win all eight rounds.

The third night was March 15, and the agent was Ullman. The target was Rousseau's *Repast of the Lion* (Plate 15), which depicts a lion feeding on its kill of a smaller animal. The flowing blood contrasts sharply with the pleasant natural surroundings of trees and flowering shrubs.

In Van de Castle's first dream,

They were saying something about this girl was the murderess...

I could now feel somebody starting to climb into bed with me. And I became very upset with this and tried to grab the person and ... put my arm around his neck and started to sort of strangle him ... And it was ... a young ... boy and he said his name ... was Doodle or Poodle ... Then it seemed like this guy was starting to sort of hop around as if he were sort of like a frog...

Van de Castle's associations to this were "There was a Rorschach study in which they investigated frog symbolism. People had recorded a frog response in the Rorschach and found as they had predicted that these people would have significantly more in the way of eating problems than people who did not, and tied it up with the psychoanalytic theory about oral impregnation..."

His second dream was long and involved.

College-age girls ... They were really going to have to get the costumes or the uniforms changed because one of them felt they were very indecent ... One girl ... was critical of the rest...

There seemed to be ... an outdoor scene. The sun was shining ... A karate machine ... You were to try to make a karate chop against it...

Now at this point, it seemed as if I was involved in a conversation with a person whose name is George Saute. One of the things I just now associated with his name is that "sauté" in French means "jump" and he seemed to be standing right next to ... a ... jack rabbit ... George ... was saying something about ... it would be nice to be back around ... the wide open spaces ... His death was announced ... George had shot himself ... It was a great tragedy...

Then I was very concerned with . . . three dogs, different breeds of dogs and different colors . . . It seemed like I could see the grass around. . .

Now, this other segment involves some person who . . . was saying something about having gotten tough with this other government . . . somehow he had gotten this foreign government to back down. . .

His third dream was "There were two puppies. One seemed to be black and one brown, and we were trying to take the picture of us holding the two puppies . . . It seemed like the two of them had been sort of fighting before. You could kind of see their jaws were open and you could see their teeth . . . they would continue to try and go on with this playful biting. . ."

Van de Castle was reminded of a target used in an earlier series, "Animals," by Tamayo. "That particular target strikes me as raw, rampant aggression. I don't recall if there is any blood in that picture, but it's almost as though blood could be dripping from their teeth. . ."

His guess for the night was

Aggression seems to . . . keep popping up . . . There was the aggression, certainly in the first awakening where I bodily picked up somebody and threw him out in the hall. There was in the second one with this little device for registering karate chops. There was the aggression of the person in the military uniform who had taken kind of a hawk-like stance with regard to the opposition. There was the kind of muted aggression with the dogs on the last awakening who had been sort of fighting. So aggression is in there . . . If you want to consider the suicide as self-aggression, that would be another kind of component in there. But the aggression would have to be in some kind of diguise. . ."

The last statement, of course, was wrong. The dream disguised the aggression but in the target it was forthright. Van de Castle chose *Repast of the Lion* as number 3 with a high correspondence of 78, another "hit."

Ullman commented on the psychoanalytic aspects of this night.

After spending several hours reviewing the dreams of the night before with Dr. Van de Castle and his associations to them, and considering the context in which they occurred as well as his relationship with me, I then tried to sift out what might be considered "normal" motivational content and what might possibly be "paranormal." Leaving the target aside for the moment, the dreamer seemed to be preoccupied with a single major theme and a number of minor counter themes. The major theme was the intrusive threat posed by intimacy with another male. The threat was of frightening proportions and even lethal in character. The minor themes focused about various defensive counter strategies designed to minimize or ward off the threat, such as transforming a frightening situation into a playful one and using animals to act out aggression.

One can only speculate as to what role ESP might have played. The painting is a highly stylized yet grim statement of the law of the jungle — the weak being destroyed by the strong. The dreams include references to murder, suicide, karate, strangling, and biting, as well as to animals. One cannot say definitely that the presence of death in the dream and the appearance of two animals, one having obviously inflicted a lethal blow by biting the neck, acted as telepathic day residues to facilitate the expression of the conflict depicted. All one can say is that the two were congruent.

The fourth night was May 17, and Barbara Lidsky took over as agent. The target was *Kathak Dancing Girls,* by an unknown artist in India. It portrays two girls in brightly striped costumes dancing in a meadow. Circling the dancers in an oval is a blue sky, and golden star-like objects form the background.

Van de Castle's first dream was about "striped black and yellow bees . . . And I was surprised that you could only see two of them . . ."

His second dream had to do with Stanley Krippner, who was monitoring the EEG.

> It seemed that when I was in the lab, I was lying there and there were some of Stan's expense account statements and I looked at one of them and felt guilty for doing so because it wasn't any of my business . . . and it seemed like it was his expense account for a trip to California . . . Down underneath something was written to the effect of, "This was not enough money. Twenty-five dollars more needed to be raised." And it seemed as if somehow I knew that he didn't need to raise the money, that the twenty-five dollars had been raised in another way . . . this problem had been corrected.

Van de Castle knew that Krippner had made a trip to California in March, but the expense accounting that was twenty-five dollars short was puzzling—until Krippner later explained that in totaling up his expenses, he found that he was twenty-five dollars short of breaking even and that the additional money was sent to him by one of his sponsors.

Van de Castle's third dream started out on a theme later found to be connected with Barbara Lidsky's associations. "I dreamed that . . . I was going on a trip some place . . . It was some foreign country . . . For some reason the thought of . . . a Caribbean Island . . . named Andros." Lidsky had been thinking about a recent trip to an island in the Caribbean named Antigua as her association of visiting a foreign country.

His third dream continued.

> People seemed to be getting up and sort of stretching . . . I looked up at the sky and it seemed to be full of stars, and the stars had a . . . sort of golden color to them . . . Then I looked over to another part of the sky . . . And it seemed as if there were millions of stars and they were very vivid and very much this golden color . . . More like the kind of gold stars you'd see from fireworks display . . ."

His guess for the night was

> The part that was very vivid was . . . seeing these golden stars, which again clearly don't belong . . . the viewing of the night sky with the gold stars in it . . .

Sort of some more light mood or more holidayish . . . when I was on the island . . . It seemed there were a few small plants here and there. . .

Bees . . . the way they did their dance, then this communicated both the direction of the hive and the distance of it. . .

I think one of the men is wearing a shirt with alternating stripes which might be like the bees and the stripes they had on. And it would be a foreign land . . . This very vivid impression of the golden stars in the starry black night. . .

Van de Castle seemed to pick up very well on the unusual elements in his dreams that corresponded with *Kathak Dancing Girls;* including the interesting association of striped bees dancing. He gave the target a number 2 rank with a rating of 52, a "hit." Another round was won.

On the fifth night, June 27, Barbara Lidsky randomly selected de Chirico's *The Enigma of Fate,* a tall, triangular painting that shows a giant red hand in the foreground touching a black and white checkerboard. In the center is a tall, brick chimney between two tall buildings that have open arches.

Van de Castle (uncharacteristically) could not remember his first dream, but his second dream "had something to do with a giant."

His third dream was about the YMCA. "There were two stories in the building and downstairs was the swimming pool . . . I must have been swimming . . . because when I came upstairs, my hands were wet . . . You told me to push this button up at the top of the stairs, and I did it. And I remember pushing and my finger being wet . . . And then you came along . . . and you were going to press the button. . ." He added later: "The button just seemed sort of black."

In his fourth dream the symbolic character of the tall brick chimney seemed to come through in explicit phallic references.

In his fifth dream, "Two guys . . . took out a picture puzzle, a jig-saw puzzle. . ." He added later: "It seemed as if I could see them picking the puzzle up out of the box and the puzzle was still sort of stuck together. . ."

His guess for the night was

Oh, that giant . . . seemed not to make any sense . . . It might have been an abstract kind of painting . . . It also seemed as if there were kinds of distortions, sizes, so that part doesn't seem as if it would be realistic. I was talking about a giant . . . which was bigger than life so something would be drawn not true to life in terms of it . . . not true to life in size. It would have to be drawn out of scale and larger than what would be the real life size. . .

Van de Castle chose the de Chirico print with the giant hand touching the black and white "puzzle" as number 3 with a rating of 76 — another "hit."

On the sixth night, September 9, Lidsky's target, Cézanne's *Trees and Houses,* was a difficult one to relate to. No people are shown in the painting, only an orange-roofed white house on a hill covered by stark, barren trees, above orange-brown earth.

In Van de Castle's first dream, "All I could remember is it was something about a house..." In his second dream he saw a brief image of "just some black and white stairs leading downward..."

By his third dream, Van de Castle was remarking, "Still this same type of theme. Either Barbara and I are blocked tonight, or else she has one helluva dull, uninspiring, affectless type of a picture to deal with."

In his fourth dream, "There was a house. It was a model house like you would use if you were building a home yourself ... There were no people involved and nothing going on but this rearranging of the interior structure of it." He added later: "It was just this isolated house that seemed very small in size..."

His fifth dream had to do with "Very tall, dingy buildings." By his sixth dream he was saying, "There was no color, no movement ... It's been a very poor yield. It may be a great yield if there's a target picture in there that's a lonely shack sitting on a hillside ... then we've been doing tremendous..."

The barren trees and the color of the ground and the roof were suggested in his seventh dream. "There was a telephone pole ... It was all dirt road ... as far as colors, I could see ... the sort of orange clay of the dirt road..."

His guess for the night seemed right on.

> Some concern with houses ... I never have had any evening that I can recall with only such brief momentary fragments without any type of continuity ... very much struck by the almost complete absence of people. Practically totally without people. There wasn't one single kind of personal interaction of any consequence ... It would have to be without people ... It would probably be dingy grays or browns or sooty color ... Maybe ... some of these kinds of building-landscapes.

Van de Castle gave the target a number 2 with a rating of 69, another "hit" and another round won. The outside judge gave it a "direct hit."

On night seven, October 23, Lidsky randomly selected the target *Gangster Funeral*, by Levine. The dead gangster lies in his coffin on the left; his wife, relatives, and his garishly dressed mob pay their respects as a police officer stands by. The dominant gangster is balding and wears a brown suit and a grayish vest. The painting's perspective makes the coffin appear oval.

In Van de Castle's first dream, he had the feeling that "There is not a great deal of motion, that something quite fixed and static would be there. I had a feeling of ovalness in the center ... A little bit of brown background."

In his second dream, "There was a conversation going on at a table between myself and two other male characters . . . One of them was Fred . . . I was sort of joshing or kidding him about the clothing he was wearing. He had on a rather garish suit . . . It seems as if he had on a vest which was not exactly matching the suit . . ." He added later, "Your other suit is lumpy too.'"

In his third dream, "This person . . . was in his early forties, and the point that I remember was the partial thinning of hair, baldness . . . And it seemed as if I had to talk to the police . . ."

The dead gangster seemed to change into a white mouse in his fifth dream. "There was a real small baby mouse . . . and I wasn't sure if it was going to survive or not, so I called to somebody to get a cigar box so we could put this in . . ."

His guess for the night was "I would say people have to be in it because this was a very people-dominated night from beginning to end . . . so I would say this was a recurrent thing that I would expect the target to have. Some people in there in some kind of interaction."

Van de Castle chose *Gangster Funeral* as number 3 with a rating of 85, another "hit," which, incidentally, the judge ranked as number 1. Seven rounds were won, but in this competition all eight have to be won.

The last night of the series was November 26. When Lidsky was handed the randomly selected target-print of Cellini's *The Perseus,* which shows Perseus with the gory head of Medusa, she said it was too gruesome to work with. When the experimenter randomly selected an alternate, it, too, turned out to be too gruesome: *The Crucifixion* by Sutherland. Rather than upset her, the experimenter chose a third target for her, *Man with Arrows and Companion* by Bichitr, which portrays three men in India sitting outdoors. One of the men is playing a musical string instrument, and the dominant figure is holding a bow and arrows. The third man has a stick over his shoulder that looks like a muzzle of a rifle. At his feet is a large bundle tied up in cloth. All three men are wearing hats or headdresses. In the background is a primitive shelter. An obscure detail of the painting is a stake with a rope tied around it.

Like an American film-maker adapting a Japanese samurai plot, Van de Castle made a western out of the target in his dreams.

In Van de Castle's first dream:

> The first image seemed to be sort of a bedroll, and that made me think of "western" . . . That faded out for a minute and then the next image seemed to be as if I were walking through some doors and standing straight ahead of me were three men. They were standing equally distant apart, maybe about six feet apart from each other. They were dressed in short-sleeved blue shirts and berets and they looked very tough. I believe they were holding rifles, but the rifles were down at their sides as if the rifle butt were resting on the ground. Then it seemed as if the word "gunslinger" came through . . . A setting that's foreign or rural or western and in which there's implied violence.

In his second dream,

It seemed like it was a short length of rope . . . then there were three or four coils of rope, then the rope came down in a straight line again . . . The short looped rope led down to an image and there was a hanging and the words came to mind, *The Oxbow Incident,* a book or a movie . . . a group of men, cowboy clothes, guns on, old withered tree with an arm branch . . . and this guy swinging from a rope . . . And there was this show . . . with country music, and guys with cowboy suits and cowboy hats on . . .

In his third dream he saw a fleeting image of someone being drowned and "being pulled out of the water by a rope around their leg . . ."

In his fourth dream he saw "a coiled spring" that "just seemed to be again like some of the rope images."

In his fifth dream he saw a "hammock in which there was an awful lot of suspended strings." And in his sixth he dreamed about a trip to Oklahoma.

His guess for the night was

There might have been some day residue for this western theme in terms of Grand Ole Opry [a country-western singing radio show], although I don't think so . . . Certainly what kept coming through time and time again was some kind of concern with rope or string or cord or strings . . . My guess would be that it was a scene of western life involved. People dressed up in cowboy suits with guns . . . that somewhere in the picture rope imagery appears in a very prominent or conspicuous way.

Van de Castle ranked the target number 1 with a 100 percent rating, a "direct hit" that was a knockout in the eighth round.

It seemed curious that the obscure detail of a rope coiled around a stake should have been so prominent in his dreams; but the rope also connects thematically with the strings of the musical instrument and the string of the bow (compare "Oxbow"). Impressive was the way that the three men sitting several feet apart came through in the dream practically unchanged except for "western" adaption.

It is possible, too, that the man being hanged ("You tend to feel sorry in a way for the victim") might have been inspired by the *Crucifixion* or the *Perseus* target that the agent had rejected. One critic has pointed out that the rejection of the two randomly selected targets was a breach of procedure and that the night should have been discarded.[2] It is certainly the case that Lidsky's response was unanticipated and that the decision could be called into question. Had this occurred again, it is likely that the night would have been discarded and a make-up scheduled.

In general, the ranks assigned by Van de Castle to the eight targets (out of the target pool of sixty-four) put him considerably ahead of Erwin's judging of his second series of eight nights. The outside judge gave Van de Castle five "direct hits" with odds against chance on the order of one thousand to one;

but when Van de Castle's guesses for the night were considered separately then he received six "direct hits" out of eight, against odds of ten thousand to one. The crown for the "Prince of the Percipients" was won by the challenger.

Some critics had claimed that a "control" series should be compared with the actual series to be sure that the correspondences were not due to a coincidental arrangement of targets. Although the judging procedure was devised to answer this charge, the Van de Castle study afforded another opportunity. Targets from the second Erwin study were randomly assigned to the Van de Castle transcripts. A judge laboriously evaluated all 64 possible combinations of transcripts and targets on this basis. The targets assigned to the transcripts for "control" purposes received almost identical ratings to all other targets, demolishing yet another proposed explanation of our results.

A different form of challenge had arisen from the psychoanalytic interviews with Ullman, which lasted upwards of two hours per session. Van de Castle comments candidly:

> These discussions led to self-confrontations that I often preferred to avoid. Not only did I have to face things that were difficult to silently acknowledge to myself, but some of these had to be verbally admitted to Dr. Ullman. This was not easy and sometimes I found my motivation to continue faltering. We had started with the goal of trying to better understand what went on during the mysterious night hours when the agent and I were attempting to telepathically communicate, as well as what might have transpired during the previous waking hours that could have an influence on that night's telepathic outcome. I therefore decided that if we were going to make any progress toward our goal, it would be necessary to continue even if it meant sandpapering a few sore spots. As I managed to survive each of these sessions and bounce back I found that my participation in the study was allowing me to reap some benefits akin to those from successful psychotherapy encounters.

Becoming the "Prince of the Percipients" had offered a greater challenge than even Dr. Van de Castle had realized.

CHAPTER 12

One-Night Stands

Dream telepathy offers a great variety of interesting possibilities in experimental designs. Not all of these may be fruitful enough to warrant the painstaking and expensive methods of the formal studies we have examined so far. Therefore a somewhat simpler method of evaluating dream–ESP correspondences was used in an informal series of pilot experiments that consisted of one-night stands. In this informal series, the Maimonides staff judges ranked each target against a target pool of art-prints (usually six) with ranks in the upper half counting as "hits" and ranks in the bottom half counting as "misses." The subjects were usually asked to rank the targets too.

The experimental precautions against sensory leakage were as tight as they were in the formal experiments. The main differences in the pilot series were the use of staff judges instead of independent judges and the simpler ranking system instead of the 100-point scale. Basically the aim of the pilot experiments was to try out new ideas and new subjects. Not everyone who is interested in dream telepathy can find time to make thousand-mile journeys, like Van de Castle, for an intensive and formal dream telepathy series.

One subject whose interest in ESP prompted him to make the trip to Brooklyn for a one-night stand was the late Chester F. Carlson, a brilliant inventor whose years of patient work brought about the development of the Xerox process. Carlson maintained an interest in the Dream Laboratory as well as other parapsychological research centers. He not only contributed financially to the American Society for Psychical Research, but he also contributed his creative thinking in planning out research programs. In September 1968 Carlson died of a heart attack in New York City, where he had come, from his home in Rochester, to attend the dedication of the Chester F. Carlson Research Laboratory of the American Society for Psychical Research.

At an ASPR lecture forum held in Carlson's memory, his widow, Dorris Carlson, told how she had shared psychic experiences with her husband that were so convincing that he changed from being a skeptic of ESP to a thought-ful inquirer. "I think they may have disturbed him at first," said Dorris Carlson, "because he recognized their implications for his theoretical outlook on the world and on the nature of man."

At the lecture Dorris Carlson related the experience she had of sharing dreams with her husband.

> There would be little differences in the dreams, of course, little distortions that would come through, but the two dreams would be recognizable as con-cerning the same person or the same incident. Dr. Montague Ullman might have planned an experiment such as the little one I will now tell you about.
>
> One morning I jotted down the things that I heard and the images that I saw; these were just disconnected fragments and they didn't mean anything at all to me. I had no idea that Chester was going to dream about them. I would often tell him what I heard or saw, but on this particular day I did not. Many hours later, Chester had a dream *so vivid* that he called out with great emotion in his sleep and I had to awaken him and ask him to tell me what was taking place. As he related the details of this moving dream-experience, I clearly recognized the material which I had received and recorded some sixteen or seventeen hours earlier. Whether this experience involved a telepathic interchange be-tween Chester and myself (as in the experiments of Dr. Ullman utilizing a sleeping percipient and a waking agent), or whether I had a precognitive awareness of what was later to appear in the content of Chester's dream, I can-not presume to say.[1]

Nor can we. When this experience, and others similar to it, had been brought to our attention, it indicated to us that Chester Carlson might make a good subject for a dream telepathy experiment. He came to the Dream Lab on the night of October 4, 1965. The telepathic agent that night was Robyn Posin. The target picture was de Chirico's *The Naval Barracks,* which portrays a large naval barracks on a stretch of sand. A large wooden planking is in the foreground.

Carlson dreamed that

> I saw a building with a sheet, with a large square hanging from it. A large porch or veranda with an awning stretching in front of it . . . I was outside, either a yard or maybe a desert. A lot of sand. There was a board fence. . .
>
> A large honeycomb, several feet across . . . perhaps like a wild honeycomb might look, only much larger than the other . . . four or five feet across. . .
>
> I was looking at a large electric generator . . . that reminds me a little of that honeycomb.

He added in the morning: ". . . the general outline was the same sort of scene as the honeycomb . . . several feet high and wide, rectangular shape. I can't understand that, but quite a similarity in the two in general outline — the two dreams."

A large building, a lot of sand, a board fence are right on, as well as the rectangular shape in the other two dreams. It is interesting that the multiple dwelling units of the barracks became a honeycomb.

His dreams' emphasis on the rectangular shape and dimensions of the barracks might correspond with an inventor's way of perceiving objects.

Another inventor who has a profound interest in parapsychology is Arthur Young. A resident of Philadelphia, he invented an important feature of the Bell Helicopter and numerous other mechanical devices. Young frequently lectures on philosophical problems such as "Cosmology and the Geometry of Meaning" and conducts his own research into parapsychological phenomena.

In December 1968 Young visited the Dream Laboratory for an experiment in clairvoyance. A target picture was randomly selected and removed from its envelope by a blindfolded assistant who placed the picture on a table without seeing it. No one knew what picture was in the target room until the room was unlocked in the morning after the experiment.

As he was going to sleep, Young reported seeing ". . . some kind of an optical instrument like a hunk of glass that had crossbars in it. A view of a circular room with a lot of things on the floor, including a round stool. . ." In the morning, he added: ". . . a globe of glass . . . I was looking down on an oval room. I said round, but it was oval and had a lot of objects in it . . . This was very clear and precise."

When the experimenter unlocked the target room, he found the same target picture that he and Young had ranked as number 1 out of six: a photograph of a communications satellite, a metal globe with crossbars. It was mounted on an oval platform, surrounded by circular mirrors.

Chance seemed to have favored the subject's interest in mechanical inventions by selecting as a target a mechanical invention that Young was able to describe in detail from a physical and dimensional point of view. This achievement was similar to Chester Carlson's ESP success in describing the dimensions of the barracks.

Another point of interest is that Young's imagery came while in the hypnagogic (leading into sleep) altered state of consciousness. This ties in with the theory of a New Jersey psychiatrist and parapsychological investigator, Dr. Berthold E. Schwarz,[2] who made a study of the reports that America's most famous inventor, Thomas Edison, used to get some of his ideas from his scientific colleagues by telepathy. Edison had the habit of catnapping between long hours of work, and according to Schwarz, this frequent entry into the hypnagogic state may have been the key to possible help by ESP for his thousands of patented inventions and innovations. Edison, incidentally, was profoundly interested in telepathy and constructed an electrical apparatus in an unsuccessful attempt to facilitate ESP.

A number of experimental studies by the Maimonides staff and others of altered states of consciousness and ESP have shown that direct clair-

voyance of a concealed target picture is facilitated by altered states of consciousness. And so Arthur Young's success at clairvoyantly describing a picture does not come as a shock to the Maimonides staff, even though it might
be a shock to someone who had decided that all ESP was due to "brain broadcasting," analogous to radio broadcasting.

Although no formal study has yet been done in comparing dream telepathy with nocturnal dream clairvoyance, a few pilot sessions have been done
with a telepathy target (with an agent) and with a clairvoyance target (without an agent). During a four-night series with a single subject, the correct
clairvoyance target was identified four times. The telepathy target was only
identified once. However, the subject had been told there would be a clairvoyance target and was not informed about the telepathy target.

On August 24, 1967, two young men, Myron Taranow and Stuart
Fischer, acted as sleeping subjects in separate sleep rooms. Both subjects were
told that there would be a telepathy target as well as a clairvoyance target.
That night Krippner and an assistant, Gayle Miree, both concentrated on the
same target picture but with completely different interpretations in their
associations. This confusion, they thought, might deflect the subjects from
the telepathy target to the clairvoyance target.

The telepathy target was *Mother and Child,* by Daumier, which shows a
woman holding a child while hurrying across a field. The clairvoyance target
was *Bijin by a Waterfall,* by Harunobu, which depicts a mythical Japanese
woman dressed in a green robe and sitting on a ledge by waterfall.

One of Fischer's dreams was about Superman's wife, "Mrs. Clark Kent,"
being arrested. "When she was released, many newsmen were around . . .
Everyone was talking about the woman being released. She was sitting in a
big chair. . . ." Later he dreamed that "I was working at the laboratory with
a Japanese guy. Suddenly he went back to Japan . . . The Japanese guy was
a lab assistant, about twenty-five years old. He had two kids."

Another of his dreams was about being with his mother for dinner at a
hotel, and he commented in the morning that there was "a lot of green in my
dreams."

Taranow dreamed about a green bird. "A penguin. Doing nothing . . .
hiding between two mountains. Talking about women. There was a young
woman there dressed in green." He expanded on his green penguin dream
in the morning. "The penguin was dead . . . There were about 50,000 penguins, all of them green. The green penguins died laughing. I thought of a
slogan, 'Oppose Discrimination Against Penguins.' There was . . . an old
woman in one of my dreams. She looked like a penguin. She was dressed in
green."

The clairvoyance target got direct "hits" of number 1 from the judge,
while the telepathy target was rated number 3 for Taranow and number 4 for
Fischer. Two mythical women, one "Mrs. Clark Kent" and the other a woman

resembling a green penguin, seemed very much like the mythical Japanese woman dressed in green. Just why Taranow should have been worried about Penguins' Liberation remains something of a comic mystery. Whether it was caused by the agents' design or the subjects' preference, the clairvoyance target came through more clearly.

When there is more than one agent the situation can be confusing, especially in experiences like the one that occurred on June 24, 1964, when Joyce Plosky was the agent. Sol Feldstein, who later alternated as agent with Plosky in the first screening study, was an experimenter that night and did not know that the target picture was Chagall's *Green Violinist* (Plate 5). It portrays a violinist with a cap on his head and a dog and horse in the background.

The subject that night was a young man named Sam. The initial dreams had no correspondence with the target.

At 3:30 A.M. Feldstein, who had been napping, wrote down the following dream. "Dream about being on an island. Horse and cart came along and I have to hide. Brother Bob is along. He can be seen but for some reason it is dangerous for me to be caught."

A little later, Sam had this dream: "There was a feeling of going around something, of maybe a horse and a carriage and a whip. . ." adding in the morning, "A carriage and a driver with a cap on, whipping the horse."

It seemed as if Sam's dream had combined Feldstein's dream report of a horse and cart with Plosky's target of a man wearing a cap and standing in front of a horse. Despite this apparent confusion, the staff judge, without knowing of Feldstein's dream, was able to pick *The Green Violinist* as the first in a pool of ten pictures.

A planned night with two agents also included an opportunity for both clairvoyance and telepathy. The subject that night was a young woman named Pam. The target was a photograph of a statue by Cellini of the ancient Greek hero Perseus. The statue is of the naked Perseus in a standing position having a sword in one hand and holding out the head of the slain Medusa in the other. To investigate whether a subject was able to supply the missing part of a telepathy target by clairvoyance, the Medusa's head was cut from the target picture and put in a separate sealed envelope. There were five other such pictures in the target pool, each with an important piece removed and placed in a separate sealed envelope. The smaller pieces remained in their unopened envelopes.

The subject, Pam, knew nothing about this procedure but was told that she was to dream about a picture that two people would be concentrating on. The two agents were Robert Nelson, a writer, and Diane Schneider, a student staff associate. The agents tried to work together to intensify the telepathic effect of their target of Perseus minus the Medusa's head.

Pam's first report was about her own head. "It's not a headache. It's dizziness . . . My head is heavy. . ."

Later she had an image of "Something bloody. There's something disturbing and I don't know what it is . . ."

She also dreamed about being in Central Park on Sunday afternoon. "There was also a man . . . and his arms were out. His head was over to the right side."

Pam's remarks in the morning included references to the odd feeling of her head. "Then I had a picture of somebody with a bandage around their skull . . . There was . . . something bloody and there was vomit around it. Something very painful, very painful. It's something very disturbing about it . . . It's kind of like a killing."

And then she added an extraordinarily accurate remark about the removal of a piece from the picture — "A separation in the right hand side of the picture."

The staff judge picked both parts of the Perseus target as a hit. However, it is not really possible to separate what might be clairvoyance from what might be telepathy. The agents knew what part of the picture was missing, and Pam might have picked that up telepathically. Or she might clairvoyantly have tuned into the picture of the head in the sealed envelope. Certainly, though, the dominant themes of a head, something bloody, killing, something disturbing, and a man with his arms thrust out seemed accurate.

The basic problem is that if the subject is able clairvoyantly to get a picture that no one sees, she should be as equally able to clairvoyantly get a picture that two people are looking at. That is one of the reasons why it is not possible to draw any conclusions from these pilot sessions on clairvoyance. An even stronger reason is that there are just not enough of these pilot sessions from which to make any generalizations.

Let us return to the theme of Perseus, this time before he slays the Gorgon Medusa. The target picture on November 1, 1968, was *Perseus and the Graiae*, by Burne-Jones. The Graiae were three old crones who shared one eye and one tooth between them. By stealing their eye and tooth Perseus persuaded them to tell him where the three Gorgons lived, of which Medusa was the only one mortal and thus capable of being killed. Having stolen a magic helmet from the Graiae, which rendered him invisible, Perseus set out to behead Medusa. The painting itself shows Perseus standing on a murky blue-green and yellow undulating surface with the three Graiae. Behind the figures are mountains, green-yellow clouds, and snow. The entire painting is done in blue-green and yellow.

The subject that night was Alan Vaughan, and the agent was his wife at that time, Iris. Although Vaughan had experienced precognitive dreams, he had not at that time been aware of any telepathic dreams. Vaughan tried to generate imagery of the target through meditation before he went to sleep. "I have an impression about the target painting. Iris has not yet opened it, though it has been selected. I get the notion of a scene—a desert, perhaps a painted desert. Flat land, colored clouds . . . There may be a human figure or two in the painting. . ."

His first dream was about "walking along a large place . . . there seemed to be some sort of activity going on. . ." In his second dream he saw some "yellow and green," and in the third dream he saw "bluish-green" with the association of Keats' poem of Madelaine, "the light is coming in the stained glass window and coloring her."

In his fifth dream he was hearing a song from *The Boys from Syracuse* (a Rodgers and Hart musical about ancient Greek twins). "'Give him the ax, give him the ax.' There are images associated with this . . . It was very hazy. Sort of a dark green." In his sixth dream he sensed being under water, "murky . . . very murky." In his seventh dream he was walking with his wife over a "grassy embankment."

In the morning, he remembered another dream about a "snow bear" and thought again of "Give him the ax." "I was thinking again about the Christ . . . crucifying, or give him the ax . . . Everything was a very peculiar green, murky color . . . I was getting emotions . . . both of joy and sadness and thinking of Christ suffering and yet there was a sense of joy. There very well might be a martyred death connected somehow at the end. . ."

Medusa, of course, had been beheaded by a sword rather than an ax. We might speculate that Perseus felt "a sense of joy." Pam's explicit images of blood and killing, when the severed head was a target, contrast with the more muted emotions of Vaughan when the picture served as an indirect suggestion of the eventual death of the Medusa.

The use of a musical tune to carry a telepathic message with its accompanying words ("Give him the ax") was seen earlier with Robyn Posin hearing a commercial song for a brand of beer when the target was Chagall's *The Drinker*. Turnabout, however, can be interesting play. On January 23, 1966, Sol Feldstein, the agent for Posin's formal series, was serving as a sleeping subject. Feldstein's agent that night was William Erwin, who had been his subject for the two formal series. The target for this night was *The Beer Drinkers,* by Daumier, which shows two men seated at a table with two glasses of beer.

In summing up his dreams in the morning, Feldstein said: "I don't know if this has anything to do with Robyn's former target. She had that target, *The Drinker*. And I had another tune which I can't remember right now. It had something to do with drinking. Oh, yes. 'Follow the Drinking Bird.'" (The actual name of the song is "Follow the Drinking Gourd," demonstrating how subjects may distort their memory in an apparent attempt to match the target material.)

This example gives Carington's association theory a good workout. Chagall's *Drinker* with Feldstein as agent reminds Posin of a singing beer commercial. Daumier's *Beer Drinkers* reminds Feldstein as subject of her target *The Drinker,* and he thinks, as she did, of a tune that has something to do with drinking, which turns out to facilitate a direct hit.

Although most ESP-dream correspondences seem to be transformed by associations, it is sometimes startling when they come through practically unchanged. In a pilot session with a psychologist named Dick, the agent, Diane Schneider, was concentrating on a collage showing two children in a museum looking at gems in a display case.

Dick's first dream was that he "was younger than I am now. In school . . . The word 'collgate' is on a white scroll. No, it's the word 'collage.'"

In his second dream he was in "a museum . . . Someone else is with me. The colors are black and brown. . ." He added in the morning: "There were only two of us in the museum dream."

The word "collage" appearing on a white scroll seems extraordinary for it is an extremely rare word to find in dreams.

By comparison, according to Hall and Van de Castle's *Content Analysis of Dreams,* the word "church" appears in 6 out of 500 male dreams. This word appeared in the dreams of a young high school student, Robert Harris, on September 27, 1968. "I was dreaming about . . . Europe. We came to this building. I think it was a dome or something. It was a very old building. It could have been a church."

Harris summarized his dreams in the morning. "We went into this great big hall and there was this little old lady speaking . . . I remember walking down a street . . . and it was cobblestone . . . I remember a lot of gray from the buildings . . . I think it was a church or something. . ." (Harris, in fact, had been in Europe recently with his parents, Dr. and Mrs. Krippner.)

The target that an agent was concentrating on that night was Van Gogh's *The Church at Auvers,* which shows a large gray church. In the foreground is a woman walking on a cobblestone road toward the church.

Although such direct correspondences are impressive, more intriguing sometimes are correspondences that seem to formulate riddles, such as "What plant is like a parasol?"

The subject on May 29, 1969, was a secretary named Vera. The agent was a staff research associate, Richard Davidson. The target was Monet's *Corn Poppies,* which depicts a meadow covered with red poppies on one side and green plants with purple blossoms on the other side. In the background a line of trees is broken by a chateau. In the foreground is a woman holding a parasol and walking with a child.

Vera's dream reports included:

> I was getting a lot of plants . . . I remember a lady, and I think she was kind of dressed up. Sort of a middle-aged lady who held out a great big branch of parsley.
>
> I was walking . . . Some kid sort of came up . . . It was a little kid . . . There

were trees all around . . . I was walking along the street again and there was a little boy . . . I think we had been walking . . . We were sort of outside of the park.

In the morning, she said, "It seems I did have a lot of leaves in different parts of my dream . . . Some green plants and . . . some flowers . . . Somebody had held a branch and somebody else held a giant sprig of parsley . . . There were trees around . . . The little boy was pleasant . . . The whole atmosphere of that dream seemed to be pleasant and sort of festive. . ." A woman holding a giant sprig of parsley seems to answer our riddle about the parasol.

Sometimes the title of the picture rather than its pictorial contents seems to come through. For instance, when the target was *The Jesters,* by Rousseau, which shows two monkeys in a jungle, the female subject dreamed about "a very funny clown. A real handsome, magnificent clown."

It is interesting, too, to see how different subjects respond to the same target. Let's examine the dreams of two women subjects, Iris Vaughan and Felicia Parise, when their target was *Departure of a Friend,* by de Chirico. The picture is of a twilight scene with many shadows and with two men standing in the background. Behind the men and extending into the foreground is a wall made up of arches and columns. A rectangular pool and a courtyard occupy the center. The two women's agent on the night of June 27, 1969, was William Thompson, a teacher.

Vaughan's dreams included: "A group scene; The Shadow Song is running through my head"; and walking outside of a building. "It was a large, municipal-type building." In another dream, "I was walking along a corridor with one other person . . . The colors were dark browns, blacks and grays. . . . I was giving flowers to my grandmother."

In the morning, she said, "There were several personal dreams about me and about my family. The dark colors were unusual . . . So was the theme of walking around and coming back. . ."

Parise's dreams were also about her family. "I was at my mother's house" and "I was playing with my niece." In her sixth dream she was on 18th Avenue in Brooklyn. "There's a bank on 18th Avenue and 65th Street. I don't know if it's a savings bank or what. Yeah, a savings bank it is, and a pretty tall building. It's gray. . ."

Common to both dreams was a large building and the color gray; each subject dreamed about being with some member of her family. When this theme of departure (but with a different painting by Beckman) had been used in the first screening study, a medical student had dreamed that he and his wife "were moving from our apartment." If there was any common link in these three dreams to the theme of departure, it was the appearance of close family members.

Recall also Erwin's dream of cars being pounded by the ocean when the target showed the savage boxing match in Bellow's *Both Members of This Club.* When a high-school student named Don had that target he dreamed about a contest between a man and a fish, and a foot race. "The trout . . . was lying on its back and . . . there was blood on its gills kind of flowing into the water. I wanted to catch some fish and . . . it was a gigantic fight, and I finally pulled it in." About the race, he said, "The person who had the fastest time would therefore be the winner. That was the kind of contest that it seemed to be . . . He's quite a scrapper. He's always slapping me around. . ."

In Chapter 15 we shall study this similarity in response to the target more closely in the formal study in which two sleeping subjects have the same targets.

Another way of studying dream telepathy is by comparing it with precognition — foreknowledge of events. On the night of January 3, 1969, the subject was a student named Gordon. Before the agent, Gayle Miree, selected the target, Krippner hypnotized Gordon and told him to try to get imagery of the target that would be selected. Gordon responded with: "Out in the distance sort of a mountain, and it must be evening or morning because . . . the light is sort of brightest out over the mountain and as I look up it gets darker blue, but down over the mountain it's sort of white and nice and clear and sunny."

Miree then randomly selected as target *Snow Mountain,* by Chang Shu-Chi. This print depicts a mountain with pine trees and boulders dotting the scene and a deer in the distance. Subdued colors of black, brown, gray, blue, and green predominate in the picture.

Gordon summed up his dreams in the morning. "Seeing mountains or mountain sort of things . . . Just a dark black in the background . . . The entire thing was rock colored . . . very dull and shadowy and dark. Sort of a steep hill and . . . very dark clouds . . . rolling in through the mist over the mountain. . ."

His precognitive imagery thus seemed as much on target as his telepathic dream imagery.

Two days later, Gordon wrote the Maimonides staff a letter.

> I had a very strange experience on the way up (to the north) on the bus. At one point further upstate . . . I was watching the side of the road when I saw a deer. What was strange was that the deer was standing in the snow up against a cliff covered by a waterfall that had frozen in a way that reminded me of a detail in the target picture . . . It is very rare to see a deer so close to a roadside during the hunting season. It is probably a coincidence but an amazing one nonetheless.

We have decided to let the Jungians figure that one out.

For comparison with the dreams of the subjects already presented, we will examine the dreams of Douglas Johnson, the celebrated British psychic. A professional medium at the College of Psychic Studies in London, he has done much experimental work with parapsychologists in the United States and had been a close friend of Eileen Garrett.

On April 9, 1969, Johnson's target was a collage depicting Mary holding the dying Jesus. Both figures have halos. Mary is wearing a blue and gold robe and, anachronistically, a wrist watch.

Johnson's first dream was about "a woman I know . . . I seem to have been talking to her and I was saying goodbye." In his fourth dream he had "the feeling of being in the company of somebody that I loved."

In the morning he remarked on "Golds and Blues . . . A very nice light." His guess for the night was "It could be a picture of . . . two figures in the painting who are either very great friends or are in love with each other . . . Some emotional relationship probably."

Both Johnson and Krippner picked the correct target as number 1. It is interesting, though, that Johnson's ESP dreams seem to be as distorted and transformed as the ESP dreams of "ordinary" individuals who have no conscious control over their psychic faculty.

In the next chapter we shall investigate the possible difference between dreams of known psychics and dreams of more "ordinary folk." To add a little excitement, a distance of fourteen miles has been interposed between the agents and the subjects.

CHAPTER 13

Long-Distance "Sensory Bombardment"

"Long distance" is self-explanatory. But what is "Sensory Bombardment"?

A technique for completely immersing a person in an audio-visual environment — bombarding his senses until a sensory "overload" is reached — was developed by Drs. Robert Masters and Jean Houston,[1] a husband and wife team who established the Foundation for Mind Research in New York. As researchers into altered states of consciousness, Masters and Houston designed an "audio-visual environment" in which sequences of slides are projected onto an 8-foot square screen that curves around a subject who is sitting between stereo loud-speakers (or wearing headphones) from which blares forth accompanying music. A computerized dual-slide projector dissolves one slide into another every twenty seconds, giving the impression of a "moving picture."

The slides, of which there are thousands, range from psychedelic paintings to thematic groupings such as Tibetan Landscapes or Moon Landings. The effect of being immersed in this audio-visual environment is quite different from "going to the movies" (with the possible exception of Stanley Kubrick's film *2001*). Subjects can become so overwhelmed by the powerful effects that they may enter an altered state of consciousness in which profound emotional feelings and even mystical or religious experience may result. Exactly what result occurs depends both on the subject and the slide program.

Stanley Krippner, who shares with Masters and Houston the research interest of altered states of consciousness, felt that the audio-visual environment might be adapted to bombard a telepathic agent with a thematic target. A somewhat similar use of thematic slide programs used as ESP targets had been pioneered by Dr. Thelma Moss at the University of California at Los Angeles.[2] The more elaborate audio-visual environment in Masters and Houston's laboratory might be expected to intensify the ESP effect.

In collaboration with Masters and Houston, the Maimonides Dream Laboratory planned a four-night pilot series, extending from April to December 1969, in which the telepathic agent would be situated in Masters and Houston's laboratory fourteen miles away from the Maimonides laboratory where two sleeping subjects would attempt to dream about the target slide program. On one of the four nights of this exploratory study, two agents were used with two different target programs, one for each agent-subject pair.[3]

This experiment also permits a look at possible differences between subjects who were "psychic" (that is, who claim to have control over their waking psychic ability), subjects who reported spontaneous ESP experiences, and subjects who had no prior ESP experiences. It also permitted a look into differences that might arise when subject and agent were sweethearts.

Once the two subjects had been wired with electrodes and put into their separate sleep rooms in the Brooklyn laboratory, a telephone call was made to Masters and Houston's Manhattan laboratory to signal that the agent should be put into the audio-visual environment. Six slide programs had been prepared for each night; one of these was randomly selected as the target.

On April 25, 1969, the agent was Richard Davidson, a staff research associate. His two subjects were his girl friend Susan, who had no prior ESP experiences, and Douglas Johnson, the English medium. On all these pilot nights, the agent and the subjects attempted to establish rapport before the experimental night.

The randomly selected slide program was "Oriental Religion," with sixty slides showing Buddhas from Burma, India, Japan, and Thailand, as well as various Indian and Tibetan deities. The accompanying sound included Sufi religious rituals and chanting by Zen Buddhist monks.

Douglas Johnson dreamed that "I saw rather a beautiful face — squarish, with slanty eyes. Eastern, I would think. Clean shaven . . . I don't know what nationality, but it was a very beautiful face."

Susan dreamed "Something about people who didn't believe in God any more and the sun came down to earth to find out why . . . And Richie came later, dressed in like these robes — white robes with blue stitchings on them . . ." and adding later, "It could have been like some sort of religious theme."

In the morning three Maimonides staff judges ranked the experimenter's notes of the two subjects' dreams against a list of six possible themes. For both Johnson and Susan, all three judges ranked "Oriental Religion" as number 1.

Did the stronger emotional rapport between Richard and Susan enable Susan to dream as telepathically as a professional psychic?

On the night of September 19, 1969, when two agents were used, one agent was Malcolm Bessent, a young English psychic sensitive who had studied for a long period under Douglas Johnson at the College of Psychic Studies in London. Bessent's subject was a student named William, who had no prior ESP experiences.

The target was a program of forty-two slides on the theme of "Ancient Egypt." Included were pyramids, sphinxes, statues, ruins, temples, paintings, and articles from the tomb of Tutankhamen.

William's dreams included references to "a semi-tropical setting" and "statuary and paintings. It was in an institute where a lot of people were studying ... something to do with death ... Beautiful art, gardens, sculpture, and fountains..."

The three judges gave "Ancient Egypt" the mean ranking of number 2 out of six. The references to statuary, paintings, and death seemed particularly appropriate, indicating that William had become "psychic" in his dreams.

On that same night, the other agent was William Thompson, a young teacher. His subject was a woman artist named Jean. The target was "Space Exploration." The slide program included views of the spacecraft and the astronauts before takeoff, the slides of the Apollo 11 flight to the moon, flight through space, the moon landing, the moon walk, and the return trip.

Jean's dreams involved "silver and bright colors"; "travel"; "futuristic designs for suits"; "getting ready for a long trip"; and "traveling to distant points." Each of three judges ranked "Space Exploration" number 1. Jean, who had previous spontaneous ESP experiences, seemed also to be able to dream telepathically.

The agent on October 9, was Gayle Miree. The two subjects were Alan Vaughan and his wife, Iris. Both Alan and Iris had been subjects for successful pilot experiments previously, and Alan had worked before with Miree as his agent. Earlier, in 1967, Vaughan spent time developing his psychic faculty at the College of Psychic Studies in London with Douglas Johnson.

The target that night was "Artistic Productions of a Schizophrenic." The slides were of abstract designs painted in primary colors by a woman patient undergoing therapy in Czechoslovakia. Miree later described the mood of the designs as "anger, confused, and chaotic." Iris Vaughan dreamed that

> The bombardment ... was ... this silly imagery and a lot of it doesn't make sense ... It was almost mental, more or less conveying a feeling rather than concrete terms as such ... They weren't really images. They were like thoughts or moods that were sent out to the person. It was sort of a projection of a whole mood ... It was weird. It was almost like some sort of psychiatric thing.

In the morning, she added: "They were throwing out all these images ... for maybe a psychological therapeutic bribe ... It was like I was watching a picture and all these kids were protesting ... They were really rioting like crazy. Really nutty. A lot of hate emanating from the mob scene..."

Alan Vaughan, after his second dream report, said: "I just had the strong impression that Gayle is behind the screen and that the images are very close to her . . . I think it's sort of a mess, actually, the stuff she's been looking at. And what I mean by that is disjointed fragments and discord, and I think it's sort of unpleasant, really."

His third dream was about talking to a teen-age boy and then meeting a woman, whose husband and infant child then entered the scene. The baby prophesied "earthquakes in Monte Carlo" and the husband kept repeating nonsensical phrases. His fourth dream was about "some images of abstract designs."

In the morning, he added: "I remember . . . a feeling of trying to help the boy with a problem, some sort of personal problem . . . A small child . . . said . . . 'There will be an earthquake soon in Monte Carlo. . .' The general feeling was of bewilderment . . . And then there appeared what seemed to be cards . . . with abstract lines on them . . . some sort of art card."

His guess for the night was "A very aggressive element—disjointed. Also, at one point I heard some rock music from *Hair,* 'Crazy for the Red, White and Blue' . . . Sort of insane. And I think I would probably find it somewhat repulsive, and I think Gayle would too . . . There might be a bit of the absurd as well . . . Something meaningless. . . ."

Both husband and wife picked "Artistic Productions of a Schizophrenic" as number 1, as did the three judges.

This experiment seemed to indicate that both subjects were "psychic equals" in dream telepathy. The wife's references to "silly imagery," "projection of a whole mood," "weird," "some sort of psychiatric thing," a "psychological therapeutic bribe," and "crazy" seemed particularly apt. The husband's references to "a mess," "disjointed fragments and discord," "abstract designs," "sort of insane," "absurd," and "meaningless" also hit the target. The primary colors of the schizophrenic's paintings were aptly described by the song "Crazy for the Red, White and Blue." The use of music as a telepathic carrier was seen in the previous chapter.

Although Miree did not know it that night, the artist's schizophrenia began with delusions about her husband and infant child, which could be interpreted as being thematically related to Vaughan's strange third dream of a woman's infant child prophesying earthquakes and her husband repeating nonsensical phrases.

On the last night of the series, December 19, the agent was Brian Washburn, a student research assistant. His subjects that night were his girl friend Jane, who had no prior ESP experiences, and Malcolm Bessent, the psychic sensitive who earlier had served as an agent. The target that night was "Birth of a Baby." The slides were explicit photographs of a woman giving birth, but the sequence was shown in reverse.

Jane dreamed about "a lot of shapes, all formed with kind of a semicurved line" and "a threat, but it wasn't to myself . . . It was directed against a French teacher . . . but they decided not to hurt her."

Her guess for the night was ". . . the threat was the uncommon thing . . . I'd say something to do with something threatening."

Malcolm dreamed that "Whatever Brian's looking at are still shots, but . . . I'm getting this moving sensation . . . I had the feeling I was in a labyrinth. . ." and of "a lot of little figures" that "seemed designed to stand." In his third dream, he was thinking of "underground tunnels . . . It was some sort of small vehicle for one or two people." In his fourth dream he thought of a girl he hadn't seen for three years, "She's probably had children by now . . . I know she wanted children very much. . ."

In the morning, he added: "I saw just the head of a man, entirely bald, and not quite life-size. Smaller than life-size. . ." About the girl, he added: "She's often told me she was really looking forward to being married and having children . . . She seemed to regard this as part of her feminine function or role in life . . . The curious thing . . . was she was standing as if under a spotlight, as if there was a light on her. . ."

The three judges gave Jane's dreams a rank of 2 and Malcolm's a rank of 3, both "hits."

Jane's dreams seem to reflect the biological difference between the sexes: Only a woman is threatened with the pain of childbirth. Malcolm's dreams show interesting symbol transformation of the birth canal to a "labyrinth" and "an underground tunnel" through which ran a "small vehicle." A baby, of course, is a "little figure" that is "designed to stand" and the baby's head-first emergence is suggested by the small, bald head. The photographer's lights on the woman also seemed to find representation in the dream.

In general, the judges' rankings of eight "hits" and no "misses" seemed to indicate that the dreaming state served as a "psychic equalizer" between people who in waking psychic experience ranged from daily use of ESP (for professionals, like Douglas Johnson) to no experience at all.

The long-distance "sensory bombardment" *may* have enhanced the dream-telepathy effect — we emphasize *may* for no control experiments were done — but it would not be possible to distinguish if this "enhancement" resulted from the excitement to the subject of a challenge to dream about something 14 miles away or from the great emotional intensity of the agent's experience.

Let's increase the distance to 45 miles and the number of agents to 2,000 and see what happens.[4]

In early 1971 a series of six concerts was scheduled to be given by a rock group, the Grateful Dead, at the Capitol Theater in Port Chester, New York, 45 miles away from the Dream Laboratory in Brooklyn. Each of the concerts was attended by an audience of 2,000 young people. The members of the Grateful Dead, who had visited Krippner at the Dream Laboratory, agreed to try an ESP dream experiment in which their audiences would be the telepathic agents (Plate 16).

To explore possible differences arising from the agents' orientation toward the sleeping subject, two subjects were used. One subject, Malcolm Bessent, who had demonstrated excellent results in other ESP dream experiments, was to sleep at the Dream Lab. His name was shown to the audiences in a series of slides preceding exposure to a target. The slides said, "Try using your ESP to 'send' this picture to Malcolm Bessent. He will try to dream about the picture. Try to 'send' it to him. Malcolm Bessent is now at the Maimonides Dream Laboratory in Brooklyn."

The control subject was Felicia Parise, who had also shown good results in earlier dream-telepathy experiments. She spent the night at her apartment and was telephoned every 90 minutes for dream reports. Her name was unknown to the audience of agents.

Both subjects went to bed early so that they would be asleep by 11:30 P.M. — the time when the audience was exposed to the target material. The targets were a group of 14 slides*; each night two of these slides were randomly selected to be the target pool. Then, at the Capitol Theater, an experimenter would toss a coin to determine which slide would be shown to the audience.

Observers at the concerts noted that the majority of the audience were already in altered states of consciousness by target time. These altered states were brought about by the music, or by the earlier ingestion of psychedelic drugs, or by contact with the other members of the audience.

After the initial slides told the audience that they were participating in an ESP experiment and they were to "send" a picture to Malcolm Bessent, the target slide was projected for 15 minutes, while the Grateful Dead continued to play.

On the second night of the study, February 19, 1971, the target slide was *The Seven Spinal Chakras,* by Scralian. This painting shows a man in the lotus position practicing yogic meditation. The seven "chakras" (purported energy centers of the body, centering around the spinal column) are vividly colored. A brilliant yellow circle of energy radiates from his head in the pattern of mosaic facets. Malcolm Bessent dreamed that

> I was very interested in . . . using natural energy . . . I was talking to this guy who said he'd invented a way of using solar energy and he showed me this box . . . to catch the light from the sun which was all we needed to generate and store the energy . . . I was discussing with this other guy a number of other areas of communication and we were exchanging ideas on the whole thing . . . He was suspended in mid-air or something . . . I was thinking about rocket

---

*More slides were selected than were actually needed so that a sufficient number would be available near the end of the study for random selection. The first dream telepathy study was criticized for only having twelve pictures in the target pool, leaving only one picture available for random selection on the final night of the study.

ships ... I'm remembering a dream I had ... about an energy box and ... a spinal column.

Less direct correspondences appeared in Felicia Parise's dream in the morning. "I had a big, fat, yellowish, green parakeet with a head like an owl. Something happened to the cage and it broke ... I also had another dream with a yellow canary ... The cage was hanging very high outside of the garage door ... I said, 'I wonder how the parakeet lives? I never feed it. God must raise his temperature so he doesn't freeze.'"

Yet her guess for the night of February 21, two nights later, seemed more on target for the 19th. "It was something bright, like a crystal with many facets of colors ... There is some sort of light or sun or a bright light. It's maybe a man, short like a Buddha ... like something Aztec, a Mexican totem pole."

When the transcripts for all six nights were sent to two independent judges to rate all six target pictures on a 100-point scale, the judges gave a mean score of 83 for Bessent's dream of February 19 with the target *The Seven Spinal Chakras,* which was the highest rating assigned to Bessent's 36 transcript-target pairs.

For Parise's dreams of the same night, when a yellow bird's temperature was being raised by God, the judges gave a rating of 28, in comparison with a 96 for her transcript of February 21.

Overall, Bessent had four "direct hits" out of six nights, whereas Parise had only one "direct hit," which was for the final night. It is interesting, however, that three of Parise's "miss" nights received very high ratings with targets used on other nights. Her fourth night's dreams received a rating of 96 for the second night's target (*The Seven Spinal Chakras*); her third night's dreams received a rating of 74 for the fifth night's target; and her fifth night's dreams received a rating of 65 for the third night's target. These are all in the Great Correspondence to the Very Great Correspondence range, and they suggest that she may have been displacing her ESP in time — both backward (postcognitively) and forward (precognitively).

If one assumes that Bessent and Parise had about the same ability at ESP dreaming, this experiment suggests that agent orientation toward the subject plays an important role in helping the subject telepathically beam in to the target. If one further assumes that both subjects were telepathically "reaching out," then the fact that the agents are attempting rapport with one subject and not the other may indicate that it is easier for the subject to make telepathic contact if there is rapport.

If, on the other hand, one assumes that the agents are "broadcasting" stimuli, then one would expect 2,000 broadcasters to heighten the effect considerably. But this did not seem to have a marked effect. Certainly no particularly striking improvement in accuracy was noted when compared with what ordinarily occurs when single agents are used. In fact, there is some evidence that one's attitude toward long-distance ESP may be more important than the actual distance. For those who find it an exciting and novel challenge, ESP may actually be enhanced; for those who feel they are attempting something impossible and do not expect success, there may be no results. An attempt to demonstrate that long-distance ESP is possible was made by Apollo 14 astronaut Edgar Mitchell,[5] who performed an ESP experiment from the Apollo craft — 200,000 miles away from his subjects on earth. His results were equivocal because a delay in lift-off delayed Mitchell's "transmission" times during his scheduled rest periods.

This inadvertent situation brings us to one of parapsychology's most formidable problems: time and ESP.

CHAPTER 14

Dreaming of Things to Come

Dreaming about things that have not yet happened is clearly impossible, or so our common sense tells us. Cicero said so, and his complaint has been echoed thousands of times through the last two millennia. Yet stubbornly, persistently, exasperatingly, people have reported precognitive dreams in all ages and cultures that we know. The majority of these spontaneous cases are premonitions of death, disaster, and danger.[1]

To adequately deal with the tremendous theoretical complexities of precognition would require, at the least, another book in itself. Here we will limit ourselves to answering Cicero's complaint that chance coincidence accounts for dreams that are apparently precognitive.

Throughout the years of dream telepathy experiments at the Maimonides Dream Laboratory there would occasionally arise a dream that strikingly corresponded with some future target or some incident in the subject's life.[2] Ullman and Dale noticed apparent precognitive dreams in the experiment described in Chapter 5.

Yet there seemed little reason to believe that someone would — or could — dream precognitively every single night of a long experimental series. Expectations became more hopeful, however, with the arrival from England of Malcolm Bessent, the young psychic sensitive who acted both as an agent and as a subject in the "Sensory Bombardment" pilot series. Bessent's training in London with Douglas Johnson seemed to have developed his psychic faculty.[3] With encouragement from Eileen Garrett, Bessent decided to explore more deeply his psychic potential. Financial assistance from Arthur Young, the Philadelphia inventor, and Donald C. Webster, a Canadian industrialist, enabled Bessent to come to the Maimonides Dream Laboratory in the summer of 1969 for a formal precognitive dream study.

Bessent had experienced apparent spontaneous precognition and this seemed to carry over to the laboratory situation. In an experiment run by Charles Honorton[4] at the Maimonides Laboratory, Bessent attempted to guess which of two colored lights would next be lighted by an electronically controlled random-number generator. Both his predictions and his "hits" were automatically registered. The total number of trials was set in advance: 15,360. There were 7,859 "hits," 179 more than expected by chance — with odds against chance on the order of five hundred to one.

In designing the "First Bessent Study in Precognition," the Maimonides team combined the past dream telepathy target procedure with an innovation suggested in 1967 by M. P. Jackson in the ASPR *Journal*[5] that a special waking experience serve as the precognitive target. The waking experience, however, would be designed *after* Bessent's dreams were recorded and mailed off to the transcriber; the person who made up the experience would have no contact with Bessent or his dreams.[6] An elaborate random-number system was used to choose a target word from Hall and Van de Castle's *Content Analysis of Dreams,* and this in turn was matched with an art-print target, which in turn was used to design the multi-sensory experience. Three outside judges would compare each night's protocol to each of the eight target experiences on a 100-point scale. There were eight nonconsecutive nights in this series. The hypothesis of the experimenters was that the independent judges would assign greater than chance ratings to the transcripts for the experiences that would follow the next morning.

To show how this works, let us follow one night's dreams and the next morning's experience that Bessent had been told to dream about precognitively.

Bessent's first dream was an "impression of green and purple . . . Small areas of white and blue."

In his second dream, "There was a large concrete building. A lot of concrete, for some reason. It seemed to have importance. But it was architecturally designed and shaped . . . and there was a patient from upstairs escaping . . . This patient from upstairs, I'm not sure it was a 'he.' It might have been a woman . . . She had a white coat on, like a doctor's coat, and people were arguing with her on the street."

Bessent's third dream was "Kind of a feeling. Not a feeling exactly, but a rumor . . . of hostility toward me by people in a group I was in daily contact with . . . I wasn't actually experiencing it, the actual hostility, I mean . . . My impression was that they were doctors and medical people. . . ."

In his fourth dream: "I was dreaming . . . about breakfast . . . The cups were all white . . . Drinking . . . Eating . . . It was all in color. . . ."

His review of the first dream was "I had the feeling that I was happy and you were happy. . . ."

His review of the second dream was "The concrete wall was all in natural color, you know, sort of sandy color . . . It's rather like a carved wall, not large . . . I felt that a Negro patient had escaped . . . or just walked out, and that to do this, he or she . . . had put on a doctor's white coat and got as far as . . . the archway."

His review of the third dream was "...I was aware of an impression of hostility ... Something I had done aroused hostility in people. It had to do with my work, and I think all the people were medical ... My impression was of having done something which caused some kind of feeling of resentment ... and it was sort of the hostility that caused them to think or say, 'Get rid of him.'"

His fourth dream review was "...all the cups and things were rattling ... They were all drinking out of glasses..."

His guess for the night was "...My impression is sort of a ... feeling of people talking..."

In the morning, the recorder (Krippner)—the staff member who was assigned to make up the experience—was given two random numbers selected by another experimenter using an elaborate random-number system. The recorder then used the numbers as a key to come up with the word "Corridor" from the Hall–Van de Castle book. He then went to the large collection of art-print targets and searched for a picture that might have a tie-in. He selected *Hospital Corridor at St. Rémy,* by Van Gogh (Plate 17).* The picture portrays a lone figure in the corridor of a mental institution, which is constructed from concrete. The predominant colors are orange, green, deep blue, and white.

The recorder (Krippner) then designed a multi-sensory target experience through which Bessent would be led. The experience was as follows:

Auditory: Rosza's "Spellbound" played on the phonograph. Recorder laughing hysterically in the background. Recorder will welcome the subject as "Mr. Van Gogh."

Visual: Paintings by mental patients will be shown by slide projector.

Taste: Subject will be given a pill (niacinamide) and a glass of water.

Smell: Subject will be "disinfected" with acetone daubed on a cotton swab.

Touch: Subject will be led through a darkened corridor of the lab to reach the recorder's office.

The experience, which the recorder led Bessent through after he awakened in the morning, served as the target description given to the judges along with seven other similarly designed target experiences. The target words selected for the other nights were "parka hood," "desk," "kitchen," "teaspoon," "body back," "leaves," and "elbow."

The judges ranked "Corridor" highest of all eight target words for the correct night—a "direct hit."

---

*As these experiments took place in a mental health center, the precognitive nature of the correspondences between Bessent's dreams and the art print might be questioned. In other words, would it be so unusual for a subject to dream about a mental patient under these conditions? One should remember, however, that statistical analysis involved all eight of the nights; none of the others mentioned hospitals or mental patients. Again, the evaluation method of comparing all the nights against all of the targets permits a correction to be made for this type of situational correspondence.

The correspondences were strikingly direct and clear and referred both to the actual target picture that Bessent saw and the actual experience.

It should be added that Krippner was wearing a white coat and was a friend of Bessent; it is not surprising that his strange treatment of Bessent evoked the precognitive dream response of being treated with hostility by people he was in daily contact with.

Of the eight nights, the judges assigned five as "direct hits" and two other nights in the top half ("hits"). The odds of this happening by chance are on the order of five thousand to one. That is, if chance were the cause of those correspondences, one would have to do 5,000 more such experiments before expecting a similar coincidence.

This seemed to answer Cicero's complaint.

Parapsychologists, however, are very critical. Although every possibility of sensory leakage had been excluded, and the random-number selection of a target word was beyond reproach, there was still the possibility that the recorder might be using his own ESP to correspond with the recorded dreams in selecting the target picture and designing the experience. While it seemed unlikely that the recorder should suddenly have turned into such a superb psychic, theoretically there should be a control for this possibility.

This is one of the many problems in designing precognition experiments that must necessarily be controlled to rule out clairvoyance and telepathy. The reason that clairvoyance and telepathy experiments are not controlled to rule out precognition is that it is apparently impossible to do, since one could always argue that if the target were known to any person in the future, then a subject could use his or her precognitive ability telepathically or clairvoyantly. If the test were run by a machine, then the subject could precognize the results, and so on. The theoretical problems, as we have said, are tremendously complex — perhaps the most complex of any study known to science.

To illustrate the kind of theoretical difficulty that precognition poses for interpretation of dream telepathy, let us consider briefly a dream that Vaughan had on April 3, 1969, during a formal dream study, which will be covered later. The dream was summed up in the post-sleep interview.

> I was lying in bed and Chuck Honorton was there and he was marking a transcript and he was using the letter "F" as a symbol for something . . . He said, "Oh, 'F' is for failure . . ." Then I looked at the television set there and this television set actually seemed to be part of the experiment as well . . . as I looked at it, the whole thing began to move and come to life, and there was a man holding a knife . . . and behind him was a monkey lying on the floor, and there may have been someone else there as well . . . I wonder if there might be sometime an experimental thing like this . . .

Later, when reviewing the transcripts of the experiment, Vaughan wrote Ullman a letter on July 17, 1969, pointing out that dream as being possibly precognitive of a future experiment.

On January 12, 1970, the Canadian television personality Norman Perry arrived at the Dream Laboratory to film an experiment for Canadian television. Perry was to be the dream subject, and Vaughan was asked to be a back-up subject in case he couldn't get to sleep. An agent in another building selected a picture from a target pool of six oversized pictures, made up specially for this experiment. The randomly selected target that night was a white monkey holding an orange. To add vividness, the agent took an orange and ripped it apart.

That night Vaughan dreamed about ripping apart a round loaf of bread. However, when he ranked the target pictures, he scored a "miss." Honorton was there as experimenter. Vaughan had "failed."

Perry chose the monkey as the "direct hit" because of his dream of a white animal that strikingly corresponded with the target, and included the correct details of a blue rug and a black window. As Vaughan watched the camera filming for television, he saw Perry put the oversized targets on the floor. Perry pointed out his "direct hit," the monkey (prone, of course, on the floor). Perry's second choice was a picture of a man holding an ax (instead of a knife).

Taken as precognitive correspondences, this dream and the subsequent events theoretically imply that the whole experiment's procedure and success—choosing a monkey as target; Perry dreaming telepathically about it and putting the monkey on the floor; and the second choice of a man holding an ax; Vaughan failing; Honorton being the experimenter; and the experiment being televised—all this somehow "existed" nine months before the experiment. To add confusion, Vaughan apparently and correctly precognized a target that he was to fail at telepathically and even precognized his failure.

Let us now concentrate on attempting to demonstrate that precognition in dreams can be experimentally controlled to such an extent that a psychic sensitive can dream more about the future than the past.

"The Second Bessent Study" in precognitive dreaming was scheduled for the summer of 1970.[7] A target pool was prepared of ten slide-and-sound sequences on the subjects of "police," "2001," "crucifixion," "loneliness," "Egyptian art," "death," "authoritarian signs," "birds," "beards," and "saints." Each target sequence, made up of from ten to twenty-two slides, was accompanied by ten minutes of appropriate music or sound that was listened to with stereophonic headphones.

The sixteen nights of this series were arranged in pairs, so that on the first night Bessent would attempt to dream precognitively about the target sequence he would see the next night, and on that night he would attempt to dream more conventionally about the sequence he had just seen as a control. Thus, on the odd-numbered nights, he would attempt to dream about the future; and on the even-numbered nights, he would attempt to dream about the past. To insure that the EEG technician who elicited his dream reports would not somehow favor one series over the other, technicians were brought in from New York University who neither knew nor cared about the experiment's design. The precognitive targets were selected by yet another experimenter more than twelve hours after the tape of Bessent's dreams had been mailed to the transcriber.

After the sixteen nights were transcribed, the transcripts were sent to three outside judges who rated them on a 100-point scale against each of the eight target sequences that had been used; the targets were viewed by the judges so as to get the target's full flavor.

After the judging forms were tallied and the means of the three judges' ratings taken, one night's transcript was rated against one target with a correspondence of 98 — the highest rating assigned to any of the 128 transcript-target pairs. That night was September 13, 1970, experimental night fifteen and therefore a precognitive night.

The target sequence Bessent saw the next evening was "birds." The slides depicted birds in the water, on the land, and in the air. No particular bird or type was emphasized. The infinite color and variety of the species was seen, matched by aviary noises of bird calls on the sound tape.

The following are some extended excerpts from the transcript of September 13.

Bessent's first dream: "I was having a nice dream. I was with some doctors. It was an informal meeting . . . We looked into the sky. There was a dark blue color in the sky."

Second dream: "I was dreaming about an analysis I had made in my previous dream. I was about to hand it over to some doctors to see what would happen . . . The color blue is very strong."

Third dream: ". . . It involved Bob Morris.* His experiments with birds. The general reaction to him would be of his interest, I felt . . . I felt that once the target was seen, it would explain everything. The target is of emotional interest to Bob Morris. The color of deep blue is important. The sea or the sky."

Fourth dream: "I don't remember anything."

Review of first dream: ". . . Dark blue colors. An informal meeting with doctors . . ."

Review of second dream: ". . . I had an enormous sack on my back which was stuffed full of letters like a mailman, and yet the sack was completely weightless . . . Something important happened around water . . . Everything was blue . . . It was as if there was a blue light, almost, so that everything, although you knew it really wasn't blue, appeared to be blue . . ."

---

*Dr. Robert L. Morris, formerly an animal-behavior psychologist (specializing in birds) at Duke University, later joined the staff of the Psychical Research Foundation in Durham, N.C. In 1985, he was selected to fill the Koestler chair in parapsychology at the University of Edinburgh, Scotland.

Review of third dream: "...Bob Morris does research on animal behavior and, more specifically, birds ... He's been doing various research and studies with birds and he's taken me out to see his sanctuary place where all the birds are kept ... I remember seeing various different kinds of doves. Ring-tailed doves, ordinary doves, Canadian geese. There were many, many different kinds of varieties ... I just said, 'Oh, well, you'll understand everything when you see the target. I don't have to explain it now. It's self-explanatory, so you'll have to wait a while.'"

Review of fourth dream: "...The only thing I think of is just water. Just a lake of water. Kind of greeny-blue ... A few ducks and things. It's fairly misty, but there are quite a lot of mandrake geese and various birds of some kind swimming around in rushes or reeds ... Birds ... I just have a feeling that the next target material will be about birds."

And Bessent added: "It's interesting also because I wrote a poem a couple of days ago about freedom and birds, and the last couple of lines were..., 'Even birds aren't free; they have gravity to contend with.'"

This stunning "direct hit" can be compared with the night following the bird experience, which was rated at 18 for little correspondence. First dream: "...I don't recall..." Second dream: "...I can't remember what I've been dreaming about..." Third dream: "...I thought about various people..." Fourth dream: "...I was reading a letter written by Irene Hall, our secretary here ... She wrote this letter saying she and Chuck had gone out one night last week and that they'd gone to this restaurant like on the top of a very high-rise building ... I had sort of a mental impression of a tremendous restaurant which is on the top of a very high building and it was nighttime and they were having dinner together in candlelight..."

His review of the main theme was "Something about communication or correspondence..."

Overall, for the eight precognition nights, there were five "direct hits"; one "hit" in second place; one "hit" in third place; and one "miss" in fifth place (on the night when the target was "beards"). There were no "direct hits" for the eight control nights. The highest rating of correspondence that any post-experience night got was 28. In seven of the eight pairs of nights the precognition night had greater correspondence to the experience than the post-experience nights. The exception was when the theme was "death."

The odds against these results happening by chance are on the order of one thousand to one.

Taken together, the two Bessent studies have lent experimental corroboration to the precognitive hypothesis. At least one psychic sensitive (Bessent) appeared to dream precognitively fourteen out of sixteen times. Additional studies as well as corroboration in other laboratories are needed to shed further light on an issue as complex and difficult as precognition.

CHAPTER 15

Finding Out More About ESP

In the formal ESP dream studies so far described, the emphasis was on demonstrating that dream telepathy (and dream precognition in the Bessent studies) could be experimentally controlled to such an extent that the dream-target correspondences could not be attributed to chance coincidence. Finally we had provided an experimental answer to "Cicero's Complaint." It was now time to find out more about dream ESP.

In a formal study that ran from January 1969 through January 1970, four sleeping subjects were used to investigate the possible differences in dream telepathy when using a single target for half the nights and a different target for each REM period for the other half. The first two subjects were Alan Vaughan and Robert Harris; the second two were Iris Vaughan and Felicia Parise. All of them had been successful in pilot experiments. (See chapters 12 and 13.) The "Vaughan Study," which was designed by our research associate, Charles Honorton, gave statistically significant results favoring the use of a different target for each REM period.

The agent for the first two dreamers, Alan Vaughan and Robert Harris, was Gayle Miree, who had been an agent for Vaughan in successful pilot experiments. In addition, she had established rapport with Harris at the Dream Lab where he frequently helped out. Harris, who is Krippner's stepson, was at the time of the experiment a fourteen-year-old high school student.

Krippner's interest in Vaughan's potential as an ESP dream subject was first sparked by a letter he received from him on June 4, 1968, written from Freiburg, West Germany, where Vaughan was studying spontaneous precognitive dreams at the Freiburg University Institute for Border Areas of Psychology. Vaughan's letter cited several of his dreams that he felt might be premonitory of Robert Kennedy being assassinated in the near future. Krippner discussed this letter with Charles Honorton, and on June 6, the day after Robert Kennedy's assassination, Honorton replied to Vaughan that parapsychology did not yet know enough about such phenomena to warrant acting on presumptive precognitive reports.

To gain further insight into these phenomena, Krippner suggested to Vaughan that he should also be on the outlook for precognitive dreams during this series. As Vaughan and Harris were not told of the experiment's novel design, they assumed that a different target would be used each night as in earlier studies, and Vaughan mistook Krippner's remarks to mean that the experiment was designed to compare telepathic and precognitive correspondences to eight targets. Because his main research interest is precognition, Vaughan directed his efforts more toward precognition than telepathy. Thus all eight of his transcripts contained many remarks singling out certain dreams as pertaining to future targets and other dreams as pertaining to life events in the future. One of the dreams singled out as precognitive of a future experiment closely corresponded to a televised pilot experiment nine months later, as noted in the previous chapter.

And so, unwittingly, the stage had been set for a contest pitting a subject's precognitive motivations against an agent's attempts to influence his dreams telepathically. As the experiment had been designed for evaluation only of synchronous ESP, this contest must be scored on the qualitative level helped by the outside judge's ratings. The dreams of Harris, who was motivated to dream synchronously, should provide a basis for comparison.

For the first four nights the agent, Gayle Miree, was to "transmit" the same target picture to both subjects every night. She was offered eight sealed envelopes that contained different pictures. She randomly selected one, leaving the others sealed. The one she chose was Dalí's *Portrait of Gala* (Plate 18), in which the sitting figure of Dalí's wife, Gala, shown from the back, is looking at a mirror image of herself facing the front. She wears a multi-colored striped jacket bearing intricate criss-cross designs. The predominant colors are shades of brown, and her hair is brown.

Harris' dreams of the first four nights bore a number of correspondences to the target, particularly the color of brown. His most direct correspondence came from the third dream on his first night. ". . .there was this girl in a fur coat . . . it was a ratty fur coat. . ." On his second night, he was looking for a girl who "had dark brown hair."

By comparison, Vaughan's dreams bore not a single correspondence to the target, as was noted on April 21, when he was asked to judge correspondences on a 100-point scale for the first four nights, dream-by-dream, against the target pool of eight pictures. He still did not know, of course, that only one target had been used, and he gave extremely high correspondences to several of the targets that were not used.

Vaughan's second night, February 14, had several striking correspondences to a non-target picture left in its sealed envelope, Evergood's *Lily and the Sparrows*. The oversized head of a little girl, with the neck and arms of her green-yellow dress showing, is looking out of a window of a red-brick apartment house at a flying flock of sparrows. The perspective is distorted in such a way that she appears to be a dwarf.

The most striking correspondence was "I think of three comedians like 'The Three Stooges' and they live in like little bird houses that are pushed next to each other with little gabled roofs and you can see through the holes in the center, and their names are Lily, Lolly, and Louie . . . I just have a sense that they are buffoons. . ." He added in the morning: "I just was aware of them being behind these holes in the houses . . . What associations this may have . . . unless it's with birds somehow, I don't know . . . Kind of a mood of mild absurdity."

Other correspondences that night included Vaughan's imagery generated during meditation before going to sleep. "There may be people . . . I also see a flock of birds." Other non-REM imagery included hearing a song from *Showboat*. "'Fish gotta swim, birds gotta fly' seem to be the lines that are important"; also included was a woman who "had either a yellow or greenish-yellow dress on." Vaughan's guess for the night was "I think this may have been a painting . . . in which there are, perhaps, birds. . ."

Vaughan reported that getting direct names, such as Lily, sometimes happens when he attempts to get psychic impressions about people in his waking state. More often, he said, he gets similar names beginning with the same letter.

Of his REM dreams that night, only one seemed to have correspondence worth noting, but not to the agent's selected target. Krippner was talking with an experimenter about altering states of consciousness in ESP experiments by using psychedelic drugs such as psilocybin. Meanwhile, in his sound-isolated sleep room, Vaughan had been dreaming about "two scientists . . . and they were trying to classify these drugs as far as their effect on consciousness . . . There's one drug that seemed to be associated with ESP, and at one point they were trying to experiment with psilocybin . . . and there seemed some frustration involved because the differences between the drugs weren't clear enough cut. . ."

For his third night, February 21, Vaughan noted many correspondences with the target *Washington and Lafayette at the Battle of Yorktown,* by Reed. As with these other apparently displaced targets, it was never taken out of its envelope. In the center is George Washington, mounted on a white horse, and the French general Lafayette is seated on a brown horse behind him. Washington is wearing a white wig, white trousers, and a black and white coat. They are looking across the grassy battlefield toward rows of infantry men who have just been hit by three exploding bombshells. On the right is a row of mounted cavalry.

Vaughan's first non-REM image was of "An out-of-doors scene. I seemed to sense animals . . . in a field . . . like an oxen or a horse. . ."

His second non-REM image seemed to emphasize the initial letter *L:*

"a song that doesn't exist . . . 'Let us lead the life of leisure, Lazarus.'" His association to this was "the word *Lazaret* refers to France. I mean, it's a French word for hospital for the wounded, usually during war time." (*Lazaret* is accented on the last syllable, like Lafayette.)

Vaughan's third non-REM image seemed like a long dream to him.

> I seemed to be in large grounds, grassy grounds and there seemed to be a hospital . . . Men there were wounded . . . They were all dressed alike; some sort of white hospital clothing, and I was helping to heal them. I went to one who had something wrong with his jaw . . . and another person had something else wrong . . . It's odd that such a dream should be located out of doors . . .

He added in the morning: "they seemed to be veterans who I felt had somehow been wounded during war . . ."

Meanwhile that night, Harris also seemed to be having some non-target oriented dreams. His second dream took place at a "sort of a farm and it was during the war . . . World War II . . . and there was this dog . . . a real hero dog . . . and it went around saving people's lives." The dominant colors were brown and white.

In Harris' fifth dream, "It was like there was a war going on . . . you could walk right up to the boat . . . and they were placing the injured there . . . they were taking people in to the army . . . Like when the guy would come around and say, 'Oh, we have someone new with a fractured leg here, move over a little bit.'" He added in the morning: "They were just putting people in it—military men, that is, and at the same time they were drafting men for the army, and as I remember, a couple of friends were getting drafted . . . And then as soon as they were drafted, they helped put the bodies of the wounded in the water . . ."

In Vaughan's second dream, Washington was not mentioned, but "I had stepped out into a washroom and was *washing up* and Chuck came in and I said, 'I thought you'd be along any minute . . .'" Later comments suggested Washington's wig: "For some strange reason I had white stuff like shaving cream in my hair which I was *washing out* . . ."

Vaughan's guess for the night was "It might be a picture painted during the war . . . I think it's likely that it will be out of doors . . ."

Harris' guess for the night was "It probably would be something about war because most of my dreams had war in them."

For the fourth night, February 28, Vaughan rated very high correspondences to another unused target, *The Engineer Heartfield,* by George Grosz. This painting shows a sinister looking German engineer drawn like a cartoon, with a green head and a blue and gray torso cut off well above the knees, about three quarters down. Little wheels and other metal machinery are shown as part of his chest. He stands like a cut-out figure in the middle of a large room with massive stone walls of gray-brown hue.

Vaughan's first non-REM image had "something vaguely sinister about it ... some sort of mythological beast, not a real one..." In his second non-REM image he saw "a corpse—a body. The head was thrown back..." This led to his third non-REM image. "I had the association first of a mass burial ... and there was also an odd scene, almost like a cartoon ... It was ... somehow symbolic because of the cartoon-like characters ... and then there was a ... scene which seemed to be carved out of great natural hewn blocks of granite." His fifth non-REM image was about shooting at targets. "They have wheels with ducks or birds ... and you try your luck with a rifle ... I just remember shooting a rifle at targets like that when I was in the army."

In his sixth non-REM image, Vaughan had been "transformed into a German doctor ... and I speak with a heavy German accent, asking directions how to get to the lab ... I guess I limp because my leg has been wounded somehow during the war, and I go limping up the corridor saying, 'Iss dis de vay to de laboratory?'"

In his eighth non-REM image, he saw a photographer. "There was something kind of disgusting about this man ... But he went into this large room ... to photograph, and someone said, 'Oh, he stood three-quarters away back.'"

His guess for the night was "I don't think it was a very pretty sort of picture at all. I think it might be sort of sinister..."

The dreams during the REM periods, by contrast, had little to do with this target or any other, except for the fourth REM period statement, "There was some person who was rather odd looking, sort of exaggerated somehow ... it was distasteful...."

Harris' dreams that night were also unrelated to "Gala." He dreamed of "the gastropedic walk" that he associated with "Doctor Scholl," "rodents," and "The kids ... we got their height checked, then the guy wrote it down and then put it in the computer...." The colors were "brown and gray." In his fourth dream, "there was this guy who my sister got to know and he was going to die ... and also we had a chameleon in our refrigerator, and it was really a distinct color—green against red...." In his fifth dream he saw gray and brown again and said, "I get an eerie feeling about the whole thing." In his sixth dream, "there was an EEG there, and everyone was sticking their fingers into it...." In his seventh dream, "I was just standing up and they were on their knees worshipping ... and they were really getting mad at me—they almost practically killed me.... There was a lot of green."

His guess for the night was "Something that would have a lot of brown and green and ... people ... like ... weighing the kids and measuring their height, and people putting their fingers in the EEG ... there was a sense of a doctor being there operating the machine ... so there probably would be something with a doctor in it in the target."

Was Harris supplying supplementary details to Vaughan's correspondences? This intriguing interplay of correspondences may be related to a question recently raised by Dr. Gertrude Schmeidler.[1] She theorizes that if a person makes contact through ESP with a distant target, he may, as it were, be creating a fold in the universe. Once he has made this fold, it could perhaps be used by others. If the target is a complex one and both persons describe the same details, the explanation could be attributed to telepathy between them; but if they describe different details, it implies that they were making independent contact with the target material, with one person using the fold made by the other person.

In this first half of the experiment, Vaughan seemed to be going to elaborate lengths to hit on pictures that the agent had not seen. Furthermore, his deflected ESP dreaming might even have influenced Harris' dreams on the third and fourth nights more than the agent's target picture. The agent, Gayle Miree, so far as it seemed, was losing the contest.

Starting on the fifth night with the multitarget condition, Gayle concentrated on a different target for each REM period, using Vaughan's REM periods as a starting point. Neither Vaughan nor Harris incorporated in their dreams much of the three targets used that night.

On the sixth night, when she used five targets, there was some correspondence to the first target for both Harris and Vaughan. The most striking correspondence that night, however, appeared in Vaughan's fourth and fifth REM periods to the target that Miree did not see until later, in his eighth REM period. The target was a photo of a twelfth-century French reliquary done in gold and enameled with figures of the saints paying homage to the Virgin Mary and the Christ child. Five saints dressed in long robes of pastel green and blue form a row on the top, and below are four other figures dressed the same way and turned toward the Virgin. A larger figure of a saint at the end holds a blue object in his hand.

In Vaughan's fourth dream, he recalled

> going to . . . some sort of sidewalk bazaar and there was someone dressed up in a costume like de Gaulle. This person was wearing a very light pastel green costume with . . . long light gloves. And then as I was watching, along came a group of French school girls who were all extremely grown up, it looked to me; very, very attractive, and they were all dressed in the same sort of green pastel color, and as each one walked by, I would say, "Mon Dieu" . . . this seemed to be actually a Catholic girls' school . . . and there was posted a listing of all the girls and what year they were going to graduate. One girl . . . her name was written, was a Sister, as if she were already ordained, or whatever it is one goes through . . . The French school girls—this seemed to be very unusual, and the color green as well as the other pastels perhaps suggest to me it might have something to do with the target . . . Certainly I have never had any experience in any girls' school like that. I've never been to one. . .

His fifth REM report was "just a little dreamlet . . . I and de Gaulle were together and we both seemed to have what almost looked like a dixie cup filled with ice cream, but on the top of it is a very ornate blue that looks like some sort of a precious stone. . . ." He elaborated later, ". . . a dixie cup with a blue pendant as an opener. Well, I opened mine . . . but de Gaulle . . . had someone else open it for him, and he said most unhumbly, I thought, 'Well, if I let them do that for me, they'll think they were God for an hour.' I was thinking, 'Well, if they think they're a God, what does he think he is?'"

Meanwhile, Harris was dreaming about de Gaulle's old arch enemy. ". . . there was somebody calling out something . . . and there was something about Hitler, something like, 'Sieg Heil!' and it just went on and on . . . Green comes to mind because every time I heard that call I thought of all those German soldiers."

The synchronous target for these dreams had been a Japanese painting of two women fishing on the green bank of a stream.

On the seventh night, the agent used five targets. The first target was *Luncheon,* by Bonnard, which shows a woman sitting across from a man at a round table that is covered by a blue and white striped tablecloth with polka dots on the side. On the table are food and a bottle of wine. Harris dreamed about bottles of mustard for hot dogs, while Vaughan was dreaming about an odd-shaped tree stuck in the snow that strikingly corresponded with the fifth target sent, *Snow Mountain,* by Chang Shu-Chi.

Harris' second dream had good correspondence with the synchronous target, which shows a group of people seeing off a stagecoach. He dreamed about a welcoming committee in the subway.

During Vaughan's fourth REM period and Harris' fifth REM period, the target was an advertisement photograph by Fagan of the Paul Bunyan Dining Room at the University of Wisconsin. Shown are brown square tables that have bottles with candles in them and two windows at an angle between paintings of Paul Bunyan. The dominant colors are brown and orange. Harris had a dream about getting "a football picture taken"; a mask "that athletes wear . . . to drink. . . ."; "orange juice. . . ." and "lots of browns."

Vaughan's fourth dream seemed to combine the target with the earlier target *Luncheon,* which had the same theme of dining. "I was watching two women talk about a place to have lunch or dinner and there was one place that seemed to be almost like a designing house or an advertising agency. It had a name and letters outside the building like Firth and 'Firth Promises First in Service.'" He added later:

> Two women had come into a patio restaurant . . . and they were sitting down at a little round table and were talking about prices . . . "If we go to thirteen dollars maybe we could get a bottle of wine," and the firm that was nearby seemed to be . . . some sort of commercial firm, of brownstone . . . and there were windows which were arranged at an angle . . . and, oh yes, one of the women was wearing a blue polka dot dress.

On the eighth and final night, April 18, Harris did very well. In his third REM period, when the target was a painting of a dejected-looking white dog, he dreamed "about being in a classroom and the other kids were really ridiculing this one kid because he wasn't as smart as them..." This became more specific in his fifth dream, in which there was a small white dog.

For his fourth REM period, the target was a bronze aquamanile (water vessel) of an armored knight mounted on a horse (Plate 19). Harris dreamed that "There was this war going on and they had these helmets on ... both representatives of this war had these kind of helmets and they were just about to fight ... their copper helmets ... were bluish, and the other guys' helmets were copper bluish ... They discovered that nobody wanted to fight..."

In his fifth REM, when the target was Leger's *Three Musicians,* Harris dreamed about being chased by the cops and acting a role in the musical *My Fair Lady.*

Vaughan's best telepathic hit came in his third REM period, when the target was an untitled painting by Bacon (Plate 20). It shows a gruesome-looking black monster holding a black umbrella and surrounded by carcasses of meat. The background is purple, and it has dark purple panels suggestive of diamond shapes. Vaughan summarized his dream in the morning:

> I recall ... being at, I think, not an actor's house, but perhaps a studio, because it was as if something was being filmed, and the actor was wearing either a mask or most intensive makeup, like Boris Karloff used to do in his Frankenstein movies, and in the story he was attacking someone else, and I told him ... "Oh, don't you recall? I did a reading for you in which I said you'd be acting like a monster and I didn't realize it would be a literal sort of thing." And he just glowered at me ... I couldn't tell really if that was the effect of the makeup ... [or] if he would really [have] liked to do me in...

Another portion of the dream supplied the color and shape of the background. "One person I met knitted sweaters that had seams on them, and he was wearing basically a purple sweater ... it had a very elaborate scene on it, sort of in a diamond shape...."

By comparison, let us look next at the last four nights of Iris Vaughan and Felicia Parise. The single target was a Dalí painting of the French philosopher Voltaire. It shows a bust of Voltaire on a pedestal that stands on a red cloth. In the background are high arches opening onto an outdoors scene. The painting is actually an optical illusion, for when viewed another way there are several human figures in gray and black robes that make up the bust. When viewed this way, it seems as if the figures are issuing in genie-like fashion from a lamp. The agent for the two women was William Thompson, who had worked with both subjects before in pilot experiments.

Parise's best correspondence occurred on November 21, 1969, the first night the target was used.

> It's all mixed up . . . but at first I saw three pictures of men . . . they looked like cut-outs from magazines . . . I think I remember seeing like a raspberry color some place . . . I remember a color, gray satin . . . I think I may have been wearing this color; and the men were photographs . . . Everyone was wearing a black robe . . . I was in a very peculiar office . . . It was just that it was very old-fashioned and the rooms were divided off by French doors . . . and these French doors had curtains. . .

She added later, "Someone was giving me a little philosophy about life." That seemed a direct hit on the philosopher Voltaire aspect of the painting, as well as its "mixed-up" quality.

On the second night the target was used, December 5, Vaughan had her best correspondence to it but from the other viewing angle, including Dalí's homeland.

> My sister Linda . . . was supposed to appear on the Johnny Carson Show in a Spanish seance, and I kept kidding her about it and saying, "I don't think you're going to get on this show, because after all, what have you done? They only have famous personalities." And she said she really liked Johnny Carson, he's really fabulous in person, much nicer than he was when he got on the shows. She said when he gets on the show he splits off his personality and becomes something different. . . .

The "split personality" of the painting seemed to be reflected in her slip of the tongue in the morning.

> I'm so sick and tired of seeing Johnny Carson, and I much prefer the David Frost show, where he really gets a lot out of the people. I mean, he's got a personality show and that's what it turns out to be, whereas Johnny Frost—it's just anybody or everybody he's got on the show is another person to exhibit how great Johnny Frost is.

The following exchange occurred:

Honorton: Johnny Carson.

Vaughan: Yes, Johnny Carson, right. I'm sorry.

Honorton: Jack Frost. (laughing)

Vaughan: And so I was doing this imitation for her, what I thought Johnny Frost looked like. . .

In the other half of the experiment, in which several targets a night were used, the women did not exhibit any of the displacements that had been so suggestive with Vaughan and sometimes Harris.

Parise's ratings of her dreams against the targets were independently significant. Vaughan's ratings were lost in the mail, and so we cannot make an adequate comparison. (An independent judge's ratings were used for getting our overall result.) There was additional difficulty with Vaughan because the tape-recording equipment malfunctioned several times and some of her dream material had to be reconstructed from the experimenter's notes.

However, for both subjects, we can give a few interesting examples of correspondences. One of Vaughan's best "hits" was on the third night when the target was an 1895 circus poster showing a buxom equestrienne balancing on top of a running black horse while a white clown looks on. The predominant colors are orange, gold, and blue. The poster says, "The Barnum & Bailey Greatest Show on Earth."

In Vaughan's second dream,

> I was having a dream about, I guess it was me, but it was a different form of me. It wasn't really me. It was just somebody similar to me . . . a girl who was . . . just doing work with something or other . . . but she was very, very, very healthy; she always had loads of vitamins and minerals and fruits and vegetables and things like this because her boss was like that . . . a health nut . . . and she had this huge Great Dane dog that she used to take for a walk every once in a while. She was a very big sports fan; liked the outdoors and things like that, and it seems she may have been working for you out here . . . then the dream sort of switched . . . and Laurie kept saying how much she liked [Mrs. Vaughan's dog] Meka, and she let her out and Meka was running around having an absolute blast; just running and running and running. . .

The colors she saw included "reds and golds and yellows."

In the morning Honorton asked if she were a sports fan. "Not really," she replied, "No. I like horse races, but aside from that I don't go to baseball games or anything."

Another target that night was *The Harvesters,* by Brueghel, which shows a family in the fields at harvest time. A group are picnicking under a tree. Vaughan dreamed about a family "out on a picnic."

On the second night, both Vaughan and Parise had some suggestive "hits," but on different targets — a pattern that generally persisted throughout their multi-target phase.

For Vaughan's seventh and eighth REM periods, the target was a painting of two heavy-set middle-aged women dressed in white and sitting at a round table in a garden having tea. A gray dog is at their feet, and a black cat is on one woman's lap.

In Vaughan's seventh dream, "A whole group of us were standing around at a bar and we were singing . . . There's a big, heavy, old woman in it — a younger heavy-set woman, and they were singing a duet . . . two cats like a cartoon . . . One cat had grasped the other cat's hands which he was shaking, and like he really twisted his thumb. The other second cat thought it was very funny until he had it done to him . . ."

In her eighth dream, "There was this old ancient man or woman — I couldn't tell which — but I think it was a man and he had funny-looking dog's teeth; his teeth looked like a dog's . . . and there was this lady, slightly younger . . ."

The target for Parise's seventh REM period was Picasso's *Man with*

Violin. Neither man nor violin are readily apparent in this cubist style of colored rectangular blocks with black angular lines. The predominant colors are brown, dark yellow, black, red, and dark orange. In her seventh dream,

> I walked into my living room, somebody had put a lot of pillows on my couch — so many pillows that the room looked crowded . . . Pillows that were very brightly colored. They were red and yellow pillows; black and white stripe; orange; orange and yellow; brown, black and white . . . all colors . . . I was just curious as to who put the pillows there and why, and I was annoyed because they left hangers all over the place, and a big paper bag . . . and I was just like annoyed because they left my apartment all upset.

The target for Parise's eighth and ninth REM periods was a portrait of a distinguished-looking gentleman who is formally dressed in a long blue coat, dark trousers, a blue hat, and bowtie. Behind him, fire springs up, and in his right hand he holds a sword. Only the thumb is visible, and a tassle hangs from the sword handle. Her eighth dream was about President Nixon's daughters at a convention hall; her ninth was about a family friend.

> In reality he has both hands, but I — I dreamt about him just a little while ago. I dreamt he had one hand. . . . His right hand was missing, and all he had was, like a thumb that was attached to the wrist . . . but this did not depress him. He was very, you know, well-adjusted, and he would joke a lot about it . . . and he showed us an artificial hand that he got and how it works. . . . And he said the only reason he needed an artificial hand was that he needed a finger to tie a string around in order to remind himself (giggling). . . .

She added later: "And then he put on the artificial hand so he could show us how it works, and I remember my mother saying . . . 'Joe, with all these things, aren't you afraid you're going to scare somebody in the subway?' And he laughed, and he said, 'No, because, look, I still have a thumb.'"

Parise also had some suggestive correspondences to the targets on the first night, and, in general, she did best. In contrast with Vaughan and Harris, Parise and Vaughan did not seem to share any themes in simultaneous dreams, not even when the same target was being used.

The overall result of the series is that all four dreamers highly favored the use of different targets for every dream against a single target for four nights, which suggests that the dreamers' attention was being engaged more by novel ESP stimuli. Another possible tie-in is that the agents, especially Miree, reported getting very bored looking at the same target every night. Perhaps the dreamers also seemed to find it very boring to dream about the same target every night.

The formal study also pointed out vividly that the dreamer's motivations and expectations emerge as the strongest factors in experimental dream telepathy, and that the agent, to be successful at telepathy, must have full cooperation from the subjects, who in turn perform better if they know more clearly what is expected of them.

PART THREE

THEORETICAL IMPLICATIONS

CHAPTER 16

What Does It Mean?

Theoretically, the "Vaughan Study" raises more questions than it answers. The question we set out to answer when we designed the experiment in 1968 was based on our experience in the Ullman-Dale experiment in controlled dream telepathy and spontaneous dream telepathy. In this experiment, ESP dream correspondences would sometimes follow the apparent target stimulus by a day or two. Much earlier, in 1922, Sigmund Freud hypothesized that the stimulus might be stored in the unconscious of the percipient to emerge later in a telepathic dream:

> ...no one has a right to take exception to telepathic occurrences on the ground that the event and the presentiment (or message) do not exactly coincide in astronomical time. It is perfectly conceivable that a telepathic message might arrive contemporaneously with the event and yet only penetrate to consciousness the following night during sleep.... Often the latent dream thoughts may have been lying ready during the whole day, till at night they find the contact with the unconscious wish that shapes them into a dream....[1]

We also wondered if the stimulus was gradually and unconsciously building up until after a day or so it became strong enough to finally emerge in a telepathic dream.

The "Vaughan Study" was designed to investigate whether telepathic stimulus does "build up" over the course of a night or nights—in which case the most striking dream-target correspondences would emerge at the end of the night or the end of the series—or if dream telepathy represented a "mutual resonance" through space between agent and subject that "flashes on and off" with an even distribution of telepathic dreams throughout the night and the series. The single-target half of the series would allow for a "building up" effect; while the multi-target phase would allow for a "mutual-resonance" effect.*

---

*This refers to the theory of telepathic rapport being based on a resonance effect between two brains. Presumably if no "build up" is noted using a single target repeatedly this would favor the alternative view of a resonance effect in response to the novelty of each individual target.

The results indicated that there was no "build-up" effect. Moreover, the agents reported being bored by having to concentrate on the same target for four nights, and it seems unlikely that they were completely successful in "emotionally charging" the target after the first or second night. The best correspondences to both agents' targets came on the first or second night. In Harris' case it was his very first dream. This suggests that the novelty of the stimulus is far more important in experimental dream telepathy than any possible "build-up" effect; it would also favor the "mutual-resonance" hypothesis.

The incidence of spontaneous precognitive dreams of the percipient's future is greater than any other type of spontaneous ESP dream. However, such dreams are, of course, the most difficult to explain. A theoretical alternative to precognition, as a basis for Vaughan's displacements, might be that he was using clairvoyance to see into sealed envelopes. Yet this alternative seems unlikely, since of the many thousands of cases of spontaneous ESP dreams, very, very few have been about an object unconnected with a person. Nocturnal clairvoyant dreaming has not yet been established experimentally though we do have some experimental evidence that clairvoyant dreams can be induced under hypnosis.[2]

That interference in the agent-subject rapport can cause displacements was noted by Dr. Robert Van de Castle[3] in the experimental dream telepathy series he did with Dr. David Foulkes in Wyoming that yielded non-significant results. A "non-target" picture that Van de Castle saw when judging the target pool the morning after a dream study experiment was a picture of a large wooden serving board with fruit and desserts on it, a glass filled with brown liquid, and a chicken that was plucked bare. In his dream the night before, he was in a drugstore requesting medicine for cancer. Across a large wooden counter he was served a brown liquid in a glass. People nearby were having ice cream desserts and for a while he was confused as to whether it was a drugstore or a restaurant. At that point a small chicken, completely plucked, walked across the floor. It was wearing a small cloth vest. Van de Castle, who had been recording his dreams for years, testifies that, "I have never before nor since dreamed of a bare, naked chicken." He adds, "This type of displacement occurred on several nights and it seemed as if I might have been precognitively picking up on the pool of eight pictures rather than zeroing in telepathically on the agent. I did pick up some of the agent's conflicts over religion and had dreams of Christ being nailed to the cross and being tortured, which had nothing to do with any pictures. The agent told me the next morning that she had become very much preoccupied with religious questions and had not been able to concentrate for that reason on the target."

A search for a general model of ESP must explore not only the dimensions of space and time, but also events that seem related and are inextricably interwoven with the human experience of psi, namely, meaningful coincidences. Jung referred to this as "synchronicity," defined as meaningful coincidences that occur without *known* causes. Basic to our everyday thinking is the premise that if effects occur there must be antecedent causes. A drawback to investigating complex occurrences such as meaningful coincidences is that, while they occur plentifully in life, they are not easily lured into the artificial situation of the laboratory.

The experimental evidence for dream telepathy buttresses clinical evidence. Its occurrence leads us to conclude that the nature and fabric of the interpersonal field, and the nature of the dynamic exchanges that it encompasses, are far more subtle and complicated than current psychoanalytic and behavioral theory suggest.

Before we develop possible theoretical perspectives, let us consider some of the implications of dream telepathy for our understanding of ESP in general. Perhaps our most basic finding is the scientific demonstration of Freud's statement: ". . . sleep creates favorable conditions for telepathy."[4] In both the formal studies and the one-night pilot studies, we have found that people who are open to the possibility of ESP, are relatively comfortable in the laboratory, and are able to remember their dreams, will more than likely dream telepathically. This becomes particularly striking when the results of 80 one-night pilot sessions, with 80 different subjects, are examined for telepathic effects. Regardless of profession, walk of life, waking psychic ability or knowledge of having ever before experienced ESP, the great majority of subjects (56 out of 80) were able to report correspondences that were suggestively telepathic.

When waking telepathy experiments were conducted by other parapsychologists, the percentage of subjects who scored "hits" was generally far less than those who scored "misses." This often leads the parapsychologist, using purely quantitative methods, to search out talented psychic sensitives who can consistently produce good results. When we used Bessent, a psychic sensitive, in the precognition studies, the dreaming state enabled him to score somewhat higher than he had in waking state experiments where an automated apparatus was used to test his precognitive ability.

We firmly believe that an important ingredient in the success of experiments in dream telepathy over waking telepathy, established by quantitative testing, is the use of potent, vivid, emotionally impressive human interest pictures to which both agent and subject can relate. If such target material were to be used in waking experiments, or in other altered states of consciousness besides dreaming (hypnotic, hypnagogic, meditative states, and states altered by sensory bombardment and psychedelic drugs), the subjects may come through with better results. Our experiments suggest this is especially so when the subject is in an altered state.[5]

As our associate Charles Honorton has pointed out, ". . . successful activation of ESP may be related to a relaxed, passive state of mind, one which is relatively devoid of visual imagery, and in which there is a decrease in externally directed attention, perhaps coupled with an increase in attention toward internal feelings and sensations. One or more of these characteristics appear in a number of mental states now called *altered states of consciousness*."[6]

An important difference between these other altered states of consciousness and dreaming is that every night, every person dreams and the dream telepathy target can be superimposed upon or incorporated into the ongoing dream action. Just what type of target material gets through most easily may be related to the type of material that appears naturally in the dream. People tend to dream about themselves and other people. It is relatively rare for anyone to dream about an unpopulated scene or a thing unconnected with a specific person. The targets which are incorporated most easily into dreams generally depict people and are often archetypal (emotional) in character (which is why we have relied so heavily on art prints rather than magazine pictures, for instance). If there is a person in the target picture with whom the dreamer can identify, a telepathic incorporation is more apt to occur. If the dreamer is male, he tends to have more dreams about sex and aggression than a female, as shown by Hall and Van de Castle[7]; therefore, we would expect males to incorporate these themes more often than females. This does indeed seem to be the case, especially with Dr. Van de Castle, who by studying the frequency of themes in dreams has become very attuned to these differences.

Themes basic to both sexes, such as oral needs, generally come through very strongly. We have seldom had a "miss" when the target shows someone eating or drinking. Religion is another theme that comes through strongly in the telepathic dreams of both sexes. It is a basic theme that makes for successful target material.

Female dreamers tend to be more sensitive to colors and details of arrangement than males, perhaps reflecting their patterns of interest in the waking state. They tend to be more accurate in picking up details from target pictures, although male dreamers, who like Van de Castle are very proficient in dream recall, are able to do as well. For both sexes, the incidence of color in dreams was generally associated with ESP success.

While listening to the subject's dream report, we can get some indication of whether or not he is likely to incorporate the target. If the dream is vivid, colored, detailed, and somewhat puzzling to the dreamer, and does not "fit" into his dream pattern or reflect recent activity, then we can be alerted to the possibility that the dream is being influenced by ESP. If, on the other hand, the dream is about being wired up with electrodes, or about the experimental laboratory situation, or identifiably derived from a day's residue, then we can be fairly confident that ESP is not operating.

In the middle ground are those dreams derived from past experience but transformed in some novel way. If the event dreamed about is very recent, within the past few days, we would be less confident that it contains ESP. If the dream relates to an incident considerably in the past — particularly an incident that seems to have had little relevance to the day's problems or current preoccupations — then there is greater confidence that ESP has influenced the choice of this material for recall. Certainly one of the strongest effects we have seen is the theme of an ESP target's triggering a percipient's memory of a related event in his past. The more the dreamer can relate his personal experience to the target theme, the more successful he will be in incorporating that target by ESP.

What role does the agent play in this incorporation? At the very least the agent provides human interest for the dreamer. His associations can come through more strongly than the actual target picture. Although this effect is very difficult to evaluate statistically, these associations appear to be a potential influence on the subject's dreams. This effect was noted earlier by Van de Castle in his series for David Foulkes.[8]

When we did a pilot study to compare results of an agent looking at a target picture with results when an agent actively involved himself in the target's theme by "multisensory experience," we found that the two sleeping subjects did much better when the multisensory experience was utilized. As an example, when the target picture was Daumier's *The Pork Butcher,* the "multisensory involvement" of the agent was to open a canned ham, slice it, and eat it. In the formal series where we utilized multisensory experience, the telepathic results were highly significant; this suggests that the active involvement of the agent is an important ingredient for success.

How important is agent-subject rapport? We would say that it is a very important factor bearing on the success rate of our various subjects. In support of this we have limited, but provocative, results with identical twins. So has Van de Castle in a dream telepathy series he inaugurated at the University of Virginia.[9] Interestingly, the results with twins as agent-subject pairs engaged in other ESP studies seems not at all to be based on their physical and genetic resemblances, but on their emotional rapport. Identical twins who dislike each other do poorly, while non-identical twins who have strong emotional rapport do better at telepathy.[10]

Given the subject's strong motivation to dream telepathically, the establishment of rapport with the agent offers a positive and supportive context for the experiment. In spontaneous telepathic dreams, the agents seem to be the initiators of the telepathy, and the percipient most often is in emotional rapport with them. The possible range of variation in the agent's contribution as compared with the subject's to dream telepathy can extend from a heavy weighting in favor of the subject's efforts at "picking up" the target to a weighting in favor of the agent's emotional involvement in "sending" the target. (In experimental dream telepathy it is rare for percipients to dream about a target that they did not realize was being sent. For an example of this kind of tangential "hit" the reader is referred back to Van de Castle's account of his dream of the boxing match and his comments about this in Chapter 11.) This wide gamut of possible interplay would seem to make the "transmitter-receiver" model of telepathy somewhat simplistic.

In many spontaneous telepathic dreams, a romantic attachment between a male agent and a female percipient seemed to be a frequent condition for spontaneous dream telepathy. Because of this we noted the possible influences of sex differences among the subjects and agents participating in the pilot sessions. In the 80 pilot sessions done with 42 male and 38 female subjects on their first night, 14 male agents alternated with 10 female agents. Altogether there were 56 "hits" and 24 "misses." The following table shows the results. A "hit" is indicated by a + and a "miss" by a − ; the figure in parentheses is the percent "hit" rate, where 50 percent is expected by chance.[11]

Comparison of Male-Female
Agent-Subject Pairings in Pilot Experiments.

	Male Agents	Female Agents
Male Subjects	16 + , 5 − (76%)	16 + , 5 − (76%)
Female Subjects	18 + , 9 − (67%)	6 + , 5 − (55%)

The first surprising finding is that, in the laboratory, men are better percipients than women. This is in strong contrast to spontaneous telepathic dreams reported in the United States, Great Britain, and Germany, where women far outnumber men in reporting their ESP dreams. This disparity may be due, in part, to a cultural climate in which women are "allowed" to talk about their "irrational" ESP experiences and where men look down upon ESP as "fit for women and children." In India, where the cultural climate is far more open to paranormal phenomena, a polled survey of spontaneous ESP·experiences of children in the eighth grade was conducted by Dr. Jamuna Prasad,[12] a prominent psychologist and educator from India. Prasad found that the boys and girls reported about the same percentages of ESP experiences: 35.8 percent for the boys and 36.9 percent for the girls. For both sexes, dreams accounted for slightly over half of their ESP experiences. Given an open cultural attitude toward ESP, the sexes would seem to have equal potential at ESP dreaming.

The total number of female-agent-to-female-subject experiments is less than the others because, by experience, we found that this was the worst possible combination. We preferred to match agents and subjects in ways that would favor more "hits" than "misses."

Why then, do the women laboratory subjects do less well than the men, especially when their agent is another woman? Women may be at a disadvantage in the laboratory setting; i.e. they may feel more nervous about sleeping in a strange bed and having male experimenters walking in and out of their "bedrooms." We have also noticed that they have a harder time than men in going to sleep in strange surroundings. It is well known, too, that women are more reluctant to volunteer as subjects for sleep laboratories. All of this suggests that the sleep laboratory situation provokes more anxiety and nervousness in women than in men subjects. Since ESP has been shown by Gertrude Schmeidler and others to be so significantly influenced by attitude and mood, then perhaps the laboratory's anxiety-producing effect on women acts to suppress their psi.

But what would account for women subjects scoring so badly when female agents are used? Here we are on even less certain grounds. In general, women seem to take longer to build up a friendly rapport with strangers; and our data are for "first nights."

Based on our experience it would seem that favorable rapport for dream telepathy includes bonds of friendship, bonds of "team spirit" in a competitive situation (trying to get telepathic "hits" is a competition of sorts to be won by cooperation), and bonds of trust and friendship with the experimenter who plays a significant role in setting the emotional tone in which the experiment is carried out. A laboratory situation where the percipient is treated coldly or indifferently by the experimenters can have a devastatingly negative effect on the results—certainly as bad as if there were no subject-agent rapport. A combined absence of subject-experimenter and subject-agent rapport would very likely predispose to failure.

When a woman is a subject for the first time, results might tend to be negative whether the agent is a stranger or a friend, but especially where the agent is a stranger. This may have been an important factor in an experiment yielding non-significant results conducted by David Foulkes in Wyoming.[13] In that study all the percipients were women, all in their first attempt at dream telepathy, and all working with an agent, Malcolm Bessent, who was a stranger to them.

In the case of this particular experiment, there was some thought that perhaps a psychic sensitive would be a better agent than anyone else. After the experiment's completion, and the results were not statistically significant, it seemed that Bessent's waking psychic abilities and his abilities as an experimental subject had little to do with his ability as an agent. What, then, are the qualities that make for being a good telepathic agent? When the staff members of the Dream Laboratory were queried as to the characteristics of a good agent, the following adjectives came to mind: interested, motivated, capable of intense concentration, capable of becoming emotionally involved in the target, open, confident, capable of and wanting to establish rapport with others quickly, being very interested in others, expressive, and perhaps even possessed of some acting ability. We could, without any hesitation, apply these adjectives to Bessent — who turned out to be a poor agent. We could also apply them to Sol Feldstein, who was a very good agent but who, unlike Bessent, made a very poor percipient. Feldstein had difficulty in getting to sleep, and he felt this might have been related to anxiety about "telepathic penetration." So, when cast in the role of percipient, Feldstein was no longer "open."

The quality of openness may well be a crucial one for a successful telepathic percipient. We saw in the experiments at the Parapsychology Foundation that a few subjects who were skeptics about ESP and therefore not "open" to it, did not have telepathic dreams. Theresa Grayeb was at first apparently resentful of being "tricked" by the experimenters and agent when she learned that no target had been used and this may have initially blocked her openness. Later, in the second half of her study, Grayeb seemed to have recovered her equanimity and also her openness. Erwin, in both of his series, was completely open. His two experiences in psychoanalysis had given him the confidence to deal with whatever revelations his dreams had in store for him. Van de Castle, too, was exceedingly open and frank, since his study of the psychology of dreaming had prepared him to come to terms with the messages of his own dreams. Of our pilot subjects, those who feared "exposing" their psyche for all to see were the least successful as telepathic subjects. They tended to repress not only telepathic material but also the memory of their dreams.

In addition to openness we would add self-acceptance as a quality making for successful telepathic dreaming. The most important qualification for being a telepathic dream percipient does not seem to depend on the person's waking psychic ability nor his previous ESP experience, but rather on his willingness to accept the dream ESP experience. All of this is said somewhat tentatively as we do not yet know the limits of ESP dreaming. Telepathy may be as much a process of "reaching out" as "letting in," and different personal qualities may be required for each of these processes.

To get an impression of the personality traits and attitudes of good dream telepathy subjects, three members of the Dream Laboratory staff made selections from a 300-adjective checklist. A fourth, Alan Vaughan, filled out the checklist for the qualities of persons who do best in ESP training classes. All four agreed on these characteristics, in alphabetical order: adaptable, adventurous, alert, appreciative, curious, enthusiastic, imaginative, individualistic, sensitive, suggestible, and varied interests. Three votes were given for: independent, insightful, original, relaxed, resourceful, spontaneous, uninhibited, and warm.

By contrast, their votes for the qualities of poor dream telepathy subjects were mostly negative. All were in agreement only on one adjective: apathetic.

A few of the 300 adjectives received three votes: aloof, anxious, argumentative, conservative, conventional, despondent, nervous, and tense.

In the following years, other researchers have attempted to repeat our results, both informally and with rigorous experimentation. At a summer camp sponsored by the Association for Research and Enlightenment (the organization devoted to studying the work of Edgar Cayce), Dr. Van de Castle organized an informal telepathic dream contest.[14] One of the young women at the camp volunteered to concentrate on a picture since she expected her infant child to wake her up frequently during the night. The subjects were about 70 young men and women attending the camp. The following morning, the campers each viewed a set of five magazine pictures and ranked them from 1 to 5 for correspondence to the dreams. Ranks of 1 or 2 for the target picture were considered to be hits. This procedure was repeated on three additional nights, with a new target picture and pool introduced each night. The overall total of 95 hits and 55 misses was statistically significant.

Each summer, from 1968 to 1972, Van de Castle administered group ESP tests to adolescent Cuna Indians in Panama.[15] The targets consisted of five colored drawings portraying familiar objects: a shark, jaguar, canoe, conch shell, and airplane. Van de Castle served as agent and each of the 461 subjects completed 50 attempts. Scores were checked and tabulated by an outside assistant. The overall scoring was at a chance level, but the girls scored significantly higher than the boys. Each subject was asked to write down his or her most recent dream and 408 did so. An outside assistant scored the dreams for the presence or absence of seven content categories. The subjects with the highest content category scores had the highest ESP scores; this finding was stastically significant for both sexes. The categories most closely associated with high ESP scoring were aggression, sexuality, animals, and parental figures.

A few studies have also examined the relationship between dream recall and ESP scores. As a part of the Maimonides studies, Charles Honorton administered precognition tests to a group of 28 students on five different occasions.[16] Subjects who remembered at least one dream per week scored significantly higher than those with less frequent dream recall. Martin Johnson found a significant positive relationship between completeness of dream recall and high scores on ESP tests given to a group of Swedish students.[17] Erlander Haraldsson administered 223 Icelandic students a precognition questionnaire and discovered a significant relationship between reported dream recall and the reported frequency of precognitive dreams.[18]

Inge Strauch served as the agent and experimenter for 12 female subjects who each slept three nights in a New York City dream laboratory.[19] The judges' evaluations did not attain statistical significance. Gordon Globus and his associates conducted a 17-night experiment at the Boston University

School of Medicine's dream laboratory with a pair of friends.[20] The judges' ratings were not statistically significant. However, the judges had also been asked to rank the confidence they had in their ratings; the scores ranked with high confidence correctly identified the correct pairs of targets and dreams at a statistically significant level.

William Dement, a prominent sleep researcher, conducted a one-night dream telepathy study with a large number of college students, none of whom reported dreams that corresponded to the selected target material.[21] However, another sleep researcher, Alan Rechtschaffen, carried out a project involving six pairs of subjects that yielded 47 "hypnotic dreams" (in which the subject was hypnotized and then suggested to imagine having a dream).[22] One judge was able to match targets and hypnotic dreams at a statistically significant level, but the other judge's matchings were at chance level. Irvin Child and his associates proposed a simplified dream telepathy experiment and conducted a pilot study that demonstrated its feasibility.[23] Both the Rechtschaffen and Child models deserve further application.

Another promising procedure is one developed by John Beloff and Betty Markwick, who conducted a 100-trial experiment between Edinburgh and London. The overall results were described as "of modest significance" obtained by "a skeptically minded subject working under an ultra-rigorous regime"; this "augurs well for a simple (and inexpensive) approach to dream research." Before each attempt, Beloff would prepare five targets and send a duplicate copy to Markwick. She would record her dreams that night, then would examine the five target possibilities, placing them in rank order according to how closely each resembled her dreams. A transcript of the dreams was prepared by Markwick and sent to Beloff with her guess as to the correct target. Beloff would inform Markwick, giving her correct feedback before the next attempt. Markwick sometimes reported "out-of-the-body" experiences during the night and was urged to continue this practice. On one occasion, she reported reaching into the box containing the target, reporting that it felt like a "tangle of tape" or a "tape measure." Indeed, the target was a typewriter ribbon with the end undone.[24]

Henry Reed arranged an imaginative pilot study in which "dream helpers" attempted to "dream for" a stranger whose problems were unknown to the dreamers. The guilt-and-dependence themes of the "dream helpers'" dreams corresponded closely to the stranger's stated problem, as did several specific dream images. This study deserves to be repeated with rigorous controls as it taps into real-life concerns that may stimulate psi processes.[25] Two students at Virginia Wesleyan University alternated as subject and agent for a 20-night study. The subject was awakened by an observer (unfamiliar with the target picture) who recorded the dream reports. Using strict standards of matching for "perfect identity" between dream and target, a judge awarded a surprising nine hits out of the 20 attempts.[26] Critics of psi research often claim that "the dream-telepathy project has been abandoned . . . because it no longer produced results."[27] It is true that the Foulkes studies, carefully patterned after the Maimonides series, did not yield significant results, but there are other studies whose data, although not convincing, are certainly compelling.

One of the most successful attempts to replicate the Maimonides findings was undertaken by William Braud, a research psychologist at the Mind Science Foundation in San Antonio, Texas. The subjects attempted to receive a telepathy target as they were falling asleep (the period of time said to contain hypnagogic imagery), while asleep and dreaming, and early in the morning while awakening and perhaps experiencing hypnopompic imagery. This procedure was followed in three different experiments that were designed to explore the feasibility of conducting long-distance dream telepathy and hypnagogic imagery experiments by mail and to compare directly the relative effectiveness of dream and hypnagogic imagery as vehicles of psi awareness.

Fifty subjects participated in the first investigation. A letter was mailed to each person describing the experiment in detail. At 2:00 A.M. on the specified date, Braud viewed a randomly selected slide, one of a collection of 1,024 that had been created by Charles Honorton and his assistants at Maimonides. Subjects mailed written records of their imagery and dream recall to the Foundation office. A subject's telepathy score consisted of the number of matches with the content of the actual target slide. There were 10 content categories (e.g., animals, body parts, nature); 5 out of 10 matches were expected by chance.

Results from the first investigation were not significant. Because the data fell in the direction of "psi-missing" (when subjects make more misses than would be expected by chance), it was decided to shift the 2:00 A.M. target time to a more convenient hour. The number of subjects was reduced to 10, half of whom turned in acceptable responses. The totals for the five participants were 19 hits, 5 misses, and 6 chance scores, yielding a statistically significant ratio. The same 10 persons participated in the third investigation. The procedure was identical except that the target exposure time was changed again. Of the 36 written reports received, 19 were hits, 9 were misses, and 8 were chance scores. When the results of the two replication attempts were combined, the hypnagogic imagery appeared to contain the most target material, the significance level being so high that there was only one chance out of 1,000 that the results could be due to coincidence.[28]

A psychologist, Judith Malamud, and a parapsychologist, Rhea White, helped us divide several Maimonides dream transcripts into "units of meaning" that consisted of sentences, phrases, explanations, and interjections that carried discrete bits of information.[29] Specifically, we used all transcripts from the studies carried out with William Erwin, Robert Van de Castle,

Robyn Posin, and Theresa Grayeb. We then had an outside judge examine the target picture that had been used on the night represented by the transcript. The judge decided whether or not enough of a correspondence existed to rate the unit of meaning "telepathic."

This procedure was followed for dream reports, the subject's associations to the dreams, pre-sleep statements that the subject made while fully awake, and imagery reported during hypnagogic and hypnopompic states. There were very few correspondences in waking reports judged to be "telepathic," but a great many in dream reports and the associations to the dreams on the following morning. However, the "twilight states" of hypnagogic and hypnopompic imagery contained a higher proportion of presumptive ESP than any of the comparative conditions.

This phenomenon was capitalized on by our associate, Charles Honorton, who had observed ESP in states of consciousness appearing to be characterized by a withdrawal of attention from the external world and a shift toward internal thoughts and images. In 1972, the U.S. National Institute of Mental Health granted Maimonides funding to explore dream telepathy over a two-year period. Forty telepathy teams were utilized in this study; short films were employed instead of target pictures. No strong evidence of ESP was obtained in this experiment.[30] Yet we feel that the money was well spent because of an ancilliary study financed by the grant. Honorton enlisted 30 volunteer subjects to take part in a telepathy experiment involving the regulation of one's perceptual input to evoke hypnagogic-like imagery.[31]

After reading about Gerald Vogel's study of thought patterns and imagery during sleep onset,[32] Honorton developed an innovative procedure in which subjects were seated in our soundproof room with halved ping-pong balls fastened over their eyes. A colored light was placed six inches in front of the subject's face and a recording of the seashore played through headphones. Before the headphones were placed on the subject's ears, instructions were given to "keep your eyes open" and to "report all the images, thoughts, and feelings which pass through your mind." In the meantime, a telepathic agent in a distant room began to look at the randomly selected target material — a reel of pictures seen in three dimensions through a hand viewer.

Following the sessions, subjects inspected a duplicate set of possible reels, choosing the one they felt corresponded most closely to their thoughts and images. As there were always four reels from which to choose, one would expect — by chance alone — seven or eight hits. Instead, there were 13 correct choices, a number that was highly significant. For example, when the reel pictured American Indian scenes, the subject reported imagery of "a long highway in Mexico" and an "American Indian arrow." When the reel contained pictures of the United States Air Force Academy, the subject reported images of "an airplane," "an army uniform," and of "flying through the mountains."

Since Honorton's original report in 1974, he has produced similar results several times and has described his work with the term "ganzfeld," a German word meaning "uniform visual field" (such as the field produced with the colored light and the ping-pong balls).[33] Furthermore, successful ganzfeld experiments have been reported from a number of different laboratories, making it one of the most frequently attempted parapsychological experiments in history.[34,35] Rex Stanford produced an in-depth study of 19 ganzfeld experiments in 1984, concluding that the approach was an extremely promising avenue to research in understanding the process of ESP.[36] Between 50 and 60 percent of the attempted ganzfeld studies have produced significant data — a result that fulfills the promise of the high ESP yield in the "twilight states" investigated at Maimonides.

Some theoretical issues about psychic dreams have been raised by research psychologists in recent years. Nancy Sondow, in a 1988 article, reported analyzing a collection of 98 of her own dreams that contained presumed precognitive elements. She found that more than half the precognized elements occurred within one day of the dream, with a steep fall-off of events through increasing time spans. Sondow hypothesized a model of "branching futures with alternate possible futures" to explain both the fall-off of events through time and the clarity of temporally distant events.[37] David Ryback examined his collection of precognitive dreams and conjectured that it suggested that reality might be better explained by a holographic model in combination with an analytic model than by an analytic model alone. In the holographic model, all available information (past, present, and future) is present at each point in the hologram. The analytic model — in which past influences present and future, and it which the future cannot be foreseen — may not be sufficient to explain psychic dreams. These dreams present a world in which locations in time and space are sometimes suspended, and in which "future memory" may be observed, at least in part.

Theoretical implications also emerge from a study in which Michael Persinger examined the first night that each of 62 subjects who participated in telepathy or clairvoyance dream experiences spent at our laboratory. The results, based on subject judging, were classified as "high hits," "low hits," "high misses," and "low misses." Geomagnetic measures of the northern hemisphere were determined for each of these nights. Although there were too few "misses" for proper statistical analysis, a significant difference was observed between "high hits" and "low hits," the former being more closely associated with the absence of sunspot activity and electrical storms. These data suggest that the psi capacities of the human brain may be sensitive to geomagnetic activity.[38]

In 1978, the Maimonides Dream Laboratory closed its doors. Stanley Krippner had moved to San Francisco to direct a graduate program in consciousness studies for Saybrook Institute. Montague Ullman had developed a highly effective method for working with dreams and was teaching the procedure both in the United States and in Sweden (see Appendix D). Charles Honorton had established the Psychophysical Research Laboratory in Princeton, New Jersey, to continue his ganzfeld work and to develop video games that would test for ESP. Alan Vaughan had moved to Los Angeles to set up an office in intuitive consulting and to take advantage of several writing and publishing opportunities.* In surveying the Maimonides work with dreams and ESP, Gardner Murphy had advised:

> It will take much time and labor, but in both quantitative and qualitative terms the experimental analysis of dream telepathy is now a problem of such urgency that a mature science can no longer handle it either by ignoring it or by denying it. Fortunately, organized science has at last begun to recognize the need to look straight at the experimental data and their interpretation.[40]

In his seminal book, *States of Mind,* British psychologist Adrian Parker notes the mixed results of the attempts to replicate the Maimonides studies but, in regard to the experiments themselves, observes that they reveal "a consistency almost unparalleled anywhere in parapsychology."[41] We are very grateful for this accolade and hope that our efforts will stimulate additional experimentation. We feel that the Maimonides work demonstrates how some anomalous phenomena can be brought into the laboratory and rigorously studied.

In 1988, Alan Vaughan and Dr. Jessica Utts, a statistician from the University of California, Davis, completed a comparative analysis of Maimonides precognition data and telepathy-clairvoyance data. Using Irvin Child's 1985 compilation of experimental and pilot sessions, they found that, overall, there were 233 hits in 379 trials, 83.5 percent accuracy, z-score = 4.47, p = 3.9 × 10 to the 6th power. Telepathy-clairvoyance sessions produced 217 hits in 361 trials, 60.0 percent accuracy, z-score = 3.84, p = 6.2 × 10 to the 4th power. Precognition sessions produced 16 hits in 18 trials, 88.9 percent accuracy, binomial p = 5.8 × 10 to the 4th power. The accuracy of the precognition sessions, of course, largely reflects the scores of one subject, Malcolm Bessent. Even so, the percentage of hits is higher than that of the combined telepathy and clairvoyance sessions.

CHAPTER 17

Sleep, Psyche, and Science

The dream state is a natural arena in which creative energies are at play. Dreams tend to arrange information in unique and emotionally related ways. They break with reality-oriented thought to group things together by "illogical" association and as a consequence new relationships emerge which can sometimes provide the breakthrough for a waiting and observant mind.

Harriet Tubman was one of several historical figures who claimed to have had anomalous dreams. Some of Tubman's "Underground Railroad" routes, which provided conduits to freedom for other escaped slaves, were said to have come to her in dreams. Another dream concerned a three-headed serpent. One head resembled John Brown, the abolitionist leader, and the others looked like those of young men; a crowd rushed in and severed the serpent's heads. Shortly afterwards, John Brown and his two sons were killed at Harper's Ferry — a raid which Tubman had been invited to join, but declined partially because of her dream.

A whole industry owes its livelihood to a more mundane, but nevertheless strikingly creative, dream that occurred to Elias Howe one night. His dreaming mind picked up his frustration at being unable to perfect the sewing machine. He dreamed that he had been captured by savages and dragged before a large assemblage. The king issued a royal ultimatum. If Howe did not produce a machine within twenty-four hours that could sew, he would die by the spear. As in life, Howe was unable to perform the frustrating task, and he saw the savages approaching to carry out the sentence. The spears slowly rose and then started to descend. Howe forgot his fear as he noticed that the spears all had eye-shaped holes in their tips. He awakened and realized that the eye of his sewing machine needle should be near the point, not at the top nor the middle. He rushed into his laboratory and fashioned a needle with a hole near the tip. It worked.

Other such striking examples could be culled from nearly every field of endeavor — science, medicine, art, writing, music, and even philosophy. Sometimes, as in the experience of the great philosopher and mathematician

René Descartes, the dream pulled together disconnected fragments into a unified and understandable whole. While he was in the army, Descartes spent a winter of inactive duty in a hotel room. He was discontent with army life and ideas spun through his brain in an angry, disconnected, and contradictory way. One night he had a dream in which all his previously clashing thoughts fell suddenly into harmony. That dream began the philosophical and mathematical formulations that were to change the course of Western thought.

On occasion the creative thinker accepts and exploits his dreams and the creative elements of his inner experience. As Friedrich Kekulé said to a group of scientists in relating his famous "snake-dream" (actually a hypnagogic image) that gave him the idea of the benzene ring: "Let us learn to dream, gentlemen, and then we may perhaps find the truth."

We have spoken quite a bit about dreaming without saying very much about dreams, their meaning, and their importance. Dreams are the remembered fragmentary residues of what goes through our minds during the regularly recurrent periods of REM activity that characterizes the normal sleep cycle. The amount and clarity of recall varies greatly from one person to another and even in the same person from time to time. In cultures where dreams have more importance than they do in the Western world, there is a greater ability to remember them. Those which occur just before awakening are more likely to be remembered. Most often, however, one is left with the frustrating and tantalizing feeling of reaching out for a dream that has already disappeared.

Despite the elusiveness of dreams there are a few simple strategies that can help to improve one's recall. These include keeping a notebook and pencil handy at the bedside so that at the time of awakening, either during the night or in the morning, a note can be made concerning any dream fragments still in the mind. Any images, feelings, or words should be set down immediately. Capturing a fragment in this way will often bring additional ones into focus. It is particularly important when the awakening occurs during the night that a written record be made of the dream fragment. The sleeping self is notoriously resistive to being disturbed, and it will often try to bypass the effort which is necessary to rouse oneself sufficiently to write the dream down. During these transitory awakenings one is perfectly capable of deceiving oneself with bland reassurances that so vivid a dream will certainly be remembered in the morning. If one doesn't resist this self-deceptive strategy the outcome is apt to be a blank mind as well as a blank sheet of notepaper.

Why go to the trouble of remembering dreams?

We live in an age of specialization. Most people feel very unconnected to their own dreams and accept this as the normal state of affairs. Dream interpretation is relegated to the domain of such highly trained professionals as psychoanalysts. Only they possess the specialized knowledge needed to decipher a dream's esoteric symbolism. The public is mystified by its own dreams and professionals unfortunately contribute their part to the mystification process.

Actually this is the converse of the way things really are. Dreamers themselves are the only real experts concerning the message of their dreams. With the help of a few simple technical aids they can learn how to meaningfully relate to their own dreams. An expert can share this technology, offer possible hypothetical notions suggested by the symbolic presentations in the dream, but only the dreamers themselves can assess the fit between dream and reality.

People can get more out of their dreams if they make the effort. An understanding of dreams is certainly essential to the additional task of identifying and evaluating possible paranormal content. In the interest of making dreams more meaningful, the remainder of this chapter is devoted to a brief theoretical exposition as well as a few basic technical considerations.

There are three intrinsic properties of dreams that make them objects of special interest to those engaged in psychotherapy, but which apply equally well for anyone seeking greater self-knowledge.

1. Dreams are concerned with unfinished emotional business, known psychiatrically as areas of unresolved conflict. An incidental event, hardly attended to at all during the day, may open up a particular area of conflict which later, as if on a slow fuse, becomes the subject matter of a dream. The triggering incident itself is often identifiable in the dream and is known as the day residue.

2. Dreamers are very active in relation to the conflict that intrudes itself into their awareness. One of the things they do is to take a backward glance over their own lives, scanning them for incidents historically related to the conflict that besets them. Long forgotten childhood episodes are woven into the dream if they can shed any light on the origins of their immediate focus of concern. It is as if the dreamer, finding oneself in a state of partial arousal in the course of the sleep cycle, asks the critical question "What is happening to me?" with the answer coming in the form of the insistently intrusive feelings triggered by the day residue.

The dreamer asks and answers a second question: "What are the historical origins of this disquieting threat to my equanimity?"

3. Having identified the emotionally intrinsic event, and its linkage to selective aspects of his past personal history, the individual now lets the dream explore the full implications of the threatening event and his or her capacity to deal with it. There then ensues an interplay between character defenses (hang-ups) and resources leading either to a resolution of the feelings mobilized by the conflict, or failing in that, leading to awakening.

The opening scene in the dream is the setting and expresses the mood, feeling, or idea triggered by the day residue. Then follows a middle portion which further develops the theme now projected. It is enriched by past, as well as additional present, experiences linked to it at the feeling level. Finally there is a terminal period of resolution which, when successful, results in the continuation of the normal sleep cycle and when unsuccessful, leads to awakening.

We have not yet spoken about either wish fulfillment or disguise, both of which play a prominent role in Freudian dream theory. In our view, dreaming serves a sentinel or vigilance function alerting dreamers to whatever may intrude into their conscious field. In the process of doing this the dreamer becomes engaged in an introspective emotional bookkeeping in which long-standing accounts come to light and attempts are made at settling them. The details of the account are minutely tracked down regardless of whether it is a large (important) or small (unimportant) account to start with. When the account is in too much disarray (too anxiety laden) to be settled by the dreamer, the waking brain is called in as a consultant.

Why are intrusive stimuli dealt with in so thoroughgoing a fashion? The answer is that the dreamer has a very important decision to make in the course of each dreaming period. We have to determine whether or not to remain asleep in the face of whatever is occupying our attention or whether to awaken. The dream is, in effect, a frank and honest pictorial statement of the issue as we experience it, of the connection of the issue with our past, of the resources as well as character defenses that are mobilized in response to it, and of our ability, in the face of all this, to cope with it. There is an essential honesty, truthfulness, and transparency to dream imagery that escapes us in waking life, mainly because we can't summon the same degrees of truthfulness about ourselves. While awake we are participants in a social drama and are called upon to enact many and often conflicting roles. While asleep our being is all that exists in the universe and we dare to look more deeply at our true selves.

Another way of noting this is to regard the dream as the nocturnal analogy of our conscience. While awake we are pushed and pulled in many different directions and sometimes we respond for reasons of expediency. Such actions have a gradually corrosive effect upon our sense of worth and self-respect. It is precisely such occasional pockets of personal compromise that are exposed in the course of the dreamer's self-scrutiny. The extent to which we become involved in dehumanizing activity during the day (the pursuit of power or pleasure at the expense of other people) is the extent to which we may be vulnerable to discomfiture in our dreams. We are social creatures whose lives have to be fulfilled through the fulfillment of others and not through the exploitation or use of others. Since this is an idea rather than an actuality in our complex society, we have much to exercise our conscience about once we close our eyes and begin to dream.

We have concerned ourselves thus far with content. There remains another very puzzling feature of dreams, namely the form in which we experience them. Dreams, for the most part, seem to occur as a sequence of visual images. These images may be regarded as metaphors, doing what metaphors generally do, condensing thought into appropriate imagery for the purpose of emphasis or creating a special effect. Dreamers may combine aspects of past and present in a single image. They may bypass logical connections as well as the conventions of time and space in the interest of the visual imagery that best expresses what they are feeling at the time. A good, although limited, analogy to depict the situation of dreamers is to imagine them viewing a radar screen, one where the scanning mechanism is picking up leftover emotional sore spots rather than external objects. Just as a small form on an actual radar screen can symbolize something as complex as a battleship or an aircraft, so an image on this subjective screen is derived from and in turn signifies a particular area of subjective concern. The radar analogy may also help us understand why any stimulus appearing on the screen engrosses us so completely and so unquestioningly. The stimulus in the dream, as on a real radar screen, appears on an otherwise quiescent field. Regardless of whether it is trivial or of overwhelming import, it becomes the sole focus of our attention and overwhelmingly compelling in its impact. We never lose interest in our own dream at the time it is occurring. It is one of the few occasions in our lives where we can be sure our attention will not wander.

Of all the altered states of consciousness investigated by parapsychologists as being favorable to ESP, dreaming is the only one which happens to each of us every day, in a regular physiological rhythm, occurring about every ninety minutes throughout the night's sleep. At these times the eyes move rapidly back and forth (periods of Rapid Eye Movement, or REM). Other physiological changes, i.e. changes in respiration, pulse rate, penile erection, also occur. The REM periods increase in duration through the night. While dreaming, the brain shows electrical activity that is closest to the waking pattern as compared with other stages of sleep. It is during this REM period that sleeping subjects are also most likely to have transitory awakenings.

These correlations are both intriguing and puzzling. Does the eye movement represent scanning activity? Or is some unknown biological mechanism at work? Do the penile erections represent a state of sexual arousal? Or is this part of a non-specific effect of generalized tissue irritability? Does the electrical activity of the brain represent arousal? Or is this a special state unrelated to the arousal mechanism?

The interpretation of these data are widely disputed, especially when considered in the context of psychoanalytic thinking. A recent contribution to the psychology of dreaming is, coincidentally, authored by our "Prince of Percipients," Dr. Van de Castle. He has this to say about the controversy:

> The new EEG findings raise questions regarding the relationship between dreaming and the discharge of instinctual urges, as well as other hypotheses

about dreaming and the discharge of instinctual urges advanced by Freud. Lack of agreement exists about the degree of fit, if any, between recent findings and Freud's viewpoints, but there is some consensus that a revision would definitely be needed in the notion that the dream acts as the guardian of sleep. Since it has been consistently found that subjects are much more likely to awaken during REM periods, it would not appear that dreaming serves to maintain sleep. Some researchers have suggested that the notion should be reversed as it seemed to make more sense to say sleep acts as the guardian of dreaming. . . .

Ullman, in the mid-1950s, postulated that dreaming states represented a heightened state of vigilance and extended the idea of vigilance to include parapsychological data. The dreamer generally dreams about a recent event that has some disturbing quality. Ullman suggested that, in addition to scanning their own past for experiences related to the theme of the dream, dreamers can on occasion span both time and space to pick up information that is of importance to them.

The experimental discovery of the REM effect was supportive of the vigilance theory of dreaming to the extent that it suggested that there was a built-in, physiologically controlled mechanism producing recurrent states of brain arousal and activity. Awakening could occur if the intensity and quality of feelings generated during these periods were great enough. During these repetitive bouts of brain activity, dreamers, focusing on the most recent disturbing experience, engage in two kinds of operations to determine whether or not the disturbance is one that would warrant awakening. They review their own past history for the historical roots of their response to the present disturbance, and they mobilize their characteristic strategies of defense against anxiety and change. Only if these mechanisms cannot contain and resolve the anxiety does awakening take place. The dreamer, in effect, has made an emotionally determined decision as to whether or not it is safe to continue sleeping. This is the central idea of the vigilance theory of dreaming.

The "psi vigilance" theory (Rex Stanford's term) postulates that during the REM dreaming state the human mind is most susceptible to psi impressions which, in turn, are incorporated into the dream. At these times, dreamers are scanning not only their internal environment but also their "psi field," to see if any hostile or threatening influences external to themselves must be dealt with. During sleep, humans are in their most helpless state and vulnerable to attack. Animals who live in constant threat of their lives may perhaps deal with this by a REM mechanism whereby they periodically come close to waking. Apparently humans have a more sophisticated system of vigilance, one that responds to symbolic threats rather than physical threats to their social existence. The dreaming state, perhaps because of its possible linkage to a primitive danger sensing mechanism, provides the most favorable altered state of consciousness for ESP.

Ullman also suggests that this dreamining state of "psi vigilance" can, in some individuals, result in creative dream solutions to problems at hand and, in the light of precognition dream studies, to problems on their way. Examples of dream creativity run the gamut from the solution of everyday problems to creative breakthroughs, although the latter are as rare as truly creative ideas themselves.

Ullman's emphasis on the factor of vigilance in dreaming and its relationship to psi effects has by no means been generally accepted by the psychological and psychiatric community. Neither has it won complete approval of the parapsychological community—which seldom reaches agreement on anything—all of which makes for stimulating controversies.

Our main surmise is that the human psyche possesses a latent ESP capacity that is most likely to be deployed during sleep, in the dreaming phase. Psi is no longer the exclusive gift of rare beings known as "psychic sensitives," but is a normal part of human existence, capable of being experienced by nearly everyone under the right conditions. It took many hundreds of thousands of years before humans learned to write language. How much longer will it take before they learn to use psi? We are optimistically inclined to say that the time lag between "discovery" and "application" will be considerably shortened in the coming years and that a deeper understanding of psi will profoundly influence our way of looking at our place in the universe. We may discover ourselves to be less alienated from each other, more capable of psychic unity and more capable of closeness in ways never before suspected.

Whether this will come about depends largely on how realistically we try to understand ourselves and the world we have created—not merely our "parapsychological" self but our whole self, our whole psyche as well as our ability to realize a planetary concern that crosses national boundaries. The future direction of humanity depends on the future direction not only of its sciences and technologies, but also of its philosophies. If technology and its concomitant philosophy of mastery over nature continue to crowd out a philosophical humanism based on a congruence between people and nature our problems will grow worse: pollution, decay, wars, alienation. If such a humanistic philosophy guides our technology, we have a chance. Humanity's psychic potential suggests that in the basic fabric of life everything and everyone is more closely linked than our discrete physical boundaries would seem to suggest. Perhaps all forms of life are vitally interrelated in ways we do not yet clearly understand.

If we can develop more insight into this linkage through parapsychological research, we will better understand the nature and extent of our interdependence and may ultimately succeed in tempering the cruelty and exploitation that exist in human affairs. To integrate parapsychology into other sciences will also require an integration of the other sciences into parapsychology. We need to develop good experimental teams on an interdisciplinary basis that will include the physical, psychologial, and biological sciences.

The investigators currently associated with this venture are helping to inch our way forward in the hope that at some point in the very near future the last remaining resistances will melt away or perhaps be blasted out of existence by further experimental data. With proper personnel and material support, this could open the way to exciting and limitless possibilities in the application of an interdisciplinary approach to the linking of parapsychological research to the basic, applied, and social sciences.

APPENDICES

APPENDIX A

Erwin's Nocturnal Tour
of the French Quarter

What follows is the full, unedited transcript of Dr. William Erwin's dreams
on November 22, 1964. The target was Chagall's *Paris Through a Window* (Plate
7). The painting shows a man observing a panorama of Paris from his window.

SUBJECT: William Erwin
DATE: November 22, 1964
AGENT: Sol Feldstein
EXPERIMENTER: Stanley Krippner
(Night number 5 in a series of 7)

FIRST DREAM REPORT

EXPERIMENTER: Bill, wake up please.
SUBJECT: *silence.*
EXPERIMENTER: Bill, are you awake?
SUBJECT: Yes.
EXPERIMENTER: Please tell me your dreams or what you have been thinking.
SUBJECT: It was ... *pause* ... It seems as though it was an experiment again ...
pause ... *sighing* ... Gosh ... *pause* ... I don't know what was happening
... *laugh* ... I did for a second. Now, let me see ... *long pause* ... It seems
like Sol was in it this time.
EXPERIMENTER: Will you repeat that please?
SUBJECT: It seems like Sol was in it this time.
EXPERIMENTER: O.K.
SUBJECT: All I'm talking about right now is just the impression I had of the dream,
because the memory ... *long pause* ... Just an impression there. No images
or anything seem to come back at the moment.
EXPERIMENTER: Well, was there anything else at all?
SUBJECT: Impression-wise ... *long pause* ... I think I'd better describe this. I have
the feeling that there was a dream — something going on, and as I was

awakened I had a slight feeling of what it was. I would say that on the one hand it was almost as though I had just gone to sleep. I mean by this that I wasn't really aware at the time that I had been asleep. Time-wise, I'm speaking of . . . that I just dozed off a short time ago. I really don't know how long ago it has been since I went to sleep, but as I was trying to recapture some sort of feeling about the dream, pictures of ships kept coming to mind. These were not ships in the sense of well-defined . . . it was almost as though there were very vivid strokes with — oh — almost a paint brush, or India ink, or something of this nature — and stroked the outline of a type of boat that existed, oh . . . the word Babylonia comes back . . . *laugh* . . . I don't know why — but that period. Phoenicians, perhaps — boats that they used. Or . . . *pause* . . . I don't quite want to say Egyptian, but it's more that type of boat, and the way that I saw it was not in its complete or well constructed or laid-out sense, rather a raw, bold type of outline. Now this was the image as I was trying to recall the dream. This was what came to mind.

EXPERIMENTER: Does this remind you of anything?

SUBJECT: *pause* . . . Well, it reminds me of a whole series . . . *long pause* . . . My own association, I was thinking of a class I took around different myths, mythologies — Egyptian, Babylonian . . . *pause* . . . Well, it was a study of these original myths — earlier writing . . . I'm thinking of the *Iliad*, Egyptian Gods . . . or whether it was the class itself . . . the instructor. . .

EXPERIMENTER: O.K. Thank you. You may go back to sleep now.

SUBJECT: Do you have a second blanket?

EXPERIMENTER: Pardon me, I didn't hear you.

SUBJECT: Do you have another blanket — an additional blanket?

EXPERIMENTER: Oh yes. Just a minute.

SECOND DREAM REPORT

EXPERIMENTER: Bill, wake up, please.

SUBJECT: *silence.*

EXPERIMENTER: Are you awake?

SUBJECT: *sighing* . . . Yes.

EXPERIMENTER: Can you tell me your dreams or what you've been thinking?

SUBJECT: Well, I was dreaming of bees — I guess it was bees . . . Sort of bees flying around flowers.

EXPERIMENTER: Could you repeat that please?

SUBJECT: Flying around flowers. Buzzing around a flower . . . *long pause* . . .

EXPERIMENTER: Was there anything more?

SUBJECT: *inaudible.*

EXPERIMENTER: I didn't catch that last comment. Could you repeat it?

SUBJECT: I was just saying, I was trying to figure out where it came from or led to . . . *sighing* . . . *long pause* . . . *mumbling* . . . I don't seem to have too much more to say about it.

EXPERIMENTER: Does this remind you of anything?

SUBJECT: *silence* . . . No. Not this time.

EXPERIMENTER: O.K. Thank you. You may go back to sleep now.

THIRD DREAM REPORT

EXPERIMENTER: Bill, are you awake?

SUBJECT: *yawning* . . . Yes.

EXPERIMENTER: Tell me what you have been thinking or dreaming.

SUBJECT: *sighing* . . . The last thing I was dreaming was about a little boy.

EXPERIMENTER: A little louder, please.

SUBJECT: The last thing I was dreaming was about a little boy, in a jewelry store, and I was walking through it, and he was saying to the other one, "Leave him alone, they just like to look," and one little boy said he wanted to . . . he wondered if the other one would hold some of the jewelry he wanted to look at. To clarify this: one boy was minding shop. The one that was visiting asked the one that was minding shop to hold a piece of jewelry. It was a shop that had a lot of very small — from very small to medium — glass art objects as well as necklaces, and things of this nature. I had, earlier . . . let me see, the dream started out in a walk. I was walking — for some reason I say the French Quarter, I don't know why I say that — through department stores . . . *pause* . . . and I was walking through different departments in a depart-ment store . . . *pause* . . . wait a minute . . . *long pause* . . . hmph . . . I can't recall . . . I had some sort of feeling that there was more before that but I can't . . . anyway . . . walking through department stores, talking with a group of Shriners. . .

EXPERIMENTER: Would you repeat that please?

SUBJECT: A group of Shriners that were having a convention . . . *pause* . . . They had on a hat that looked more like a French policeman's hat — you know the French — I would say that would be the nearest way to describing it.

EXPERIMENTER: Would you describe it please?

SUBJECT: It was sort of like a French policeman's hat. Not quite, but it seemed to me . . . I mean this was the general idea. It seemed to me it fitted more . . . let me see, the French . . . no, no, no . . . *pause* . . . I take that back. I don't know why I said French. It would be more like the Vatican guard, so I guess, in a way if I think back, it would be earlier French . . . yes . . . yes . . . if I think back perhaps . . . er . . . before the French Republic . . . this type of hat. It wasn't quite three-cornered, but it was the boat-shaped hat. I forget what they're called, if I ever knew. They had hats of that nature and I was commenting on it. A few had fezzes, and then I was commenting on some that had regular oversea caps on, and which I said they looked like a troop of boy scouts . . . *laughing* . . . This group happened to be from Ohio . . . *laughing*.

EXPERIMENTER: From where?

SUBJECT: Ohio . . . I think that's interesting . . . *pause* . . . I was talking to two of them. In thinking back, let me see . . . a little earlier I was walking through a bar . . . I walked near to a women's bar; a men's bar — this is all through these stores and things ... *pause* ... but as I say, the earlier part of the dream has been lost. All I can remember was a feeling of oldness. I wouldn't say antiquity. I would say old ... like an ... I said French Quarter earlier, but I was using that and get a feel ... *pause* ... type of thing makes me think of an early village of some sort. Even the idea of a mission-type church comes to mind ... *musing* ... A mission ... maybe I should say in this instance I'm thinking primarily of Spanish architecture ... *pause* ... but generally it would be some sort of a blend of this romantic type of architecture — buildings, village, quaint ... *pause* ...

EXPERIMENTER: Is there anything else?

SUBJECT: I'm thinking. At the moment ... *sighing* ... *pause* ... I can't seem to have any further thoughts.

EXPERIMENTER: All right. Thank you. You can go back to sleep now.

FOURTH DREAM REPORT

EXPERIMENTER: Yes?

SUBJECT: Much of the dream I don't remember.

EXPERIMENTER: Could you speak a little louder please?

SUBJECT: Much of this dream I don't remember. Just sort of feelings and highlights. Sort of thoughts that are mingled. One thought that seems to come back — keeps coming back — is a bagel ... *laughing* ... I don't really know what it really means ... Somebody asked for one; somebody wanted one; somebody was eating one — I don't know; but the imagery of costumes comes back. In this instance, I have thoughts of biblical type costumes — flowing ... *pause* ... I have a feeling ... I can't go any further than this, but I have a feeling that you were in this dream some way ... *pause* ...

EXPERIMENTER: You have a feeling that what?

SUBJECT: That you were in the dream. I can't recall how, in this bagel thing. The feeling is that you were there, a feeling is that you were there — a feeling also that in the dream there were other elements of food involved. As I said, these were just the highlights I could remember. I was quite aware that as I was awakening I knew what it meant ... actually what I wanted to say was that I knew what was going on.

EXPERIMENTER: Is there anything more?

SUBJECT: That's all I can glean at the moment.

EXPERIMENTER: Does this remind you of anything?

SUBJECT: *pause* ... Well, in a strange way it reminds me of what I was saying earlier — in the earlier dream, but different. It's a village again. Yes, it does. It reminds me of a picture that we have. I don't remember the artist. It's a reproduction. No, it isn't a reproduction ... it's a photograph or a printed reproduction-type of it, and as you look at it, it would make you think of a town in Morocco. Well, the first one made me think of a town in the northern coast of Africa with the Arabic influence or the Moslem influence, but I would say more like some of the villages of Spain or Italy that would be on a hill ... so that would be a gradual ... almost like one on top of the other—one behind the other as it went up the hill. I'm sure that when he did this particular piece, this particular work, it was done with that view in mind.

EXPERIMENTER: Will you repeat that last statement please?

SUBJECT: When he did this piece of art work, the picture that I have in mind, I'm sure that he had one of these villages in mind. This particular one—it was not white—whitewashed, like in Greece or . . . *yawning* . . . or some of the areas I have noticed in pictures, but in this instance, it had gray and reddish tones in the houses. That's all.

EXPERIMENTER: Thank you. You can go back to sleep again.

FIFTH DREAM REPORT

EXPERIMENTER: Are you awake?

SUBJECT: Yes. Another brief dream image. Some sort of conversation. But the image—the memory I remember is a man, once again walking through one of these villages—these towns . . . it would definitely be in the early nineteenth century . . . *pause* . . . attire . . . French attire . . . and he would be walking through one of these towns as though he would be in a higher . . . as though he were walking up the side of a hill above other layers of the town . . . *long pause* . . . That's all I remember now. Some of the other slipped away. That's all.

EXPERIMENTER: Is there anything else at all?

SUBJECT: No, that's all I can pull out. There's something else, but I don't . . . *pause* . . .

EXPERIMENTER: Does this remind you of anything?

SUBJECT: No. No more than the others did.

EXPERIMENTER: Well, that's very good. You can go back to sleep for awhile.

POST-SLEEP INTERVIEW

FIRST DREAM REVIEW

EXPERIMENTER: How well do you think you slept?

SUBJECT: How what?

EXPERIMENTER: How well did you sleep?

SUBJECT: Oh, I slept pretty good.

EXPERIMENTER: How many dreams do you think you had?

SUBJECT: Four or five—something like that.

EXPERIMENTER: Which ones do you remember?

SUBJECT: *pause* . . . The things that stand out are the ones where I described the village . . . *pause* . . . Let me see . . . *pause* . . . I remember the one describing the journey through the stores, the Shriners, and all that. A couple, in describing villages . . . *pause* . . . the first dream . . . hmph . . . I can't remember the first, but . . . *long pause* . . . That's about all I can remember . . . *laughing* . . .

EXPERIMENTER: Was there anything different in these dreams or about these dreams as compared with your usual dreams?

SUBJECT: *long pause* . . . One thing — usually I can remember them better . . . *yawning* . . .

EXPERIMENTER: O.K. Here are the dreams as they came through: Feel free to tell me any associations, additions, or changes that you may have to them. Your first dream went something like this: There was an experiment and Sol was in it. I have a feeling that I just dozed off a short time ago. Pictures of ships kept coming to mind, almost as if one took very vivid strokes with a paint brush or India ink and painted the outline of the type that existed in Babylonia, or the Phoenicians. I don't want to say Egypt, but of that time. It reminds me of a class I took; different myths — Egyptian, Samarian, Babylonian, in which the original myths were studied — Egyptian gods, the class itself, and the instructor. O.K.?

SUBJECT: Um . . . I still have the feeling . . . As I think of it now, even though I described these boats as a period piece, it makes me think of a . . . *pause* . . . boat . . . I won't say a gondola, but . . . *pause* . . . there is a . . . *pause* . . . picture. I've never seen a picture. This is a . . . what I'm thinking of is a reproduction of a piece of wallpaper of a — I don't know what you call it — an over-sized gondola or some sort of a boat . . . it's a festive thing . . . that reminds me of the one in the dream . . . the images that I saw. But it would be the one that had the elegantly dressed clowns, the Mardi Gras-ish type that makes you think, in this instance of the Italian, perhaps, courts of . . . Shakespeare's Romeo and Juliet, something of that sort — nevertheless, the boat was what stands out. That's all.

SECOND DREAM REVIEW

EXPERIMENTER: All right. Here's the next one: I was thinking about a bee flying around a flower, and there's no more to say. O.K.?

SUBJECT: *laughing* . . . There is no more to say . . . *pause* . . . *yawning* . . . Let's see . . . a bee around a flower . . . *musing* . . . I have no idea . . .

THIRD DREAM REVIEW

EXPERIMENTER: All right. Here's the next one: A little boy is in a jewelry store. He is saying, "Leave him alone," about another boy. "They like to look." One boy was minding shop. The shop had a lot of medium-sized glass objects in it. O.K.?

SUBJECT: Is that all you have about the shop part of that dream?

EXPERIMENTER: There are some more things to come, but I thought I'd pause right there.

SUBJECT: About the shop, I mean.

EXPERIMENTER: Yes.

SUBJECT: As I think back, the shop — one of the things — the objects in it had small trinkets, bracelets, jewelry, and one of the boys wanted to touch something; wanted to pick up and look, but instead of doing it himself, he asked the boy that had the shop—the boy who was minding shop . . . he asked him to do it for him, and he was commenting to this visitor (the boy was commenting to the other little boy) that most people in the shop like to look around and didn't want to be disturbed . . . *pause* . . .

EXPERIMENTER: No, I don't have that aspect of the dream. Thank you very much. Then you made the following statement: Earlier I dreamed I was walking in the French Quarter through a department store. I was walking through different departments in the store. A group of Shriners were having a convention. They had on a hat that looked like a French policeman's hat, rather, like the Vatican guard—earlier French style. It was a boat-shaped hat. A few had fezzes on. They looked like a group of boy scouts. This group happened to be from Ohio. I was talking with two of them. I was walking through a bar; a women's bar, then a men's bar. O.K.?

SUBJECT: *pause . . . slowly . . . musing . . .* I think that's it pretty much.

EXPERIMENTER: And then you said: All I can remember about the earlier part of the dream is a feeling of antiquity; of oldness, which makes me think of an early village with a mission-type church or Spanish architecture. Romantic-type architecture and buildings. O.K.?

SUBJECT: I guess that was the first one in which I was having these villages, but I have nothing to add to that portion.

FOURTH DREAM REVIEW

EXPERIMENTER: All right. Here's your next dream: One thing that keeps coming to mind is a bagel. Someone is asking for one or eating one. I have the feeling that you were in the dream somehow. There are other elements of food involved. In a strange way, it reminds me of a village—of a photograph we have of a painting. As you look at it, it makes you think of a town in Spain or Italy that would be on a hill. The other dream made me think of a town in North Africa with the Moslem influence. When the painter did this piece of art work, I'm sure he had one of those villages in mind. It had gray and reddish tones. O.K.?

SUBJECT: *pause . . .* I have nothing more to add.

FIFTH DREAM REVIEW

EXPERIMENTER: All right. Here's the next dream: I remember a man walking through one of those villages or towns in early nineteenth-century attire— French attire—walking up a hill above other layers of towns. O.K.?

SUBJECT: Oh, yes . . . um . . . um . . . *pause* . . . All these would be closely resembling one another . . . *pause* . . .

EXPERIMENTER: Now is there anything else that you can add about your dreams for the night?

SUBJECT: *pause* . . . No.

GUESS FOR THE NIGHT

EXPERIMENTER: Then, make a guess at what you think the target for the night was.

SUBJECT: Well ... *yawning* ... On the aspect of repeating things so much, it would have to do with the village and the period, and this costume area. Actually, perhaps something of this nature ... All of these, if I think back, all of them were dealing with the same period. Even this boat, as I mentioned, placed it back and it talked about the earlier period, the boats themselves, as I referred to them in additional notes and feelings, seemed to fit in with the period in which I was talking about the village and the costume; so far as the feel of what the target might be, it might be in this area.

EXPERIMENTER: Can you be more specific?

SUBJECT: Well the area must be — I mean, just basing it on the costumes and all, the nineteenth century, early nineteenth century ... and in the ... either the Italian or French or Spanish or even coastal area — not necessarily the coastal area, but the villages of this ... a town of this area. Yes, well, it would be this quality, because I ... as I think of the dream ... although the dreams themselves — they didn't have the feeling that it was by the sea ... there was water, or a river ... maybe that's what I'm thinking of, or maybe the canals of Venice. I don't know. I'm not sure. But still this doesn't work out with the impressions of the dreams, so I've got a little problem trying to make all these things fit in ... except that the village seemed to be in hilly country. But it would be a period of the nineteenth century, I think. Reflecting much older architecture, of course ... the structures being of an older period, and not of the castle-type, necessarily. No, it wouldn't be of the castle-type. It would be of the ... *pause* ... of this village type. It might be ... *pause* ... a church involved; but it would be a village or town with these rock, stone, or adobe type houses very close together covering the hills ... *pause* ...

EXPERIMENTER: O.K. Thank you.

APPENDIX B

Psychology and Anomalous Observations:

The Question of ESP in Dreams*

by Irvin L. Child

In recent years, evidence has been accumulating for the occurrence of such anomalies as telepathy and psychokinesis, but the evidence is not totally convincing. The evidence has come largely from experiments by psychologists who have devoted their careers mainly to studying these anomalies, but members of other disciplines, including engineering and physics, have also taken part. Some psychologists not primarily concerned with parapsychology have taken time out from other professional concerns to explore such anomalies for themselves. Of these, some have joined in the experimentation (e.g., Crandall & Hite, 1983; Lowry, 1981; Radin, 1982). Some have critically reviewed portions of the evidence (e.g., Akers, 1984; Hyman, 1985). Some, doubting that the phenomena could be real, have explored nonrational processes that might encourage belief in their reality (e.g., Ayeroff & Abelson, 1976). Still others, considering the evidence substantial enough to justify a constructive theoretical effort, have struggled to relate the apparent anomalies to better established knowledge in a way that will render them less anomalous (e.g., Irwin, 1979) or not anomalous at all (e.g., Blackmore, 1984). These psychologists differ widely in their surmise about whether the apparent anomalies in question will eventually be judged real or illusory; but they appear to agree that the evidence to date warrants serious consideration.

Serious consideration of apparent anomalies seems an essential part of the procedures of science, regardless of whether it leads to an understanding of new discoveries or to an understanding of how persuasive illusions arise. Apparent anomalies — just like the more numerous observations that are not anomalous — can receive appropriate attention only as they become accurately known to the

*Reprinted by permission from American Psychologist, Vol. 40, No. 11, November 1985.

scientists to whose work they are relevant. Much parapsychological research is barred from being seriously considered because it is either neglected or misrepresented in writings by some psychologists — among them, some who have placed themselves in a prime position to mediate interaction between parapsychological research and the general body of psychological knowledge. In this article, I illustrate this important general point with a particular case, that of experimental research on possible ESP in dreams. It is a case of especially great interest but is not unrepresentative of how psychological publications have treated similar anomalies.

The Maimonides Research

The experimental evidence suggesting that dreams may actually be influenced by ESP comes almost entirely from a research program carried out at the Maimonides Medical Center in Brooklyn, New York. Among scientists active in parapsychology, this program is widely known and greatly respected. It has had a major indirect influence on the recent course of parapsychological research, although the great expense of dream-laboratory work has prevented it from being a direct model.

None of the Maimonides research was published in the journals that are the conventional media for psychology. (The only possible exception is that a summary of one study [Honorton, Krippner, & Ullman, 1972] appeared in convention proceedings of the American Psychological Association.) Much of it was published in the specialized journals of parapsychology. The rest was published in psychiatric or other medical journals, where it would not be noticed by many psychologists. Most of it was summarized in popularized form in a book (Ullman, Krippner, with Vaughan, 1973) in which two of the researchers were joined by a popular writer whose own writings are clearly not in the specific tradition, and the book departs from the pattern of scientific reporting that characterizes the original research reports.

How, then, would this research come to the attention of psychologists, so that its findings or its errors might in time be evaluated for their significance to the body of systematic observations upon which psychology has been and will be built? The experiments at Maimonides were published between about 1966 and 1972. In the years since — now over a decade — five books have been published by academic psychologists that purport to offer a scholarly review and evaluation of parapsychological research. They vary in the extent to which they seem addressed to psychologists themselves or to their students, but they seem to be the principal route by which either present or future psychologists, unless they have an already established interest strong enough to lead them to search out the original publications, might become acquainted with the experiments on ESP in dreams. I propose to review how these five books have presented knowledge about the experiments. First, however, I must offer a summary of the experiments; without that, my review would make sense only to readers already well acquainted with them.

The experiments at Maimonides grew out of Montague Ullman's observations, in his psychiatric practice, of apparent telepathy underlying the content of some dreams reported by his patients — observations parallel to those reported by many other psychiatrists. He sought to determine whether this apparent phenomenon would appear in a sleep laboratory under controlled conditions that would seem to exclude interpretations other than that of ESP. He was joined in this research by psychologist Stanley Krippner, now at the Saybrook Institute in San Francisco, and a little later by Charles Honorton, now head of the Psychophysical Research Laboratories in Princeton, New Jersey. Encouraged by early findings but seeking to improve experimental controls and identify optimal conditions, these researchers, assisted by numerous helpers and consultants, tried out various modifications of procedure. No one simple description of procedure, therefore, can be accurate for all of the experiments. But the brief description that follows is not, I believe, misleading as an account of what was generally done.

The Experimental Procedure

A subject would come to the laboratory to spend the night there as would-be percipient in a study of possible telepathic influence on dreams. He or she met and talked with the person who was going to serve as agent (that is, the person who would try to send a telepathic message), as well as with the two experimenters taking part that night, and procedures were explained in detail unless the percipient was a repeater for whom that step was not necessary. When ready to go to bed, the percipient was wired up in the usual way for monitoring of brain waves and eye movements, and he or she had no further contact with the agent or agent's experimenter until after the session was completed. The experimenter in the next room monitored the percipient's sleep and at the beginning of each period of rapid eye movements (REM), when it was reasonably certain the sleeper would be dreaming, notified the agent by pressing a buzzer.

The agent was in a remote room in the building, provided with a target picture (and sometimes accessory material echoing the theme of the picture) randomly chosen from a pool of potential targets as the message to be concentrated on. The procedure for random choice of a target from the pool was designed to prevent anyone else from knowing the identity of the target. The agent did not open the packet containing the target until isolated for the night (except for the one-way buzzer communication). Whenever signaled that the percipient had entered a REM period, the agent was to concentrate on the target, with the aim of communicating it telepathically to the percipient and thus influencing the dream the percipient was having. The percipient was oriented toward trying to receive this message. But of course if clairvoyance and telepathy are both possible, the percipient might have used the former — that is, might have been picking up information directly from the target picture, without the mediation of the agent's thoughts or efforts. For this reason, the term *general extrasensory perception (GESP)* would be used today, though the researchers more often used the term *telepathy*.

Toward the approximate end of each REM period, the percipient was awakened (by intercom) by the monitoring experimenter and described any dream just experienced (with prodding and questioning, if necessary, though the percipient of course knew in advance what to do on each awakening). At the end of the night's sleep, the percipient was interviewed and was asked for impressions about what the target might have been. (The interview was of course double-blind; neither percipient nor interviewer knew the identity of the target.) The dream descriptions and morning impressions and associations were recorded and later transcribed.

The original research reports and the popular book both present a number of very striking similarities between passages in the dream transcripts and the picture that happened to be the night's target. These similarities merit attention, yet they should in themselves yield no sense of conviction. Perhaps any transcript of a night's dreaming contains passages of striking similarity to any picture to which they might be compared. The Maimonides research, however, consisted of carefully planned experiments designed to permit evaluation of this hypothesis of random similarity, and I must now turn to that aspect.

Results

To evaluate the chance hypothesis, the researchers obtained judgments of similarity between the dream content and the actual target for the night, and at the same time obtained judgments of similarity between the dream content and each of the other potential targets in the pool from which the target had been selected at random. The person judging, or course, had no information about which picture had been randomly selected as target; the entire pool (in duplicate) was presented together, with no clue as to which picture had been the target and which ones had not. That is, in the experimental condition a picture was randomly selected from a pool and concentrated on by the agent, and in the control condition a picture was left behind in the pool. Any consistent difference between target and nontarget in similarity to dream content, exceeding what could reasonably be ascribed to chance, was considered an apparent anomaly.

The data available for the largest number of sessions came from judgments made by judges who had no contact with the experiment except to receive (by mail, generally) the material necessary for judging (transcripts of dreams and interview and a copy of the target pool). For many sessions, judgments were also available from the dreamer; he or she, or course, made judgments only after completing participation in the experiment as dreamer (except in some series where a separate target pool was used for each night and the dreamer's judgments could be made at the end of the session). For many sessions, judgments were made for the dream transcripts alone and for the total transcript including the morning interview; for consistency I have used the latter, because it involved judges who had more nearly the same information as the subjects.

The only form in which the data are available for all series of sessions is a count of hits and misses. If the actual target was ranked in the upper half of the target pool, for similarity to the dreams and interview, the outcome was considered a hit. If the actual target was ranked in the lower half of the pool, the outcome was considered a miss. The hit-or-miss score is presented separately in Table 1 for judges and for subjects in the first two data columns. Where information is not supplied for one or the other, the reason is generally that it was impossible for the researchers to obtain it, and for a similar reason the number of cases sometimes varies.*

Each data row in Table A refers to one segment of the research, and segments for the most part are labeled as they were in the table of Ullman et al. (1973, pp. 275–277). Segments that followed the general procedure I described— all-night sessions, with an agent concentrating on the target during each of the percipient's REM periods—are gathered together in the first eight lines, A through H (in five of these segments, all but A, C, and H, a single percipient continued throughout a series, and in four of these the percipient was a psychologist). Other types of segments are presented in the rest of the table. Lines I, J, and K summarize precognitive sessions; here the target was not selected until after the dreaming and interview had been completed. The target consisted of a set of stimuli to be presented directly to the percipient after it had been selected in the morning. Lines L and M represent GESP sessions in which the percipient's dreams were monitored and recorded throughout the night, but the agent was attempting to transmit only before the percipient went to sleep or just after, or sporadically. Line N refers to a few clairvoyance sessions; these were like the standard GESP sessions except that there was no agent (no one knew the identity of the target). Finally, Line O reports on some GESP sessions in which each dream was considered separately; these formed a single experiment with four percipients, comparing nights involving a different target for each REM period with nights involving repeated use of a single target.

Regardless of the type of session (considering the five types I have described), each session fell into one of two categories: (a) pilot sessions, in which either a new dreamer or a new procedure was being tried out; these appear in lines H, K, and N, or (b) sessions in an experimental series, planned in advance as one or more sessions for each of two or more subjects, or as a number of sessions with the same dreamer throughout. Most of the researchers' publications were devoted to the results obtained in the experimental series, but the results of the pilot sessions have also been briefly reported.

A glance at the score columns for judges and for subjects is sufficient to indicate a strong tendency for an excess of hits over misses. If we average the outcome for judges and for subjects, we find that hits exceed misses on every one of the 15 independent lines on which outcome for hits and misses differs. (On Line E hits and misses occur with equal frequency.) By a simple sign-test, this outcome would be significant beyond the 0.0001 level. I would not stress the exact value here, for several reasons. There was no advance plan to merge the outcomes for

---

*Of course, usable judgments could not be obtained from the subject in precognitive sessions, because at the time of judging he or she would already know what the target had been. For Line F, the single subject was unable to give the extra time required for judging, and for Line O one of the four subjects failed to make judgments. In a few of the pilot sessions (Lines H, K, and N) only the subject's judgment was sought, and in some sessions only that of one or more judges; in a few the mean judges' rating was neither a hit nor a miss but exactly at the middle.

Table 1
Summary of Maimonides Results on Tendency for Dreams to Be Judged More Like Target Than Like Nontargets in Target Pool

Series	Judges' score		Subjects' score		z or t resulting from judgments		Sources
	Hit	Miss	Hit	Miss	Judges	Subjects	
GESP: Dreams monitored and recorded throughout night; agent "transmitting" during each REM period							
A. 1st screening	7	5	10	2	$z = 0.71^b$	$z = 1.33^b$	Ullman, Krippner, & Feldstein (1966)
B. 1st Erwin	5	2	6	1	$z = 2.53^b$	$z = 1.90^b$	Ullman et al. (1966)
C. 2nd screening	4	8	9	3	$z = -.25^b$	$z = 1.17^b$	Ullman (1969)
D. Posin	6	2	6	2	$z = 1.05^c$	$z = 1.05^c$	Ullman (1969)
E. Grayeb	3	5	5	3	$z = -.63^c$	$z = 0.63^c$	Ullman, Krippner, & Vaughan (1973)
F. 2nd Erwin	8	0			$t = 4.93^a$		Ullman & Krippner (1969)
G. Van de Castle	6	2	8	0	$t = 2.81^a$	$t = 2.74^a$	Krippner & Ullman (1970)
H. Pilot sessions	53	14	42	22	$z = 4.20^b$	$z = 2.21^b$	Ullman et al. (1973)
Precognition: Dreams monitored and recorded throughout night; target experience next day							
I. 1st Bessent	7	1			$t = 2.81^a$		Krippner, Ullman, & Honorton (1971)
J. 2nd Bessent	7	1			$t = 2.27^a$		Krippner, Honorton, & Ullman (1972)
K. Pilot sessions	2	0			$z = 0.67^c$		Ullman et al. (1973)

GESP: Dreams monitored and recorded throughout night; agent active only at beginning or sporadically

L. Sensory bombardment	8	0	4	4	$z = 3.11$[b] $z = 0.00$[c]	Krippner, Honorton, Ullman, Masters, & Houston (1971)
M. Grateful Dead	7	5	8	4	$z = 0.61$[c] $z = 0.81$[c]	Krippner, Honorton, & Ullman (1973)

Clairvoyance: Dreams monitored and recorded throughout night; concealed target known to no one

N. Pilot sessions	5	3	4	5	$z = 0.98$[b] $z = 0.00$[b]	Ullman et al. (1973)

GESP: Single dreams

O. Vaughan, Harris, Parise	105	98	74	79	$z = 0.63$[c] $z = -.32$[c]	Honorton, Krippner, & Ullman (1972)

Note. GESP = general extrasensory perception. Italics identify results obtained with procedures that preserve independence of judgments in a series. For some series, the published source does not use the uniform measures entered in this table, and mimeographed laboratory reports were also consulted. Superscripts indicate which measure was available, in order of priority.
[a] Ratings. [b] Rankings. [c] Score (count of hits and misses).

judges and subjects. Moreover, the various series could be split up in other ways. Although I think my organization of the table is very reasonable (and I did not notice this outcome until after the table was constructed), it is not the organization selected by Ullman et al. (1973); their table, if evaluated statistically in this same way, would not yield so striking a result. What is clear is that the tendency toward hits rather than misses cannot reasonably be ascribed to chance. There is some systematic — that is, nonrandom — source of anomalous resemblance of dreams to target.

Despite its breadth, this "hitting" tendency seems to vary greatly in strength. The data on single dreams — Line O — suggest no consistency. At the other extreme, some separate lines of the table look impressive. I will next consider how we may legitimately evaluate the relative statistical significance of separate parts of the data on all-night sessions. (I will not try to take exact account here of the fact that the single-dream data are not significant, though it is wise to have in mind that the exact values I cite must be viewed as slightly exaggerated, in the absence of any explicit advance prediction that the results for all-night sessions and for single dreams would differ greatly.)

Two difficulties, one general and one specific, stand in the way of making as thorough an evaluation as I would wish. The general difficulty is that the researchers turned the task of statistical evaluation over to various consultants — for the most part, different consultants at various times — and some of the consultants must also have influenced the choice of procedures and measures. The consultants, and presumably the researchers themselves, seem not to have been at that time very experienced in working with some of the design problems posed by this research nor in planning how the research could be done to permit effective analysis. Much of the research was not properly analyzed at the time, and for much of it the full original data are no longer available. (The researchers have been very helpful in supplying me with material they have been able to locate despite dispersal and storage of the laboratory's files. Perhaps additional details may be recovered in the future.) The result is that completely satisfactory analysis is at present possible only for some portions of the data.

The specific difficulty results from a feature of the research design employed in most of the experimental series, a feature whose implications the researchers did not fully appreciate at the time. If a judge is presented with a set of transcripts and a set of targets and is asked to judge similarity of each target to each transcript, the various judgments may not be completely independent. If one transcript is so closely similar to a particular target that the judge is confident of having recognized a correct match, the judge (or percipient, of course) may minimize the similarity of that target to the transcripts judged later. Instructions to judges explicitly urged them to avoid this error, but we cannot tell how thoroughly this directive was followed. Nonindependence would create no bias toward either positive or negative evidence of correspondence between targets and transcripts, but it would alter variability and thus render inappropriate some standard tests of significance. I have entered in the two succeeding columns of the table a t or a z that can be used in evaluating the statistical significance of the departure from chance expectancy (t is required when ratings are available, and z must be used when only rankings or score counts are available, because sample variability in the former case is estimated from the data but in the latter case must be based conservatively on a theoretical distribution). If ratings were available, they were used; if not, rankings were used if available; otherwise, score count was used.

Is there likely to have been much of this nonindependence in the series where it was possible? A pertinent fact is that the hits were not generally direct hits. That is, there was no overwhelming tendency for the correct target to be given first place rather than just being ranked in the upper half of the target pool. This greatly reduces the strength of the argument that ordinary significance tests are grossly inaccurate because of nonindependence. Because certainty is not possible, however, we need to separate results according to whether the procedures permitted this kind of nonindependence. In the table, I have italicized results that cannot have been influenced by this difficulty (either because each night's ratings were made by a different person or because each night in a series had, and was judged in relation to, a separate target pool) or that closely approximate this ideal condition.

The outcome is clear. Several segments of the data, considered separately, yield significant evidence that dreams (and associations to them) tended to resemble the picture chosen randomly as target more than they resembled other pictures in the pool. In the case of evaluation by outside judges, two of the three segments that are free of the problem of nonindependence yield separately significant results: The pilot sessions (Line H) yield a z of 4.20, and thus a p of .00002. An experiment with distant but multisensory targets (Line L) yields a z of 3.11 and a p of .001. If we consider segments in which judgments may not be completely independent of each other and analyze them in the standard way, we find that the two series with psychologist William Erwin as dreamer are also significant (if nonindependence of judgments does not seriously interfere), Line B with a z of 2.53 ($p < .01$) and Line F with a t of 4.93 and 7 df ($p < .01$). The two precognitive series (Lines I and J), each with 7 df, yield ts of 2.81 and 2.27, with p values slightly above and below .05, respectively.

Segment results based on the subjects' own judgments of similarity are less significant than those based on judgments by outside judges. Only two segments reach minimal levels of statistical significance: Line G, where the t of 2.74 with 7 df is significant at the .05 level, and Line H, where the z of 2.21 is significant at the .05 level.

The statistical evaluation of the separate segments of the Maimonides experiments also permits a more adequate evaluation of their overall statistical significance. For judgments by outside judges, three segments are free of the potential nonindependence of successive judgments (Lines H, L, and N). Putting these three together by the procedure Mosteller and Bush (1954, pp. 329–330) ascribed to Stouffer (recommended by Rosenthal [1984, p. 72] as the "simplest and most versatile" of the possible procedures), the joint p value is $< .000002$. For the subjects' own judgments, six segments are available (Lines A, C, G, H, L, and N), and their joint p value is less than .002. The other segments of the data have the problem of potential nonindependence of successive judgments, and even if the exaggeration of significance may be small for a single line, I would not want to risk compounding it in an overall p. Their prevailing unity of direction, however (direction not being subject to influence by the kind of nonindependence involved here), and the substantial size of some of the differences, justify the inference that the overall evidence of consistency far exceeds that indicated by only those selected segments for which a precise statistical statement is possible. The impression given by the mere count of hits and misses is thus fully confirmed when more sensitive measures are used.

Parapsychological experiments are sometimes criticized on the grounds that what evidence they provide for ESP indicates at most some very small effects detectable only by amassing large bodies of data. Those to whom this criticism has any appeal should be aware that the Maimonides experiments are clearly exempt from it. The significant results on Lines F and G of the table, for example, are each attributable basically to just eight data points.

If replications elsewhere should eventually confirm the statistically significant outcome of the Maimonides experiments, would the fact of statistical significance in itself establish the presence of the kind of anomaly called ESP? Of course not. Statistical significance indicates only the presence of consistency and does not identify its source. ESP, or the more general term *psi,* is a label for consistencies that have no identifiable source and that suggest transfer of information by channels not familiar to present scientific knowledge. A judgment about the appropriateness of the label, and thus about the "ESP hypothesis," is complex. It depends on a variety of other judgments and knowledge—how confidently other possible sources of the consistent effect can be excluded, whether other lines of experimentation are yielding results that suggest the same judgment, and so on.

I believe many psychologists would, like myself, consider the ESP hypothesis to merit serious consideration and continued research if they read the Maimonides reports for themselves and if they familiarized themselves with other recent and older lines of experimentation (e.g., Jahn, 1982, and many of the chapters in Wolman, 1977).

Some parapsychological researchers—among them the Maimonides group—have written at times as though a finding of statistical significance sufficiently justified a conclusion that the apparent anomaly should be classified as ESP. I can understand their choice of words, which is based on their own confidence that their experiments permitted exclusion of other interpretations. But perhaps psychologists who in the future become involved in this area may prefer to use a term such as *anomalies,* so as to avoid variable and possibly confusing connotations about the origin of the anomalies. Zusne and Jones (1982) wisely prepared the way for this usage in speaking of *anomalistic psychology.* But meanwhile, psychologists need not cut themselves off from knowledge of relevant facts because of dissatisfaction with the terminology surrounding their presentation.

Attempted Replications Elsewhere

The Maimonides pattern of controlled experiment in a sleep laboratory, obviously, is extremely time consuming and expensive, and replication seems to have been attempted so far at only two other sleep laboratories. At the University of Wyoming, two experiments yielded results approximately at mean chance expectation — slightly below in one study (Belvedere & Foulkes, 1971), slightly above in the other (Foulkes et al., 1972). In a replication at the Boston University School of Medicine (Globus, Knapp, Skinner, & Healey, 1968), overall results were not significantly positive, though in this instance encouragement for further exploration was reported. The researchers had decided in advance to base their conclusions on exact hits — that is, placing the target first, rather than just in the upper half; by this measure, the results were encouraging, though not statistically significant. Moreover, to quote the researchers, "*Post hoc* analysis revealed that the judges were significantly more correct when they were more 'confident' in their judgments.... Further conservatively designed research does seem indicated because of these findings" (Globus et al., 1968, p. 365).

A study by Calvin Hall (1967) is sometimes cited as a replication that confirmed the Maimonides findings; in truth, however, although it provided impressive case material, it was not done in a way that permits evaluation as a replicaton of the Maimonides experiments. Several small-scale studies, done without the facilities of a sleep laboratory, have been reported that are not replications of even one of the more ambitious Maimonides experiments but each of which reports positive results that might encourage further exploration (Braud, 1977; Child, Kanthamani, & Sweeney, 1977; Rechtschaffen, 1970; Strauch, 1970; Van de Castle, 1971). In the case of these minor studies — unlike the Maimonides studies and three systematic replications — one must recognize the likelihood of selective publication on the basis of interesting results. Taken all together, these diverse and generally small-scale studies done elsewhere do, in my opinion, add something to the conviction the Maimonides experiments might inspire, that dream research is a promising technique for experimental study of the ESP question.

The lack of significant results in the three systematic replications is hardly conclusive evidence against eventual replicability. In the Maimonides series, likewise, three successive replications (Lines C, D, and E in Table 1) yielded no significant result, yet they are part of a program yielding highly significant overall results.

If results of such potentially great interest and scientific importance as those of the Maimonides program had been reported on a more conventional topic, one might expect them to be widely and accurately described in reviews of the field to which they were relevant, and to be analyzed carefully as a basis for sound evaluation of whether replication and extension of the research were indicated, or of whether errors could be detected and understood. What has happened in this instance of anomalous research findings?

Representation of the Maimonides Research in Books by Psychologists

It is appropriate to begin with E.M. Hansel's 1980 revision of his earlier critical book on parapsychology. As part of his attempt to bring the earlier book up to date, he included an entire chapter on experiments on telepathy in dreams. One page was devoted to a description of the basic method used in the Maimonides experiments; one paragraph summarized the impressive outcome of 10 of the experiments. The rest of the chapter was devoted mainly to a specific account of the experiment in which psychologist Robert Van de Castle was the subject (the outcome is summarized in Line G of my Table 1) and to the attempted replication at the University of Wyoming (Belvedere & Foulkes, 1971), in which Van de Castle was again the subject. Another page was devoted to another of the Maimonides experiments that was also repeated at the University of Wyoming (Foulkes et al., 1972). Hansel did not mention the replication by Globus et al. (1968), whose authors felt that the results encouraged further exploration. Hansel gave more weight to the two negative outcomes at Wyoming than to the sum of the Maimonides research, arguing that sensory cues supposedly permitted by the procedures at Maimonides, not possible because of greater care taken by the Wyoming experimenters, were responsible for the difference in results. He did not provide, of course, the full account of procedures presented in the original Maimonides reports that might persuade many readers that Hansel's interpretation is far from compelling. Nor did he consider why some of the other experiments at Maimonides, not obviously distinguished in the care with which they were done from the two that were replicated (e.g., those on Lines E, M, and O of Table 1) yielded a close-to-chance outcome such as Hansel might have expected sensory cuing to prevent.

Hansel exaggerated the opportunities for sensory cuing — that is, for the percipient to obtain by ordinary sensory means some information about the target for the night. He did this notably by misinterpreting an ambiguous statement in the Maimonides reports, not mentioning that his interpretation was incompatible with other passages; his interpretation was in fact erroneous, as shown by Akers (1984, pp. 128–129). Furthermore, Hansel did not alert the reader to the great care exerted by the researchers to eliminate possible sources of sensory cuing. Most important is the fact that Hansel did not provide any plausible account — other than fraud — of how the opportunities for sensory cuing that he claimed existed would be likely to lead to the striking findings of the research. For example, he seemed to consider important the fact that at Maimonides the agent could leave his or her room during the night to go to the bathroom, whereas in Wyoming the agent had a room with its own bathroom, and the outer door to the room was sealed with tape to prevent the agent from emerging. Hansel did not attempt to say how the agent's visit to the bathroom could have altered the details of the percipient's dreams each night in a manner distinctively appropriate to that night's target. The only plausible route of influence on the dream record seems to be deliberate fraud involving the researchers and their subjects. The great number and variety of personnel in these studies — experimenters, agents, percipients, and judges — makes fraud especially unlikely as an explanation of the positive findings; but Hansel did not mention this important fact.

It appears to me that all of Hansel's criticisms of the Maimonides experiments are relevant only on the hypothesis of fraud (except for the mistaken criticism I have mentioned above). He said that unintentional communication was more likely but provided no evidence either that it occurred or that such communication — in any form in which it might have occurred — could have produced such consistent results as emerged from the Maimonides experiments. I infer that Hansel was merely avoiding making explicit his unsupported accusations of fraud. Fraud is an interpretation always important to keep in mind, and it is one that could not be entirely excluded even by precautions going beyond those used in the Wyoming studies. But the fact that fraud was as always, theoretically possible hardly justifies dismissal of a series of carefully conducted studies that offer important suggestions for opening up a new line of inquiry into a topic potentially of great significance. Especially regrettable is Hansel's description of various supposed defects in the experiments as though they mark the experiments as being carelessly conducted by general scientific criteria, whereas in fact the supposed defects are relevant only if one assumes fraud. A reader who is introduced to the Maimonides research by Hansel's chapter is likely to get a totally erroneous impression of the care taken by the experimenters to avoid various possible sources of error. The one thing they could not avoid was obtaining results that Hansel considered a priori impossible, hence evidence of fraud; but Hansel was not entirely frank about his reasoning.

An incidental point worth noting is that Hansel did not himself apply, in his critical attack, the standards of evidence he demanded of the researchers. His conclusions were based implicitly on the assumption that the difference of outcome between the Maimonides and the Wyoming experiments was a genuine difference, not attributable to random variation. He did not even raise the question, as he surely would have if, in some parallel instance, the Maimonides researchers had claimed or implied statistical significance where it was questionable. In fact, the difference of outcome might well have arisen from random error; for the percipient's own judgments the difference is significant at the 5% level (2-tailed), but for the outsiders' judgments it does not approach significance.

Another 1980 book is *The Psychology of Transcendence,* by Andrew Neher, in which almost 100 pages are devoted to "psychic experience." Neher differed from the other authors I refer to in describing the Maimonides work as a "series of studies of great interest" (p. 145), but this evaluation seems to be negated by his devoting only three lines to it and four lines to unsuccessful replications.

A third 1980 publication, *The Psychology of the Psychic,* by David Marks and Richard Kammann, provides less of a general review of recent parapsychology than Hansel's book or even Neher's one long chapter. It is largely devoted to the techniques of mentalists (that is, conjurors specializing in psychological rather than physical effects) and can be useful to anyone encountering a mentalist who pretends to be "psychic." Most readers are not likely to be aware that parapsychological research receives only limited attention. The jacket blurbs give a very different view of the book, as do the authors in their introductory sentences:

> ESP is just around the next corner. When you get there, it is just around the next corner. Having now turned over one hundred of these corners, we decided to call it quits and report our findings for public review. (Marks & Kammann, 1980, p. 4)

Given this introduction to the nature of the book, readers might suppose it would at least mention any corner that many parapsychologists have judged to be an impressive turning. But the Maimonides dream experiments received no mention at all.

Another volume, by psychologist James Alcock (1981), quite clearly purports to include a general review and evaluation of parapsychological research. Alcock mentioned (p. 6) that Hansel had examined the Maimonides experiments, but the only account of them that Alcock offered (on p. 163) was incidental to a discussion of control groups. By implication he seemed to reject the Maimonides experiments because they included no control groups. He wrote that "a control group, for which no sender or no target was used, would appear essential" (p. 163). Later he added, "One could, alternatively, 'send' when the subject was not in the dream state, and compare 'success' in this case with success in dream state trials" (p. 163). The first of these statements suggests a relevant use of control groups but errs in calling it essential; in other psychological research, Alcock would have doubtless readily recognized that within-subject control can, where feasible, be much more efficient and pertinent than a separate control group. His second statement suggests a type of experiment that is probably impossible (because in satisfactory form it seems to require the subject to dream whether awake or asleep and not to know whether he or she was awake or asleep). This second kind of experiment, moreover, has special pertinence only to a comparison between dreaming and waking, not to the question of whether ESP is manifested in dreaming.

Alcock, in short, did not seem to recognize that the design of the Maimonides experiments was based on controls exactly parallel to those used by innumerable psychologists in other research with similar logical structure (and even implied, curiously enough, in his own second suggestion). He encouraged readers to think that the Maimonides studies are beyond the pale of acceptable experimental design, whereas in fact they are fine examples of appropriate use of within-subject control rather than between-subjects control.

The quality of thinking with which Alcock confronted the Maimonides research appeared also in a passage that did not refer to it by name. Referring to an article published in *The Humanist* by Ethel Grodzins Romm, he wrote,

> Romm (1977) argued that a fundamental problem with both the dream telepathy research and the remote viewing tests is that the reports suffer from what she called "shoe-fitting" language; she cited a study in which the sender was installed in a room draped in white fabric and had ice cubes poured down his back. A receiver who reported "white" was immediately judged to have had a "hit" by an independent panel. Yet, as she observed, words such as "miserable", "wet", or "icy" would have been better hits. . . . Again, the obvious need is for a control group. Why are they not used? (p. 163)

What Romm described as "shoe fitting" (misinterpreting events to fit one's expectations) is an important kind of error that is repeatedly made in interpretation of everyday occurrences by people who believe they are psychic. But the dream telepathy research at Maimonides was well protected against this kind of error by the painstaking controls that Alcock seemed not to have noticed. Surely Romm must be referring to some other and very sloppy dream research?

Not at all. The details in this paragraph, and even more in Romm's article, point unmistakably, though inaccurately, to the fifth night of the first precognitive series at Maimonides. The actual details of target and response would alone deprive it of much of its value as an example of shoe fitting. As reported by Krippner, Ullman, and Honorton (1971), the target was a morning experience that included being in a room that was draped with white sheets. The subject's first dream report had included the statement, "I was just standing in a room, surrounded by white. Every imaginable thing in that room was white" (p. 201). There is more similarity here than Romm and Alcock acknowledged in mentioning from this passage only the single word "white."

More important, however, is the fact that the experiment they were referring to provided no opportunity for shoe fitting. The procedures followed in the experiment were completely misrepresented in a way that created the illusion that the possibility existed. There was no panel, in the sense of a group of people gathered together and capable in influencing each other. The judges, operating independently, separately judged every one of the 64 possible combinations of target and transcript yielded by the eight nights of the experiment, not just the eight correct pairings, and they had no clues to which those eight were. Their responses are hardly likely to have been immediate, as they required reading the entire night's transcript. Because each judge was working alone and was not recording times, there would have been no record if a particular response had been immediate, and no record of what particular element in the transcript led to an immediate response.

I looked up in a 1977 issue of *The Humanist* the article by Romm that Alcock cited. The half page on shoe-fitting language gave as examples this item from the Maimonides research and also the SRI remote-viewing experiments (Puthoff & Targ, 1976) done at SRI International. In both cases what was said was pure fiction, based on failure to note what was done in the experiments and in particular that the experimenters were well aware of the danger of shoe-fitting language and that the design of their experiments incorporated procedures to ensure that it could not occur. Romm's ignorance about the Maimonides research and her apparent willingness to fabricate falsehoods about it should be recognized by anyone who had read any of the Maimonides research publications. Yet Alcock accepted and repeated the fictions as though they were true. His presentation in the context of a book apparently in the scientific tradition seems to me more dangerous than Romm's original article, for anyone with scientific orientation should be able to recognize Romm's article as propaganda. Its title, for example, is "When You Give a Closet Occultist a PhD, What Kind of Research Can You Expect?" and it repeatedly speaks of "cult phuds," meaning people with PhDs who are interested in parapsychological problems. Alcock's repetition of Romm's misstatements in a context lacking these clues may well be taken by many a reader as scholarly writing based on correct information and rational thought. Paradoxically, both Alcock's paragraph and Romm's article are excellent examples of the shoe-fitting error that both decry in others who are in fact carefully avoiding it.

The last of the five books that bring, or fail to bring, the Maimonides research to the attention of psychologists and their students is *Anomalistic Psychology: A Study of Extraordinary Phenomena of Behavior and Experience,* a 1982 volume by Leonard Zusne and Warren H. Jones. This is in many ways an excellent book, and it is also the one of the five that comes closest to including a general review of important recent research in parapsychology. Its brief account of the Maimonides dream experiments, however, misrepresented them in ways that should seriously reduce a reader's interest in considering them further.

Zusne and Jones's description of the basic procedure made three serious errors. First, it implied that one of the experimenters had a chance to know the identity of the target. ("After the subject falls asleep, an art reproduction is selected from a large collection randomly, placed in an envelope, and given to the agent" p. 260). In fact, precautions were taken to ensure that no one but the agent could know the identity of the target. Second, the authors stated that "three judges . . . rate their confidence that the dream content matches the target picture" (p. 260), leading the reader to suppose that the judges were informed of the identity of the target at the time of rating. In fact, a judge was presented with a dream transcript and a pool of potential targets and was asked to rate the degree of similarity between the transcript and each member of the pool, while being unaware of which member had been the target. Third, there was a similarly, though more obscurely, misleading description of how ratings were obtained from the dreamer.

This misinformation was followed by an even more serious misrepresentation of the research and, by implication, of the competence of the researchers. Zusne and Jones (1982) wrote that Ullman and Krippner (1978) had found that dreamers were not influenced telepathically unless they knew in advance that an attempt would be made to influence them. This led, they wrote, to the subject's being "primed prior to going to sleep" through the experimenter's

> preparing the receiver through experiences that were related to the content of the picture to be telepathically transmitted during the night. Thus, when the picture was Van Gogh's Corridor of the St. Paul Hospital, which depicts a lonely figure in the hallways of a mental hospital, the receiver: (1) heard Rosza's *Spellbound* played on a phonograph; (2) heard the monitor laugh hysterically in the room; (3) was addressed as "Mr. Van Gogh" by the monitor; (4) was shown paintings done by mental patients; (5) was given a pill and a glass of water; and (6) was daubed with a piece of cotton dipped in acetone. The receiver was an English "sensitive," but it is obvious that no psychic sensitivity was required to figure out the general content of the picture and to produce an appropriate report, whether any dreams were actually seen or not. (pp. 260–261)

If researchers were to report positive results of the experiment described here by Zusne and Jones and were to claim that it provided some positive evidence of ESP, what would a reader conclude? Surely, that the researchers were completely incompetent, but probably not that they were dishonest. For dishonesty to take such a frank and transparent form is hardly credible.

Incompetence of the researchers is not, however, a proper inference. The simple fact, which anyone can easily verify, is that the account Zusne and Jones gave of the experiment is grossly inaccurate. What Zusne and Jones have done is to describe (for one specific night of the experiment) some of the stimuli provided to the dreamer the next morning, *after* his dreams had been recorded and his night's sleep was over. Zusne and Jones erroneously stated that these stimuli were provided *before* the night's sleep, to prime the subject to have or falsely report having the desired kind of dream. The correct sequence of events was quite clearly stated in the brief reference Zusne and Jones cited (Ullman & Krippner, 1978), as well as in the original research report (Krippner, Honorton, & Ullman, 1972).

I can understand and sympathize with Zusne and Jones's error. The experiment they cited is one in which the nocturnal dreamer was seeking to dream in response to a set of stimuli to be created and presented to him the next morning. As may be seen in Table 1, results from such precognitive sessions (all done with a single subject) were especially strong. This apparent transcendence of time as well as space makes the precognitive findings seem at least doubly impossible to most of us. An easy misreading, therefore, on initially scanning the research report, would be to suppose the stimuli to have been presented partly in advance (because some parts obviously involved a waking subject) and partly during sleep.

This erroneous reading on which Zusne and Jones based their account could easily have been corrected by a more careful rereading. In dealing with other topics, they might have realized the improbability that researchers could have been so grossly incompetent and could have checked the accuracy of their statements before publishing them. Zusne and Jones are not alone in this tendency to quick misperception of parapsychological research through preconception and prejudice; we have already seen it in Alcock's book. Alcock (1983) wrote the review of Zusne and Jones's book for *Contemporary Psychology,* the book-review journal of the American Psychological Association, and he did not mention this egregious error, even though very slight acquaintance with the Maimonides research should suffice to detect it.

Discussion

The experiments at the Maimonides Medical Center on the possibility of ESP in dreams clearly merit careful attention from psychologists who, for whatever reason, are interested in the question of ESP. To firm believers in the impossibility of ESP, they pose a challenge to skill in detecting experimental flaws or to the understanding of other sources of error. To those who can conceive that ESP might be possible, they convey suggestions about some of the conditions influencing its appearance or absence and about techniques for investigating it.

This attention is not likely to be given by psychologists whose knowledge about the experiments comes from the books by their fellow psychologists that purport to review parapsychological research. Some of those books engage in nearly incredible falsification of the facts about the experiments; others simply neglect them. I believe it is fair to say that none of these books has correctly identified any defect in the Maimonides experiments other than ones relevant only to the hypothesis of fraud or on inappropriate statistical reasoning (easily remedied by new calculations from the published data). I do not mean that the Maimonides experiments are models of design and execution. I have already called attention to a design flaw that prevents sensitive analysis of some of the experiments; and the control procedures were violated at one session, as Akers (1984) pointed out on the basis of the full information supplied in the original report. (Neither of these genuine defects was mentioned in any of the five books I have reviewed here, an indication of their authors' general lack of correct information about the Maimonides experiments.)

Readers who doubt that the falsification is as extreme as I have pictured it need only consult the sources I have referred to. Their doubt might also be reduced by familiarity with some of James Bradley's research (1981, 1984). In his 1984 article, he reported similar misrepresentations of fact on a topic, robustness of procedures of statistical inference, on which psychologists would not be thought to have nearly the strength of preconception that many are known to have about ESP. How much more likely, then, falsification on so emotionally laden a topic as ESP is for many psychologists! In the earlier article, Bradley (1981) presented experimental evidence (for college students, in this case, not psychologists) that confidence in the correctness of one's own erroneous opinions is positively correlated with the degree of expertise one believes oneself to have in the field of knowledge within which the erroneous opinion falls. This finding may help in understanding why the authors of some of these books did not find it necessary to consider critically their own erroneous statements.

A very considerable proportion of psychologists have a potential interest in the question of ESP. In a recent survey (Wagner & Monnet, 1979) of university professors in various fields, 34% of psychologists were found to consider ESP either an established fact or a likely possibility, exactly the same proportion as considered it an impossibility. In this survey, psychologists less frequently expressed a positive opinion than did members of other disciplines, a finding that may be attributable to psychologists' better understanding of sources of error in human judgment. There seems to be no equally sound reason for the curious fact that psychologists differed overwhelmingly from others in their tendency to consider ESP an impossibility. Of natural scientists, only 3% checked that opinion; of the 166 professors in other social sciences, not a single one did.

Both of these groups of psychologists have been ill served by the apparently scholarly books that seem to convey information about the dream experiments. The same may be said about some other lines of parapsychological research. Interested readers might well consult the original sources and form their own judgments.

ESP in Dreams:
Comments on a Replication "Failure"
by the "Failing" Subject

by Robert L. Van de Castle

Child (1985) documents that the fairly impressive data base substantiating the presence of ESP in dreams, particularly that produced at Maimonides Medical Center, has been seriously neglected by psychologists and has been inaccurately described or distorted by some authors discussing the topic. The necessity to objectively examine the evidence for dream telepathy was stressed by Gardner Murphy (1971):

> It will take much time and labor, but in both quantitative and qualitative terms, the experimental analysis of dream telepathy is now a problem of such urgency that a mature science can no longer handle it either by ignoring it or by denying it (p. 3).

My own contributions to the exploration of dream telepathy have involved authoring a review chapter on clinical and experimental dream telepathy studies (Van de Castle, 1970), acting as an experimenter in dream telepathy studies (Van de Castle, 1971a, 1971b), co-developing a therapeutic paradigm for utilizing telepathic dreams (Reed, 1985), and serving as an experimental subject in three different laboratories where dream telepathy was investigated. Since my role in this field has been a unique one, I would like to briefly review my experiences in other laboratory settings prior to the "failure to replicate" experiment at Wyoming (Belvedere & Foulkes, 1971), and provide some additional details about that experiment to place the outcome in a more balanced perspective. The Wyoming experiment is being emphasized because Hansel (1980), a leading critic of parapsychology, in his chapter on "Telepathy in Dreams" limited his discussion of the overall successful outcome of 10 investigations at Maimonides Hospital to a single paragraph, but devoted nearly eight pages to his description and discussion of the "unsuccessful" Van de Castle replication.

Montague Ullman, the senior investigator at Maimonides, had visited Calvin Hall and me at the Institute of Dream Research in Miami, Florida, and encouraged us to explore whether telepathic stimuli might influence dream content. The first experimental attempt occurred on March 12, 1964. Hall, serving as the experimenter and EEG monitor, had concentrated on imagery of a boxing match and I gave a subsequent REM report about "a large auditorium and there was a boxing match going on." Hall's next effort was five nights later. He concentrated upon skiing imagery and my subsequent REM report involved "a girl high in the air on skis." Sometimes the correspondences were questionable. Two REM periods later, Hall concentrated upon an imagined tattoo on his skin and my REM report described a woman's legs and "if one looked closely at her legs, these very ugly varicose veins were apparent and the flesh looked sort of segmented."

Hall continued his explorations with me and with five other subjects. In his judgment, a representation of the target material was detectable in 13 of my 17 dreams that he attempted to influence (76 percent). The corresponding figures for the other five subjects ranged from 65 percent to 25 percent. Overall, he concluded that some features of the telepathic stimulus had appeared in 56 percent of the 121 targeted dreams. When Hall utilized a multiple choice format to match target stimuli and dream themes, the matching dream theme was correctly selected by a group of about 100 undergraduate students, at a statistically significant level, in 29 of the 36 cases judged.

Since these six subjects had reported dreams from several nights of REM awakenings as well as home recalled awakenings (range 34–97 dreams), it was possible to calculate how frequently a designated theme was dreamed about when a telepathic stimulus was not involved. For example, some form of punching activity occurred in 4 of my 97 dreams, but the only time I reported a boxing match was when Hall had concentrated upon such imagery. Hall summarized his positive results in an article entitled "Experiments on Telepathically Influenced Dreams" (Hall, 1967).

My experimental sessions at Maimonides Medical Center began on January 5, 1967, and continued on seven subsequent nights spaced from 4 to 11 weeks apart. Although the dates of my participation during this 44 week period are clearly noted in Chapter 11 of the original edition of *Dream Telepathy* (Ullman, Krippner, & Vaughan, 1973), which provides a brief summary of each of my night's results, Hansel (1980) indicates I "slept in the [Maimonides] Dream Laboratory on eight *successive* [italics added] nights" (p. 245).

An important psychological difference exists when one is repeatedly awakened at every REM period and has a month to recuperate rather than a single day, as happened on four occasions under the time constraints imposed at Wyoming. The entire eight sessions were completed there within a 14 day period. However, when Hansel (1980) describes "the essential differences in procedure" (p. 246) between the two laboratories, he fails to mention this temporal difference and focuses exclusively on the additional safeguards imposed by the Wyoming experimenters.

At Maimonides I ranked the pool of eight pictures for possible correspondences on the morning after each session and also rated them on a 100 point scale. Using a binomial criterion, I obtained eight "hits" (rank of 1–4) and no "misses" (rank of 5–8) for the eight nights ($p = .004$) and my average rating for target pictures was 74.5 and for nontarget pictures was 32.6, a difference significant at $p = .003$ by Mann-Whitney U test. Hansel (1980) notes only that I ranked each picture but gives no indication of my success level. Hansel reports the outside judge placed the target in the top half of each night's rankings but fails to mention that when my concluding guess of the target's presumed content was utilized by the judge, a total of six direct correspondences (rank of 1) was obtained ($p = .0001$). These statistical analyses appear on page 275 of Ullman et al. (1973) and on pp. 100–101 of Ullman and Krippner (1970).

Child's (1985) article contains further examples of Hansel's (1980) misleading account of the Maimonides research and results. In Hansel's reference notes (1980, p. 253), he indicates that the foreword to (the 1973 edition of) *Dream Telepathy* was written by Murphy Gardner. Hansel (1980) also displayed an inventive style in identifying the Wyoming experimenters: "Replication of the experiment was attempted by Edward Belvedere of the Maimonides Laboratory and David Roulkes of the University of Wyoming" (p. 246). Belvedere was a graduate student who had worked extensively in Foulkes' laboratory and the academic affiliation of both authors was listed as the University of Wyoming in their article (Belvedere & Foulkes, 1971).

A bona fide experimenter from Maimonides would have been a welcome touch on the scene at Wyoming. The psychological climates at the two laboratories were distinctly different. In his *Psychological Bulletin* review of "Some Unintended Consequences of Rigorous Research," Argyris (1968) provides several examples of research where the nature of the laboratory setting changed and distorted the phenomena under study. J. B. Rhine (1964), reviewing some cases of exceptionally high ESP scoring, noted that an atmosphere of contagious enthusiasm and of intense "audience appreciation" for the successful scorer was an important feature. This audience appreciation was definitely present from Hall and from Ullman and Krippner. My perception of the Maimonides ambiance was "The staff always gave me the feeling that I was a visiting sultan and the red carpet was rolled out with a royal flourish" (Ullman et al., 1973, p. 141). At Wyoming, however, not only was the weather cold in midwinter but the reception was also; there were no social interactions with the staff until the study was over.

Gardner Murphy personally funded the replication effort. My original preference for the experimenter was Rechtshaffen (1970), because he had reported some impressive examples of telepathic REM dream responses to hypnotic dream targets. When the Maimonides staff found that his lab was unavailable, they made arrangements to utilize Foulkes' lab. I wrote a letter dated December 2, 1969, to Foulkes with the following comments and requests for the study:

> The date of January 22 would seem to be a good starting one. I'm not sure how long it will take us to complete the eight-night series. . . . My usual morning-after reaction at Maimonides was that of experiencing a headache and a feeling of being a little giddy or becoming unglued.
>
> Glad to hear you have a potential agent lined up. I hope that it will be arranged to have more than just this one person as a possible agent.
>
> As you know, reproductions of paintings were used in the Maimonides series but we have also found it acceptable to use *colored photographs* [italics added] from such magazines as *Life* and *Look*. . . . I would have a strong preference for a system in which the potential stimuli . . . are selected so that each one will be as different as possible from each other.

A special attempt is made to try and differentiate the type of emotionality that might be expected from each picture. . . . With such a method, it makes it much easier for a judge to evaluate possible correspondences.

I'm hoping that there will be some opportunity for discussion during the day time hours of your recent projects and to swap some ideas about scoring dreams and related topics.

This letter was apparently received because of the specificity of the details replied to in my letter from Foulkes dated January 6, 1970.

We look forward to your arrival on the 22nd.

About the study: (1) We hope to have 3 female potential agents for your selection.

(2) Targets are being selected with an eye to systematic heterogeneity of content. Our selector, who has done it before (for a pilot study) has the idea, and did a good job of getting qualitatively different pictures the first time around.

(3) The only problem with unlimited flexibility [for scheduling] is that none of us is a full time sleep researcher. We have classes to teach or take and other day time responsibilities. [The study occurred during between-semesters vacation.]

When awakened for my third REM report on my first experimental night at Wyoming, I described an interaction with Foulkes:

We were . . . discussing the planning of this experiment. . . . He was saying things about the important role that the persons who made up the random numbers could play. And I was saying something about, "Yes, these experiments get to be very complicated and that it can be all sorts of unconsciously motivated mistakes and that the person in that role could be a fairly critical one."

These remarks about the critical role of the picture selector turned out to be very prophetic. When presented the pool of pictures to judge the next morning, I felt it was not very heterogeneous and it also contained four black and white photos. When I complained that they had not followed my instructions regarding the use of colored photographs, I was told they had never received such instructions.

I was particularly distressed by the lack of emotionality and content differentiation in the picture pool and suggested another night's unofficial trial to see if more heterogeneity of material would appear. When it didn't, I requested a rearrangement of the subsequent pools so that greater heterogeneity of themes would be present and also asked to have all the pictures in color. Foulkes assigned this task to the original selector who was preparing to leave that day for vacation. I was informed that the selector had subsequently rearranged the pictures in an improved heterogenous manner but that my request for all colored pictures could not be honored because of time constraints. By including five additional art prints at that point, a total of 22 or the 56 (39 percent) subsequent pictures used in the experiment contained color.

Was the objective of improved heterogeneity achieved? This is obviously a matter of subjective judgment, so several examples will be given for the reader to judge. For example, one night, the target pool contained two slides showing hands and grids, a slide of a figure with his hands over his head, and a slide of workmen with their hands prominently displayed.

On night 6, the target picture was a black and white close-up of a nursing mother nude to the waist. One picture was a man nude from the waist up holding and kissing a woman; another was of several people drinking at a cocktail party with some whiskey bottles nearby; another was a farmer holding a bushel basket full of corn at his waist. All four pictures could be considered to represent some form of oral imagery.

On night 7, the target picture was again a black and white close up of a nursing mother nude to the waist. One picture was a close up view of a young man's face with his lips parted and his hands encircled in the hair of a woman facing him; another was a waterfront dock with a jug of wine, fruit, and a basket full of corn; another was a dragonfly eating a leaf; another was a young girl on a round rock playing a flute; another was a pom-pom waving crowd with many open mouthed spectators yelling. An oral theme seemed quite prominent in six of the pictures and, in addition to a nearly identical target picture, the pool associated with it again contained pictures with kissing imagery, bottles of alcoholic beverages, and round baskets of corn.

My first REM report on night 7 referred to "a big argument about . . . two different contracts." My second REM report was about using pieces of paper to "leave a false trail" and a prison sentence for "mal-tampering" with someone's correct identity. My third REM report mentioned "a complaint letter where somebody was writing in to express their dissatisfaction." My fourth REM period involved "a sporting proposition" that turned out to be "a bad deal" and also it being "hard to tell what time it was because I looked at about four different clocks and every one of the four had a different time." There was also a concern about others tolerating an abusive assemblyman and I was getting ready to make a complaint to "the general manager" of the night-time factory shift "to see that this be stopped immediately" because "If I was a psychologist there, then I should be making recommendations about psychological situations."

These REM reports, made before I saw another repeat of a nonheterogeneous pool of pictures, reflected considerable frustration on my part and a sense of injustice because of different contracts, false trails, bad deals, confusing messages, an abusive assemblyman being tolerated, and my psychological recommendations being ignored.

The experiment now had one more night to go. Since I had achieved two direct hits (rank of 1) on nights 3 and 4, one more direct hit on that final night would have yielded statistically significant results in favor of an ESP hypothesis. Besides my frustration over the lack of previous heterogeneity in the picture pools, I was informed that the agent (sender), an undergraduate working in Foulkes' laboratory with whom I had achieved the two direct hits, had decided to withdraw from the experiment. As a consequence, I had to utilize a former agent, with whom I had previously been completely unsuccessful, for that last decisive night.

The pool of pictures on that final night contained seven thematically similar pictures that showed people from a foreign culture or an ethnically distinct subculture in America. The eighth showed a geographically distant location (galaxy). One was a postcard from Austria showing a child being held by a bare breasted woman in peasant costume, standing by a house with a thatched roof; another was a street scene in the French Quarter of New Orleans with black musicians entertaining tourists holding a pitcher of juice; another was a street scene in a ghetto with two black teenagers in shorts holding each other in front of a spraying fire hydrant; another was a street scene in Latin America with a priest wearing a long lace cassock and a man holding a fringed umbrella over him; another was of two dark skinned women, with many bracelets on their arms, wearing saris or long shawls over their heads and shoulders; another was a crowd of Orientals with the men wearing long gowns slit at the side; another was a young man wearing a black leather jacket, carrying a guitar case, walking down some railroad tracks with a companion wearing a plaid jacket; the remaining picture was of the Milky Way or some astronomical galaxy.

My guess about the target pictures was that it would:

> deal with a foreign culture or people from a foreign culture . . . it may be something like a hippy culture within America which would be sort of like a foreign culture. . . . If I were to look for the unifying ones [themes], it would be the element of exotic or foreign culture, far-away places kind of thing. . . . I think the clothing is going to be somewhat unusual . . . somewhat distinctive and different.

Although my guess that a foreign culture or subculture and distinctive clothing was involved should have enabled me to fairly readily select a single corresponding picture if the pool had been sufficiently heterogeneous, the pictures in the pool were too thematically similar to make a correct differentiation. I did not get the necessary direct hit and the study was published as a failure to replicate my previously successful results.

Were the apparent stonewalling defenses erected at Wyoming impenetrable? I will ask the reader to judge whether the following material sounds like random responses to each nights' stimuli or whether it might represent some brief breakthroughs of ESP.

My first REM report on night 3 mentioned "some thing to do with a football game . . . there were a lot of girls playing . . . one of the girls on the team was somebody way back from grammar school."

My second REM report mentioned "some small steel balls with a horn . . . a lot of the ones who were pursuing this guy . . . were younger kids. . . . I had used it [horn] like a baseball bat and hit a small, round metal ball . . . toward a small girl."

My third REM report described

> a baseball game . . . these were a bunch of kids that were playing . . . . The team up at bat hit a real long ball . . . and the kid in front of me just caught that one beautifully
>
> Teenagers . . . there were maybe four or five of them in a row.
>
> A shift in scene, and it seemed like there was a bunch of teenagers again. . . . I was a teenager myself . . . and went out in the front yard.
>
> The scoutmaster . . . of the troop my kids are in . . . walked through . . . where all these kids were. . . . I was coming up and joking around with him.

My fourth REM report mentioned "something to do with the project with kids that you are all involved with here in the lab. . . . There was one image of a girl . . . parading around."

My fifth REM report mentioned "a bunch of kids cutting the grass. . . . One kid had just made one long swath through the grass."

My guess about the target picture was:

> The over-riding thing during the night was the constant kid reference, they were

either as boy scouts or as young kids or as teenagers . . . or this last one of young kids who were perhaps nine or ten years old. . . . So I would look for the picture then that involved a group of boys either playing baseball or some other sport . . . there should be quite a few boys not just an isolated one, there should be at least a half a dozen of them or so.

The target picture was a black and white photo showing six boys and a girl, probably aged about 8–12, laughing and strutting in sort of drum-major fashion across a large grassy area. They are in single file and several are carrying a baton with a small ball on the end. One boy has apparently thrown his baton into the air and is waiting to catch it.

My REM reports had repeatedly referred to a group of children, usually boys, but with an occasional reference to a girl, one of whom was "parading around." There was a reference to "four or five of them in a row," "joking around," one of them making "a beautiful catch," "small, round metal balls," a "yard" and "grass." All of these details were portrayed in the target picture.

Rechtschaffen's (1970) observations from his laboratory study of telepathic dreams was, "When they were hits, they were quite good. . . . A simple matching procedure does not take into account the very unlikely probability of such a specific correspondence" (p. 92).

I gave the target picture a rank of 1 and so did both judges. Foulkes also gave it a high rating in my fourth REM report that night. I dreamed he came into my room and said "Well, I thought I'd let you know, you really have been doing well tonight . . . then he was saying something like he thought I'd be pleased when I saw the pictures because he knew it was going extremely well."

The next experimental session was three nights later, the longest time interval between sessions. The target picture was a black and white photo of a woman, apparently a mental patient, sitting with her head and arms on top of her knees, which are drawn up to her chest. She is sitting on a very wide, wooden bench in front of a high plaster or cement wall with paint peeling from the ceiling.

My first REM report mentioned "an old, wooden chair. . . . I had the Negro girl try and sit on this and it just wasn't a very good fit. . . . Underground subway tracks . . . with the high, like concrete sides, along either side."

My second REM report mentioned

submitting articles for professional journals . . . specifically the *Journal of Consulting Psychology.*

We entered into this building and it turned out that it was a huge one inside and there were various kinds of seats possible . . . this girl said that she would like to sit in these other kinds, which looked like church pews and she sat there.

My third REM report mentioned "we are sort of looking around inside the house. There were some problems with it, it was an older house and there were some cracks in the ceiling."

My prediction about the target picture was:

it would be a somewhat unusual building . . . the interior of the one dream had the church pews. . . . I would look for something maybe to do then with houses or a little bit of an unusual something in the way of buildings or the interior of them. . . . As far as people . . . I see it more as one anticipated more people arriving but as yet they had not . . . you'd notice the number of empty seats more than you would the full ones. I don't think the picture would convey any set emotion in and of itself.... I think the picture would not be particularly unusual as far as the color ... there isn't very much activity in there ... the people are either just sitting there, or perhaps implied conversation, but I don't get any feeling of great motoric activity at all.

I and another judge gave a rank of 1 to the target picture but the other judge gave it a rank of 6. In view of my reasonably specific summary comments that the target picture would probably involve a relatively inactive scene like people sitting inside a building, the rating of 6 was surprising because the alternative pictures in the pool were: a colored photo of watermelon and other fruit; a colored photo of a boat crossing an expanse of water; a photo of a dead Civil War soldier lying on the ground next to a rifle; a photo of two bushmen getting ready to spear a gazelle surrounded by dogs; a colored postcard of a Chagall painting showing a couple, a large chicken, a blue Eiffel Tower, a musical instrument, and a goat's head all floating in the sky; a photo of some peasants in an outdoor setting dropping ballots into a large box; a photo of a young girl, about 5 or 6 years old, using a paint brush to color on a piece of paper with the name "Barbrah" written on it.

The familiar problem of nonheterogeneity also exists in this pool. Three pictures show foreign or ethnic themes (Eiffel Tower, bushmen, peasants); two show several animals; two show weapons (gun, spear) and a dead or soon to be dead figure; two show pieces of paper playing a central role in the picture (ballots, girl's drawing).

As predicted in my dream on that first night in Wyoming, "these experiments get to be very complicated" and "all sorts of unconsciously motivated mistakes" may be involved. Foulkes' later reflections on this study seem relevant.

> The replication attempt was unsuccessful. In retrospect, we may have erred too much on the side of "scientism" to the exclusion of creating conditions in which telepathy might reasonably (if it exists at all) be expected to flourish. It proved hard to escape the role of protector of scientific purity or guardian of the scientific morals. Were we sympathetic and encouraging observers, or scientific detectives out to prevent a crime from being committed before our very eyes? ... Particularly revealing personally was a brief moment of intrapsychic panic when it seemed as though some telepathic influence might be "coming through"—how could it be? Where had I failed to prevent a sensory leakage? Our subject [Van de Castle] clearly felt himself "on trial" before a not entirely sympathetic jury, and we also could not totally avoid the feeling that we too were on trial, with a favorable verdict for the subject raising doubts as to the scrupulosity of our judgment process.
>
> There is no place for sloppy dream research, whether on telepathy or anything else. But being rigorous is a different matter from insecurely flaunting one's rigor as we may have done in our first study (Ullman et al., 1973, p. 236).

When the experiment at Wyoming is referred to in assessing the status of ESP in dreams, I hope the previously unpublished information provided in this report will be useful in evaluating the appropriateness of labelling it as a "replication" or as a "failure."

APPENDIX D

A Group Approach
to the Anomalous Dream

by Montague Ullman

While awake, our view of ourselves is one in which we see and stress our autonomy, our individuality, our discreteness. We define our own boundaries and we try to work with them. What I'm suggesting, and which is not at all novel, is that our dreaming self is organized along a different principle. Our dreaming self is more concerned with the nature of our connections with *all* others. There is some part of our being that has never forgotten a basic truth, that in our waking lives throughout history we seem to have continuously lost sight of. The history of the human race, while awake, is a history of fragmentation. It's a history of separating people and communities of people in every possible conceivable way — geographically, nationally, religiously, politically.

Our sleeping self, I am proposing, is connected with the basic truth that we're all members of a single species and that while dreaming our concerns have to do with what has happened in the course of waking experience that interferes with, damages, impedes, obstructs or enhances these connections. While asleep, we seem about to drastically alter the way we experience space and time. While awake, we move through our lives in a sequential, linear moment-by-moment fashion with a point representing birth and another point the present moment. But when we go to sleep and begin to dream we create pictures of what's going on in our psyche from a point that, in terms of space and time, seems to be outside of our waking organization. We are able to recall events going deep into our past. The amount of information that can be gathered from the past is often greater than anything we're able to recall while awake. With this information available we can project much more accurately the implications of a present concern. If parapsychological data are valid, this scanning process does not seem to be limited to the individual.

We experience the dream as a series of images that move in relation to each other and seem to develop in some kind of a sequential pattern. Where do these images come from? We have to go back and define how we look upon the substrate. If the substrate has to be broader than the individual, then, to use an analogy, we're talking about some kind of psychic black hole of highly condensed information about ourselves and others that, under the conditions of sleep, we seem able to tap into and extract what we need to know about ourselves and others that is relevant to our immediate life situation. We have no way of processing that much information as quickly as is necessary under the conditions of dreaming, unless we process some of it all at once in terms of an image, and then process the images sequentially to capture all the information that's available to us. The dream is this first transformation out of an undefined information source. At times we come upon information that we have no right to know about in terms of waking causality and the natural space and time order of events.

When we awaken, this information undergoes a second transformation into what Shakespeare referred to as "words, words, words." Each of these transformations involves information loss. The dream has no way of capturing all the information in that original source. The waking state has no way of capturing all the information in the dreaming source. It is simply a remembrance, but a rich and significant one. Without going into all of the interesting qualities of our dream life, I'm going to emphasize what I think are the most important.

In the first place the imagery of our dreams comes out of feelings that reflect what is really going on in our lives at that time. Honesty is a quality of the images we create. Secondly, the images are concerned with the issues of connectivity, how human beings are connected with each other. Dreams deal with events that interfere with these connections. They reflect our concerns with maintaining and preserving these connections.

Dreams take as their starting point a recent emotionally intrusive event in our lives. At some time during the night the feeling residue of this event seems to trigger a backward scanning into the deepermost recesses or our remote memory system to retrieve those aspects of our past experience that are emotionally related to the current situation. As we have noted, the pictures that we come up with and that are experienced as our dream are honest reflections of our feelings at the moment and of their connection to events in our past. In effect, we have taken a series of true-to-life photographs of the relational field we find ourselves in at the time we are dreaming. It is a field that includes much more information about ourselves than is readily available to us in the waking state. The existence of psi in the dream suggest that, under certain circumstances, the scanning process extends beyond our spatial borders to pick up information clairvoyantly or telepathically and beyond our temporal limits to pick up information precognitively.

The pictures we form in our dreams are remarkable in a number of respects. We project ourselves out of our accustomed space-time ordering of events and seem able to view the entire range of our existence from a point outside our waking system. Whatever that perspective is, it is outside space and time as we experience those categories while awake. Furthermore, the images we come up with tend to be metaphorical rather than literal or direct reflections of our situation. While asleep, we transform our primitive imaging capacity into the distinctly human capacity for metaphor. We will refer to the metaphor of the dream image as the oneiric metaphor, in contrast to the metaphor of waking speech. The reason our dream images take this form has been dealt with elsewhere (Ullman, 1969, 1973). In brief, it derives from the vigilance hypothesis of dreaming, which holds that the dream images we form are primarily self-confrontational and function as emotional regulators of the state of arousal during the REM or dreaming period. While asleep we exist in a state of social isolation. It is important for us while in this state to assess what it is we feel in terms of the relative safety in remaining asleep. Metaphors express feelings and the metaphorical images of the dream mobilize and express a level of feeling appropriate to the nature and importance of the particular issue we are grappling with. The intensity of the feelings aroused by their metaphorical expression determines the outcome of the REM stage. Awakening occurs when the feelings mobilized cannot be contained within the sleep state and necessitate the return of the waking state and the protective social cushioning we experience in that state.

When psi effects occur during dreaming they will influence this monitoring process and if intense enough will produce awakening. Our model suggests that psi can enter the dream by way of metaphorical expression as well as enter directly.

What follows in this presentation is a consideration of the implications of these features of the dream for psi research. The views of the human condition awake and asleep are quite different and experimental strategies might be more productive if both dimensions of our existence were taken into account. In this appendix I will discuss a beginning investigation along these lines. My other three types of close encounters with psi in dreams (spontaneously, clinically and experimentally) have convinced me of the validity of this approach. Each of these experiences sheds a different kind of light on the paranormal dream but, taken together, they suggest that the properties of the dreaming phase of our existence are largely unexplored in their potential significance for the manifestation of psi. More specifically, the occurrence of psi in dreams suggests experimental approaches that are qualitatively different from those in general use.

Psi events seem to register changes in the same emotional field that the dreamer is preoccupied with. Were the focus of investigation to shift to this field, then efforts might be devoted to identifying and developing a psi favorable field. A psi effect that occurred within such a field would be spontaneous and unpredictable. Subject, agent and target could not be specified in advance. The subject, agent and target status would be identifiable only after the fact and would be derivative factors from an even larger field, all operating beyond the control of any one individual. Psi would then enter the dream as another means at the disposal of the dreamers for learning about and managing the state of their emotional connectedness to significant others. Psi derived imagery, as well as more intrinsically personal imagery, would be set in motion by the existence of the social disconnect that characterizes the dreaming state.

In our dreams we are presenting and transforming imagery. Let us look more closely at the oneiric image and explore some of its features that may have a bearing on the occurrence of psi. Imaging itself is a concrete mode of presentation that relies on form, color and, in general, the transmission of information at a sensory level. The transformation of the simple or literal image into a visual metaphor extends the range and heightens the informational impact of the image at a feeling level. In lower animals, if imagery does occur, and there is some indirect evidence that it does, the literal image probably suffices to monitor the level of arousal during the REM state. In humans, with sources of potential threat arising more in connection with more subtle changes in an emotional field, rather than the recall of actual danger in a physical field, the image transformed into metaphor serves as a more versatile adaptive mechanism for registering such effects. We have generally relied on the literal reflection of psi perceived events in dreams as a mode of detecting them. The possible relationship of psi events to the metaphorical transform is still to be explored.

The attributes of the oneiric image possibly related to psi events include:

(1) The source of the images in feelings. It is our feelings which mobilize the information we need either from our past or, paranormally, from external sources, to shed light on a current predicament. The feelings are then reflected back as metaphorically expressive imagery. The feeling tone now conveyed by these developed images assesses emotionally the relevance of the matter before us to our immediate future.

(2) Our dreams are future oriented and serve as indicators of what lies ahead emotionally as a consequence of certain recent events in our life. Psi events, especially as manifest in dreams, seem to have a predilection for future events.

(3) Our dreams are fundamentally concerned with the assessment of damage to, repair of, and enhancement of our connections to significant others. The same concern with connectedness may be said to hold for many manifestations of psi.

The Metaphorical Transform

The most interesting feature of our dream life, to my way of thinking, is the way that significant information is encoded in highly personal and often ingeniously crafted metaphors. Our dream life becomes manifest to us figuratively through the use of the visual metaphor. This involves the selection and restructuring of serially available imagery so that it can serve as a metaphorical carrier of meaning. The visual metaphor of the dream serves this purpose through the selection of an image or sequence of images that have an implicit similarity to events in the life of the dreamer. Our dreams may be thought of as metaphors in motion.

In general, metaphor links two separate domains and achieves its expressive power by the implied similarities involved in the linkage. The oneiric or dream metaphor does this by linking imagery generated in an imaginative domain in a sleeping subject to specific constellations of events that took place in the recent and past life of the dreamer. We usually assume that the memory of these events and the feelings associated with them are the starting point of the dream image. In fact we don't know where and when the metaphorical process begins. What we do know is that the oneiric metaphor is immediately available to the dreamer and with effortless skill the succeeding images unfold, adding depth and range to the original statement. There is no laborious search for the proper image, no hunting through the files to select the most appropriate one. It is simply there when it is needed, or so it seems. While most of the imagery emerges out of the recent and remote past of the dreamer the existence of the telepathic and precognitive dream suggests that any event anywhere in time and place can, on occasion, be recruited into metaphorical service for the dreamer.

The ready availability of appropriate visual metaphors for the dreamer suggests the possibility that not only do we experience events in our waking life, but we also screen them unconsciously for their metaphorical value. The ones we end up with in our dreams are those with either the greater metaphorical valence or the most recent or some combination of both. Perhaps the hypnagogic image has a bearing on this question. At one moment we are closer to the waking state and are aware of a succession of thoughts going through our mind. At the next instant we are closer to the sleeping state and there is the immediate appearance of the image metaphorically expressing the last thoughts we had. It seems to have come into being at the moment as a transformation of the waking event that stimulated that particular train of thought. The image then forms part of the visual metaphor repertoire of the dreamer that is available for use any time it may be needed.

Stated another way, there are two simultaneous ways of processing the passing streams of sensations we are subjected to. One is the familiar waking mode, the end point of which is the sense of order and understanding we come to about the world. The second way is to extract from the happenings around us their metaphorical potential and to express the result in the form of imagery which becomes available when we surrender the waking mode. The first mode is structured in and therefore limited by time and space. The second is structured more as a field extending in time and space with the greatest concentration of force being around the limited space-time frame of the individual, but with no sharp boundaries between that frame and the frame of others nor between past, present and future frames.

What we refer to as ESP would then be the manifestation of this force field as it manages to transcend the individual and reach into someone else's space-time or the future space-time of the same individual. A limited but suggestive analogy might be that of the electromagnetic field generated by an electrical current, the latter being the palpable structure of reality as we assume it to be and the former, what we might call the metaphorical psi field, being continuously generated by real events. Paranormal cognition is rarely, if ever, precisely on target. There is enough similarity to the real event to classify it as paranormal, but it is generally embedded in the idiosyncratic productions of the particular percipient.

What I am suggesting is that what we all recognize as the elusive aspect of the psi event may simply represent the emergence of a metaphorical statement in which the psi factor is one among many in the creation of the metaphor. Its frustrating elusive character then becomes an interesting allusive one. If the connection to metaphor is valid, the task of the investigator becomes somewhat more difficult. He or she has to use a double-barreled approach that will identify both psi and the metaphor.

A point worthy of note is how remarkably articulate we are in the figurative domain. We have the necessary visual metaphor immediately on hand. They are incredibly apt, ingeniously constructed and remarkably comprehensive. We are less articulate when we rely on words alone to describe our state of being (unless we revert to a metaphorical mode as the poet does). Perhaps we should modify our analogy and view the metaphorical psi field as primary and the linguistic discursive mode as secondary. Metaphors, which often originate in dreams, do provide the rich and fertile soil of language. Metaphor is the initial way of grasping on to something felt and something in need of gaining expression. When a metaphor is newly created it is alive in contrast to the dead ones which have already passed into everyday speech. The live metaphor offers a creative jolt to the literalness of language. It makes use of our versatility with language but is never quite reducible to the literalness of language. There remains something ineffable about the metaphor whether it be of the poet or of the dreamer. The same is true when we deal with a metaphor that encapsulates a psi event. We know it is true but we know it is not true in a literal sense and cannot be reduced to a state of literalness.

The newly generated metaphor has a creative, living thrust. There are two processes that came together in its birth. There would have to be a selection process to ascertain what it is that has to be expressed, and then a choice has to be made of the most suitable vehicle. Both these processes have potential theoretical linkages to the operation of psi. A psi effect can be thought of as a kind of information scanning process and one that often uses imagery as the vehicle. There are shared end-points in each instance; namely, a heightened feeling response and a sense of an opening to larger vistas—a sense of moving into unexplained territory and going beyond the self. A powerful and original metaphor, when it first arrives on the scene, does seem to connect the creator and all those affected by it to a universe larger than the self. It propels us deeper into that universe in an ineffable and feeling way rather than in a rational and logical way. If science carried us into the future in discrete steps, the metaphor does it by setting off an unending set of ripples that may diminish in amplitude, but never quite fades out. Shakespeare offered us a supply that will last for an eternity.

Dreaming is the metaphor-creating state *par excellence*. It is also a state quite conducive to the spontaneous generation of psi. We have made very little of the possible relationship between the two. Is our capacity to zero in on just the right image to serve our metaphorical needs cut from the same cloth as our ability to paranormally apprehend an event that would otherwise be beyond our reach? I have suggested that to some extent a psi event is a psi event because of its metaphorical potential. Perhaps when a reality constellation is as good a metaphor for both subject and agent, a psi event occurs. Or, perhaps the psi connections are ever-present, but it takes a metaphorical spark to make them explicit.

In summary, what I am saying about the connection of the oneiric image and psi is that it has to be viewed as part of a more general metaphorical way of processing ongoing events. Our feelings are the starting point for this flow of imagery. It is our feelings which mobilize—and on the basis of emotional rather than logical contiguity—the information we need either from our past or, paranormally, from external sources, in the construction of the metaphorical image. In the course of dreaming those metaphorical images emerge which express, reflect and shed light on our current predicament. The creation and deployment of the visual metaphor is a remarkably powerful way of revealing, at a feeling level, where we are in relation to these issues and the impact of recent events in our lives upon them. In our dreams we give visibility to the emotional components of the interpersonal fields of greatest importance to us. The potential for psi events is intrinsic to this field but hardly ever actualized, perhaps because of our underdeveloped sense of the reality of psi.

The Use of the Experiential Dream Group as a Psi Facilitating System

Based on the point of view developed above it seemed essential to address the task of working out a waking approach to dreams that could help both to stimulate and to identify psi effects. The goal was to take into account the nocturnal and the diurnal dimensions of human existence and the varying degree of openness to psi that characterized each state. In recent years I have been developing and exploring a small group approach to experiential dream work as a way of bringing people into a close, honest and helpful relationship to the images they create at night. The question to be explored was whether or not, in bringing people closer to their dreams, we could at the same time generate psi effects and bring them closer to this recognition.

The Experiential Dream Group

The process involved in experiential dream group work is not given in detail in this paper. In brief, it rests on the principle that an interested and concerned social response system is necessary to help dreamers connect with the images they have created. The group carries out this task by assuming the role of a helping agency, rather than as an outside authority with access to specialized knowledge about the dream.

In its way of functioning the group follows the natural contours of the dream. These include (1) Respecting the dreamer's authority over his or her dream. (2) Respecting the privacy of the dreamer and the private realms touched on by the dream. (3) Respecting the uniqueness of each dream and of the dreamer.

In practice this means (1) That the dreamer controls the process and is the final judge of any meanings given to the image. (2) That the dreamer controls the level of self-disclosure one feels comfortable with and is not pushed beyond that level. (3) That no a priori categories of meanings are superimposed on the dreamer. Only the meanings felt by the dreamer to be true are true.

Rationale

Experiential dream work generates emotional closeness among the participants. It is expected that this developing rapport in combination with the natural psi facilitating effect of the dream itself, would result in an increasing number of identifiable psi occurrences among the members of the group. It represents, in effect, a two-pronged approach that attempts to generate psi through sharing waking and dreaming experiences. We rely on the orientation and interest of the group in psi to capture psi events in the nondual mode of the dream state and then to heighten the possibility of interactive psi events among members of the group through experiential dream work and the sharing of dreams. The emotional set of the group and the challenging novelty of each dream heightens the expectancy level of the possibility of psi occurring in dreams and prevents the process from ever lapsing into a stereotyped or repetitive pattern. The procedure lacks any formal experimental design features and maintains an air of challenge, curiosity and spontaneity. At the same time deep and significant motivational patterns are exposed and shared.

Procedure

Every member of the group has had prior exposure to the experiential group approach to dreams. Meetings of the group occur weekly for approximately one and a half hours. There has been a nucleus of five, although at times as many as seven or eight have participated. Dream diaries are kept by each member. The dreams of each week are typed, copied and distributed at each meeting. Time is set aside to review and compare the dreams of others to his or her own dreams as well as to look for correspondence among the dreams of others. From this point on the process evolves quite informally. It may move into an experiential process around a particular dream or we may begin by pointing up and exploring what strikes us as interesting correspondence. We tend to move into the experiential work with a dream if someone feels some urgency to get help from the group with a particular dream; otherwise, we would be more involved in checking each other's dreams for correspondences, noting any correspondences between the dreams of others and events in our own lives and any correspondences between our dreams and paranormally apprehended events in our own lives.

In the process of exploring such correspondences we might shift into the experiential mode to deepen our understanding of the imagery in question. The experiential work exposes any correspondence at a metaphorical level; the dream sharing any correspondences at a literal or manifest content level, and the dream recording any psi correpondences between the dreaming and waking life of the dreamer. We are engaged in a collective fashion in a process that maximizes the psi retrieval aspects of dreaming. Just as the Toronto group (Owen with Sparrow, 1976) seemed to get physical effects with a table through their collective expectations that, somehow or other, they could get Philip's ghost to produce such effects, so we developed a collective set with regard to the occurrence of ESP effects. A light and informal spirit prevailed and excitement mounted whenever we seemed to be in pursuit of a suggestive correspondence. Our judgments of correspondences remain purely subjective. No blind or objective judging procedure has been introduced. No target is stipulated in advance nor are percipient-agent relationships designated in advance. While this leaves wide open the possibility of reading the likelihood of some extra-chance factors into the correspondences, it was our hope that a few of them would be striking enough or occur often enough to survive this bias. At any rate, at this exploratory stage no design features for blind judging have been introduced.

Results

Since there was no advance structuring of what kind of correspondence to look for, we were using a wide net to capture correspondences along a variety of axes, such as, for example:

(1) Correspondences among the dreams of two or more group members.

(2) Correspondences between the dream and the lives of one or more members of the group other than the dreamer.

(3) Correspondences, telepathic or precognitive, between the dream and events in the life of the dreamer.

The correspondences at this stage in the evolution of the group are no more than suggestive. When noted, they would provoke interest and further exploration with the goal in mind, not of pinpointing their evidential value, but as a way of maintaining a high level of excitement about and engagement with work we were doing. We were inviting psi occurrences, so to speak, in a relaxed, playful way, rather than with a quantitative concern with the evidentiality of the data. Our hope is that, if the group can continue to generate enough data, the qualitative results would speak for themselves.

Example I. Dream to dream

On April 9, 1978, I had the following dream:

> There were preparations for a large scale dinner meal for 150 people. Some people felt the meal would be stereotyped and wanted more variety than could be arranged for so many.

The same night Barbara had this dream:

> Food is laid out on several tables — varied gourmet foods. It seems as though this has been done in Tom's honor. I am there as his guest. I am sampling foods and they are delicious. It occurs to me that this is wasted as far as Tom is concerned as he is a picky eater. I then see an image of Tom with a sort of webbing (iridescent) going out from him all around. This is to symbolize the way his eating pickiness is related to many other areas of his life. I wake up thinking how true this is.

While references to food are not uncommon in dreams, they were not particularly characteristic of Barbara's or my dreams.

The suggestive points here are:

(1) The dreams occurred the same night.

(2) They both involve or imply a large scale meal.

(3) In each case there was some kind of complaint or implied complaint.

Example II. Dream to reality involving the group

In this instance the correspondence was a bit more unusual. It linked a dream occurring on the morning the group met to an unexpected event involving the group later that day.

Barbara's dream of Dec. 1, 1977:

> It was just like a scene. I didn't have the feeling of being inside. There was a man talking to me from behind a counter. There were bare shelves. Nothing was finished off. There were three pair of eyeglasses. All had the right lens removed, like a monocle. One pair had very small hexagon lenses, down low like Thomas Edison's. Also a jeweler's eye piece. There was something about an Oriental who sounded Italian giving an explanation or directive.

Shortly before (half an hour) the group was to come together for its regular weekly meeting at the American Society for Psychical Research, I ran into John Cutten, the former executive secretary of the British Society. Cutten had spent the night at the Society. I hadn't known he was in town. I extended an invitation to join our research group meeting and he accepted. His ears perked up on hearing Barbara recount her dream. He confided that the left lens of his eyeglasses was a dummy so that, in effect, he had only one lens. He also remarked that he had recently given a talk to foreign students, among whom were several Chinese students. One of them asked him why there were more haunted houses in England than anywhere else.

Barbara was listening to his account with growing interest and then commented: "England has always had a certain fascination for me. I feel somehow that their attitude and their history is more connected with psi. I visited England three years ago and it is as if one were surrounded by old souls. Psi is in one's consciousness more than here."

Barbara then amplified some of the elements of her dream: "The man was someone of great wisdom, a guru type with knowledge to give me. The glasses were smoked. You couldn't see very much with them, but it was as if you had second sight. The monocle-like three pair of glasses and the jeweler's eyepiece were all connected. The man could see whatever he wanted to see. I connect the hexagonal lens with Edison, the inventor who shed light."

She added more about England: "I watched the British Jubilee and saw the Queen of England. The old buildings there were revered. I admired the places I visited, places where people had lived so long ago."

Barabara was questioned about the events in her life prior to the dream. "Last night an incident occurred in which I was teased about being a witch. My supervisor said to someone in my presence: 'She dreams of what goes on in your head.' I was very eager to get back to our meetings after the Thanksgiving vacation. Last night I was also thinking about the research on schizophrenia that I'm doing and the relevance of the right brain-left brain work."

In the dream Barbara had no feeling of being in the store, yet she was aware of the counter in front of her and the man on the other side. In the actual situation, as it turned out, Barbara was seated at a table directly opposite Mr. Cutten.

Here, of course, the most striking feature was related to the unusual eyeglasses in the dream and, in reality, with a number of less striking supporting features. Barbara has been the one in the group most consistently involved in presumptive psi effects.

None of the presumptively psi exchanges between Barbara and myself were directly on target. They were all tantalizingly suggestive, feeling truer to the participants than they are apt to strike an outside observer. I think this is so because, however slight the surface correspondences may seem, they set off resonating effects at deeper levels in the involved parties. While that is hard to evaluate with any degree of objectivity it is a definite felt reaction that has to be taken into account in judging whether the seeming coincidence is or is not meaningful. The following is an example:

Example III
My dream: Thursday, January 7, 1982
Something about Groucho Marx and surprised to see him looking so young.

Life events:
The Marx Brothers have always been favorites of mine, particularly Groucho. I could think of no reason why he turned up in my dream that night. Here are Barbara's comments on Thursday, January 8th, when we met to review our dreams.

> On the evening of January 6th (the night I had the dream — M.U.) I was talking to my neighbor and telling him of a birthday party I had had four years ago. I had decided to give myself a birthday party and to invite whomever I wanted. At the time I invited them I also told each guest what I wanted each one to bring, something I felt was appropriate for that person to do or bring. I asked one young friend to write a poem, which he did. He also came in with a package. It was a framed picture of Groucho Marx which was taken when he was much younger. This gift referred to a special incident that had occurred between us. There is a hole in the wall beside the door in my house which had originally housed an intercom. He had earlier noticed that unseemly sight and had brought the picture so that I could hang it over the wall to cover the hole. Last night I was telling my neighbor about it and having a good laugh over it. This morning (January 8th) I had noticed a thick layer of dust on the frame of Groucho's picture. I took it down. With the picture off I could hear what was said in my neighbor's living room.

This incident, including Groucho as a metaphor, was replete with possibilities for me, possibilities that I just hint at, since they are too private to be explicit about. In his films Groucho usually had a way with women or thought he did. The relationship of the location of the picture to an old and unused communicational channel is also of interest. The link to a communication device has often been associated with the appearance of psi in a dream.

Discussion

The approach described is only a beginning in the use of dreams as a psi retrieval mechanism under conditions which are in keeping with the nature of dreams themselves. This involves working along lines that link the dream to waking life and providing the kind of social support system that helps the dreamer get at the meanings embedded in the imagery. Work carried out in this manner results in emphatic and intimate bonding among the people involved and creates conditions that stimulate psi interactions among the participants.

Since dream images are metaphorical in intent, it has been of some interest to observe how the psi data related to the metaphorical structure of the dream images. In the work on experimental dream telepathy there were many examples of how one or another property of the target would find its way into the dream of the percipient in a metaphorically amplified way, e.g., the bronze color of Gauguin's native women appearing in the dream of the percipient as the danger of becoming too sunburned or where the free hand drawing of an acute angle appeared metaphorically elaborated as canes in the shape of hockey sticks in the hands of men at a cocktail party (Ullman, Krippner, with Vaughan, 1973). In Example II, the single lens and concern with single eyepieces and glasses with one lens were metaphorically conveying a different or second sight way of knowing. These examples from our dream group are remarkably similar to examples that emerged in our laboratory work at Maimonides Medical Center.

There are many problems to be overcome before this can be said to be a workable technique. Uppermost is the problem of dealing with the level of complexity of the data that are reviewed each week. This includes the dreams of all the participants during the prior week and the personal disclosure stimulated by the dream sharing. Secondly, the evidentiality of the data themselves will have to be established on a firmer basis.

In the anecdotal literature there is often evidence of the existence of a highly charged field involved in the psi event. The same is true, but for different reasons, in the field that characterizes the appearance of psi clinically. Working in the laboratory we are generally dealing with low level effects as far as the field is concerned, which is perhaps the reason the data appear so much less striking qualitatively. We have much to learn about the evolution of a psi conducive emotional field and the factors that determine the critical psi event. The approach we have described is one way of integrating the sleeping and waking dimensions of our experience in the interest of generating this field.

Conclusions

Psi has long been considered an unconscious form of communication that often undergoes some degree of distortion before reaching consciousness. There have been efforts to test the notion of unconscious psi effects, but these have generally been designed within the framework of the traditional agent-target-subject test situation. Assuming that psi is not only an unconscious process, but also a field effect, as Murphy and others have proposed, an investigative procedure has been followed in which the emphasis is placed on the generation of a psi facilitating emotional field. Dream sharing and experiential work with dreams in a group setting were used as the means of generating such a field. This paper reports on a pilot study that was designed to explore the use of dream work in a small group setting as a way of establishing natural psi linkages. The group has worked together over the past two years, meeting weekly, sharing dreams through an experiential process designed by the author. Psi linkages were noted as they occurred spontaneously, and examples of such linkages are given.

Note: Much of this material has been adapted from two previous articles (Ullman, 1979, 1984).

REFERENCES

Chapter 1

Cicero's Complaint

1. H. Brughsch-Bey, "The Dream of King Thutmes IV," R. L. Woods (ed.), *The World of Dreams* (New York: Random House, 1947), pp. 48–50.

2. J. Ehrenwald, "Precognition, Prophecy, and Self-Fulfillment in Greco-Roman, Hebrew, and Aztec Antiquity," *International Journal of Parapsychology* **9** (1967): 228.

3. R. Hill (ed.), *Such Stuff as Dreams* (London: R. Hart-Davis, 1967), p. 30.

4. H. L. Cayce, *Dreams: The Language of the Unconscious* (Virginia Beach, Va.: A.R.E. [Association for Research and Enlightenment] Press, 1962), pp. 26–27.

5. Hill, *op. cit.,* p. 7.

6. Cicero, "Argument Against Taking Dreams Seriously," Woods, *op. cit.,* pp. 203–204.

Chapter 2

Sifting the Evidence

1. L. L. Vasiliev, *Mysterious Phenomena of the Human Psyche,* translated by S. Volochova (New Hyde Park, N.Y.: University Books, 1965), pp. 11–34.

2. E. Gurney, F. W. H. Myers, and F. Podmore, *Phantasms of the Living,* 2 vols. (London: Trubner, 1886; reprint edition Gainesville, Fla.: Scholars' Facsimiles & Reprints), vol. 1, pp. 299–300.

3. *Ibid.,* vol. I, pp. 343–344.

4, *Ibid.,* vol. I, pp. 383–385.

5. *Ibid.,* vol. I, p. 385.

6. *Ibid.,* vol. II, p. 700.

7. G. B. Ermacora, "Telepathic Dreams Experimentally Induced," *Proceedings SPR* **11** (1895):235–308.

8. F. W. H. Myers, *Human Personality and Its Survival of Bodily Death,* 2 vols. (London: Longmans, Green, 1903).

9. G. N. M. Tyrrell, *Science and Psychical Phenomena* (New Hyde Park, N.Y.: University Books, 1961), pp. 24–25.

10. Compare with the cases recorded by J. C. Barker in "Premonitions of the Aberfan Disaster," *Journal SPR* **44** (1967): 169–180.

11. I. Stevenson, "Telepathic Impressions: A Review and Report of Thirty-Five New Cases," *Proceedings ASPR* **29** (1970): 172–178.

12. *Ibid.*, pp. 1–2. L. E. Rhine, *Hidden Channels of the Mind* (New York: William Sloane, 1961).

Chapter 3

ESP on the Couch

1. S. Freud, *Psychopathology of Everyday Life,* translated by A. A. Brill (New York: New American Library Mentor Books, reprinted 1956), p. 156.

2. S. Freud, "Psychoanalysis and Telepathy," G. Devereux (ed.), *Psychoanalysis and the Occult* (New York: International Universities Press, 1953), pp. 58–60.

3. S. Freud, "Dreams and Telepathy," Devereux, *op. cit.,* pp. 69–86.

4. S. Freud, "Dreams and the Occult," Devereux, *op. cit.,* p. 108.

5. C. Tabori, *My Occult Diary* (1951), as quoted by M. Ebon, *They Knew the Unknown* (New York: World, 1971), p. 153.

6. J. Eisenbud, "Telepathy and Problems of Psychoanalysis," Devereux, *op. cit.,* p. 259.

7. The letters exchanged between Ferenczi and Freud are unpublished but available on microfilm at the Freud Archives in Washington, D.C.

8. N. Fodor, *Between Two Worlds* (New York: Paperback Library, 1967), pp. 45–46.

9. C. G. Jung, "Synchronicity: An Acausal Connecting Principle," C. G. Jung and W. Pauli, *The Interpretation of Nature and the Psyche* (New York: Pantheon Books, 1955), p. 38.

10. *Ibid.,* p. 41.

11. *Ibid.,* p. 44.

12. M. L. von Franz, "Time and Synchronicity in Analytical Psychology," J. T. Fraser (ed.), *The Voices of Time* (New York: Braziller, 1966), p. 222.

13. G. Pederson-Krag, "Telepathy and Repression," Devereux, *op. cit.,* p. 259.

14. N. Fodor, *New Approaches to Dream Interpretation* (New York: Citadel, 1952).

15. G. Devereux, "The Eisenbud-Pederson-Krag-Fodor-Ellis Controversy," *op. cit.,* Part V, pp. 223–372.

16. A. Ellis, "Comments on the Discussants' Remarks," Devereux, *op. cit.,* p. 337.

17. J. Ehrenwald, *New Dimensions of Deep Analysis* (New York: Grune & Stratton, 1954), p. 241.

18. *Ibid.*, pp. 37–50.

19. *Ibid.*, pp. 247–249.

20. *Ibid.*, pp. 248–249.

21. J. Eisenbud, *Psi and Psychoanalysis* (New York: Grune & Stratton, 1970), p. 329.

22. E. Servadio, "Psychoanalysis and Parapsychology," J. R. Smythies (ed.), *Science and ESP* (New York: Humanities Press, 1967), p. 260.

Chapter 4

The Alcoholic Cat

1. K. E. Bates and M. Newton, "An Experimental Study of ESP Capacity in Mental Patients," *Journal of Parapsychology* **15** (1951): 271–277.

Chapter 5

Early Explorations: From "Raf" to Ralph

1. L. A. Dale, Letter, *Journal ASPR* **37** (1943): 95–101.

2. W. Carington, *Thought Transference* (New York: Creative Age Press, 1946).

3. J. T. Fraser (ed.), *The Voices of Time* (New York: Brazillier, 1966).

Chapter 6

Moving Eye Witnesses

1. E. Aserinsky and N. Kleitman, "Regularly Occurring Periods of Eye Motility and Concomitant Phenomena During Sleep," *Science* **118** (1953): 273–274.

2. L. L. Vasiliev, *Experiments in Mental Suggestion* (Church Crookham, England: Institute for the Study of Mental Images, 1963).

3. C. Trillin, "The Third State of Existence," *The New Yorker,* September 18, 1965: 65.

4. H. Keller, "The World I Live In," R. L. Woods (ed.), *The World of Dreams* (New York: Random House, 1947), p. 930.

5. J. M. Stoyva, "Posthypnotically Suggested Dreams and the Sleep Cycle," C. S. Moss (ed.), *The Hypnotic Investigation of Dreams* (New York: John Wiley, 1967), pp. 255–268.

6. C. Tart, "The Control of Nocturnal Dreaming by Means of Posthypnotic Suggestion," *International Journal of Parapsychology* **9** (1967): 184–189.

7. R. Berger, "Experimental Modification of Dream Content by Meaningful Verbal Stimuli," *British Journal of Psychiatry* **109** (1963): 722–740.

8. E. Green, *Biofeedback for Mind-Body Self-Regulation: Healing and Creativity* (Los Altos, Calif.: The Academy of Parapsychology and Medicine, 1972).

Chapter 7

A Dream Comes to Life

1. E. J. Garrett, *Telepathy* (New York: Creative Age Press, 1941), pp. 70–71.

2. This and subsequent quotations from dreams are taken from transcripts on file at the Maimonides Dream Laboratory.

3. H. Carrington, *The Case for Psychic Survival* (New York: Crown, 1957), pp. 136–137.

4. G. R. Schmeidler, "Separating the Sheep from the Goats," *Journal ASPR* **39** (1945): 47–49.

Chapter 8

A Dream Grows in Brooklyn

1. C. Tart, "The Control of Nocturnal Dreaming by Means of Posthypnotic Suggestion," *International Journal of Parapsychology* **9** (1967): 185.

Chapter 9

"Color His Wounds Red"

1. C. S. Hall and R. L. Van de Castle, *The Content Analysis of Dreams* (New York: Appleton-Century-Crofts, 1966).

Chapter 11

"The Prince of the Percipients"

1. C. S. Hall, "Experimente zur Telepathischen Beeinflussung von Träumen" ("Experiments with Telepathically Influenced Dreams"), *Zeitschrift für Parapsychologie und Grenzgebiete der Psychologie* **10** (1967): 18–47.
2. C. Akers in S. Krippner (ed.), *Advances in Parapsychological Research, Vol. 4* (Jefferson, N.C.: McFarland, 1984), pp. 112–164.

Chapter 12

One-Night Stands

1. D. Carlson, "The Beginnings of Chester Carlson's Interest in Parapsychology," Lecture Forum Honoring the Memory of Chester F. Carlson, *Proceedings ASPR* **28** (1969): 5–10.
2. M. Ebon, *They Knew the Unknown* (New York: World, 1971), p. 135.

Chapter 13

Long-Distance "Sensory Bombardment"

1. A. Vaughan, "Psychenauts of Inner Space: R. E. L. Masters and Jean Houston," *Psychic* **1** (1970): 9–13.
2. T. Moss and J. A. Gengerelli, "Telepathy and Emotional Stimuli: A Controlled Experiment," *Journal of Abnormal Psychology* **72** (1967): 341–348.

3. S. Krippner, C. Honorton, M. Ullman, R. Masters, and J. Houston, "A Long-Distance 'Sensory Bombardment' Study of ESP in Dreams," *Journal ASPR* **65** (1971): 468–475.

4. S. Krippner and R. Davidson, "The Use of Convergent Operations in Bio-Information Research," *Journal for the Study of Consciousness* **5** (1972): 64–76.

5. E. Mitchell, "An ESP Test from Apollo 14," *Journal of Parapsycholgoy* **35** (1971): 89–107.

Chapter 14

Dreaming of Things to Come

1. I. Stevenson, "Precognition of Disasters," *Journal ASPR* **64** (1970): 187–210.

2. These dreams have been reviewed by Krippner in his article "The Paranormal Dream and Man's Pliable Future," *Psychoanalytic Review* **56** (1969): 28–43.

3. H. Greenhouse, *Premonitions: A Leap into the Future* (New York: Bernard Geis Associates, 1972), p. 20.

4. C. Honorton, "Automated Forced-Choice Precognition Tests with a 'Sensitive,'" *Journal ASPR* **65** (1971): 476–481.

5. M. P. Jackson, "Suggestions for a Controlled Experiment to Test Precognition in Dreams," *Journal ASPR* **61** (1967): 346–353.

6. S. Krippner, M. Ullman, and C. Honorton, "A Precognitive Dream Study with a Single Subject," *Journal ASPR* **65** (1971): 192–203.

7. S. Krippner, C. Honorton, and M. Ullman, "A Second Precognitive Dream Study with Malcolm Bessent," *Journal ASPR* **66** (1972): 269–279.

Chapter 15

Finding Out More About ESP

1. G. R. Schmeidler, personal communication, March 18, 1972.

Chapter 16

What Does It Mean?

1. S. Freud, "Dreaming and Telepathy," G. Devereux (ed.), *Psychoanalysis and the Occult* (New York: International Universities Press, 1953), p. 86.

2. C. Honorton, "A Preliminary Investigation of Hypnotically-Induced 'Clairvoyant' Dreams," *Journal ASPR* **63** (1969): 69–82.

3. R. L. Van de Castle, personal communication.

4. S. Freud, "Dreaming and Telepathy," Devereux, *op. cit.,* p. 86.

5. C. Honorton, "Tracing ESP Through Altered States of Consciousness," *Psychic* **2** (1970): 18–22.

6. *Ibid.,* p. 19.

7. C. S. Hall and R. L. Van de Castle, *The Content Analysis of Dreams* (New York: Appleton-Century-Crofts, 1966).

8. E. Belvedere & D. Foulkes, "Telepathy in Dreams: A Failure to Replicate," *Perceptual and Motor Skills* **33,** (1971): 783–789. Because this study is frequently cited in the literature, an account of its design and execution by Dr. Van de Castle is included in Appendix C.

9. R. L. Van de Castle, personal communication.

10. C. Burt, *Psychology and Psychical Research,* 17th F. W. H. Myers Memorial Lecture (London: SPR, 1968), p. 50.

11. S. Krippner, "Electrophysiological Studies of ESP in Dreams: Sex Differences in Seventy-four Telepathy Sessions," *Journal ASPR* **64** (1970): 277–285.

12. J. Prasad and I. Stevenson, "A Survey of Spontaneous Psychical Experiences in School Children of Uttar Pradesh, India," *International Journal of Parapsychology* **10** (1968): 241–261.

13. D. Foulkes, E. Belvedere, R. E. L. Masters, J. Houston, S. Krippner, C. Honorton, & M. Ullman, "Long-Distance 'Sensory Bombardment' ESP in Dreams: A Failure to Replicate," *Perceptual and Motor Skills* **35** (1972): 731–734.

14. R. L. Van de Castle, "The Study of GESP in a Group Setting by Means of Dreams," *Journal of Parapsychology* **35** (1971): 312.

15. R. L. Van de Castle. "An Investigation of Psi Abilities among the Cuna Indians of Panama," A. Angoff & D. Barth (eds.), *Parapsychology and Anthropology* (New York: Parapsychology Foundation, 1974), pp. 80–97.

16. C. Honorton, "Reported Frequency of Dream Recall and ESP," *Journal of the American Society for Psychical Research* **66** (1972): 369–374.

17. M. Johnson, "Relationship between Dream Recall and Scoring Direction," *Journal of Parapsychology* **32** (1968): 56–57.

18. E. Haraldsson, "Reported Dream Recall, Precognitive Dreams, and ESP," J. D. Morris, W. G. Roll, & R. G. Morris (eds.), *Research in Parapsychology 1974* (Metuchen, N.J.: Scarecrow Press, 1975), pp. 47–48.

19. I. Strauch, "Dreams and Psi in the Laboratory," R. Cavanna (ed.), *Psi Favorable States of Consciousness* (New York: Parapsychology Foundation, 1970), pp. 46–54.

20. G. G. Globus, P. H. Knapp, J. C. Skinner, & G. Healy, "An Appraisal of Telepathic Communication in Dreams," *Psychophysiology* **4** (1968): 365.

21. Dement, W. (1974). *Some Must Watch While Some Must Sleep,* San Francisco: W. H. Freeman.

22. A. Rechtschaffen, "Sleep and Dream States: An Experimental Design," R. Cavanna (ed.), *Psi Favorable States of Consciousness* (New York: Parapsychological Foundation, 1970), pp. 87–120.

23. I. L. Child, H. Kanthamani, & V. M. Sweeney, "A Simplified Experiment in Dream Telepathy," J. D. Morris, W. G. Roll, & R. L. Morris (eds.), *Research in Parapsychology 1976* (Metuchen, N.J.: Scarecrow Press, 1977), pp. 91–93.

24. B. Markwick & J. Beloff, "Dream States and ESP; A Distance Experiment with a Single Subject," W. G. Roll, J. Beloff, & R. A. White (eds.), *Research in Parapsychology 1982* (Metuchen, N.J.: Scarecrow Press, 1983), pp. 228–230.

25. H. Reed, (1985, September/October), "Dreaming for Mary," *Venture Inward,* pp. 14–19.

26. R. L. Van de Castle, "Sleep and Dreams," B. B. Wolman (ed.), *Handbook of Parapsychology* (New York: Van Nostrand Reinhold, 1977), pp. 493–494.

27. R. Hyman, "Maimonides Dream-Telepathy Experiments," *Skeptical Inquirer,* (Fall, 1986), pp. 91–92.

28. W. Braud, "Long-Distance and Presleep Telepathy," J. D. Morris, W. G. Roll, & R. L. Morris (eds.), *Research in Parapsychology 1976* (Metuchen, N.J.: Scarecrow Press, 1977), pp. 154–155.

29. R. A. White, S. Krippner, & M. Ullman, "Experimentally-Induced Telepathic Dreams with EEG-REM Monitoring: Some Manifest Content Variables Related to Psi Operation," H: Bender (ed.), *Papers Presented for the Eleventh Annual Convention of the Parapsychological Association* (Freiburg, West Germany: Institute für Grenzgebiete der Psychologie, 1968), pp. 431–433.

30. C. Honorton, M. Ullman, & S. Krippner, "Comparison of Extrasensory and Presleep Influences on Dreams," J.D. Morris, W. G. Roll, & R. L. Morris (eds.), *Research in Parapsychology 1974* (Metuchen, N.J.: Scarecrow Press, 1975), pp. 82–84.

31. C. Honorton & S. Harper, "Psi-Mediated Imagery and Ideation in an Experimental Procedure for Regulating Perceptual Input," *Journal of the American Society for Psychical Research* **68** (1974): 156–168.

32. G. Vogel, D. Foulkes, & H. Trosman, "Ego Functions and Dreaming During Sleep Onset," *Archives of General Psychiatry* **14** (1966), 238–248.

33. C. Honorton. "Psi and Internal Attention States." B. B. Wolman (ed.), *Handbook of Parapsychology* (New York: Van Nostrand Reinhold, 1977), pp. 435–472.

34. R. Hyman, "The Ganzfeld Psi Experiment: A Critical Appraisal," *Journal of Parapsychology* **49** (1975), pp. 3–49.

35. C. Honorton, "Meta-Analysis of Psi Ganzfeld Research: A Response to Hyman," *Journal of Parapsychology* **49** (1985), pp. 51–91.

36. R. G. Stanford, "Recent Ganzfeld-ESP Research: A Survey and Critical Analysis," S. Krippner (ed.), *Advances in Parapsychological Research, Volume 4* (Jefferson, N.C.: McFarland, 1984), pp. 83–111.

37. N. Sondow, "The Decline of Precognized Events with the Passage of Time: Evidence from Spontaneous Dreams," *Journal of the American Society for Psychical Research* **82**, 33–51, 1988.

38. D. Ryback, "Future Memory as Holographic Process: A Scientific Model for Psychic Dreams," *Journal of Creative Behavior* **20**, 283–295, 1986.

39. M. Persinger & S. Krippner, "Experimental Dream Telepathy-Clairvoyance and Geomagnetic Activity," D. Weiner & R. G. Nelson (eds.), *Research in Parapsychology 1986* (Metuchen, N.J.: Scarecrow Press, 1987), pp. 85–87.

40. G. Murphy, "Techniques and Status of Modern Parapsychology." Paper presented at the 137th Annual Meeting of the American Association for the Advancement of Science, Chicago, 1970.

41. A. Parker, *States of Mind: Altered States of Consciousness and ESP* (New York: Taplinger, 1975), p. 89.

Chapter 17

Sleep, Psyche, and Science

1. R. L. Van de Castle, *The Psychology of Dreaming* (New York: General Learning Press, 1971), p. 31.

Appendix B

Akers, C. (1984). Methodological criticisms of parapsychology. In S. Krippner (Ed.), *Advances in parapsychological research* (Vol. 4, pp. 112–164). Jefferson, NC: McFarland.

Alcock, J. E. (1981). *Parapsychology, science or magic? A psychological perspective.* New York: Pergamon Press.

Alcock, J. E. (1983). Bringing anomalies back into psychology. *Contemporary Psychology, 28,* 351–352.

Ayeroff, F., & Abelson, R. P. (1976). ESP and ESB: Belief in personal success at mental telepathy. *Journal of Personality and Social Psychology, 34,* 240–247.

Belvedere, E., & Foulkes, D. (1971). Telepathy and dreams: A failure to replicate. *Perceptual and Motor Skills, 33,* 783–789.

Blackmore, S. J. (1984). A psychological theory of the out-of-body experience. *Journal of Parapsychology, 48,* 201–218.

Bradley, J. V. (1981). Overconfidence in ignorant experts. *Bulletin of the Psychonomic Society, 17,* 82–84.

Bradley, J. V. (1984). Antinonrobustness: A case study in the sociology of science. *Bulletin of the Psychonomic Society, 22,* 463–466.

Braud, W. (1977). Long-distance dream and presleep telepathy. In J. D. Morris, W. G. Roll, & R. L. Morris (Eds.), *Research in parapsychology 1976* (pp. 154–155). Metuchen, NJ: Scarecrow.

Child, I. L., Kanthamani, H., & Sweeney, V. M. (1977). A simplified experiment in dream telepathy. In J. D. Morris, W. G. Roll, & R. L. Morris (Eds.), *Research in parapsychology 1976* (pp. 91–93). Metuchen, NJ: Scarecrow.

Crandall, J. E., & Hite, D. D. (1983). Psi-missing and displacement: Evidence for improperly focused psi? *Journal of the American Society for Psychical Research, 77,* 209–228.

Foulkes, D., Belvedere, E., Masters, R. E. L., Houston, J., Krippner, S., Honorton, C., & Ullman, M. (1972). Long-distance "sensory-bombardment" ESP in dreams: A failure to replicate. *Perceptual and Motor Skills, 35,* 731–734.

Globus, G., Knapp, P., Skinner, J., & Healey, J. (1968). An appraisal of telepathic communication in dreams. *Psychophysiology, 4,* 365.

Hall, C. (1967). Experimente zur telepathischen Beeinflussung von Träumen. [Experiments on telepathically influenced dreams]. *Zeitschrift für Parapsychologie und Grenzgebiete der Psychologie, 10,* 18–47.

Hansel, C. E. M. (1980). *ESP and parapsychology: A critical reevaluation.* Buffalo, NY: Prometheus.

Honorton, C., Krippner, S., & Ullman, M. (1972). Telepathic perception of art prints under two conditions. *Proceedings of the 80th Annual Convention of the American Psychological Association, 7,* 319–320.

Hyman, R. (1985). The ganzfeld psi experiment: A critical appraisal. *Journal of Parapsychology, 49,* 3–49.

Irwin, H. J. (1979). *Psi and the mind: An information processing approach.* Metuchen, NJ: Scarecrow.

Jahn, R. G. (1982). The persistent paradox of psychic phenomena: An engineering perspective. *Proceedings of the Institute of Electrical and Electronics Engineers, 70,* 136–170.

Krippner, S., Honorton, C., & Ullman, M. (1972). A second precognitive dream study with Malcolm Bessent. *Journal of the American Society for Psychical Research, 66,* 269–279.

Krippner, S., Honorton, C., & Ullman, M. (1973). An experiment in dream telepathy with "The Grateful Dead." *Journal of the American Society of Psychosomatic Dentistry and Medicine, 20,* 9–17.

Krippner, S., Honorton, C., Ullman, M., Masters, R., & Houston, J. (1971). A long-distance "sensory-bombardment" study of ESP in dreams. *Journal of the American Society for Psychical Research, 65,* 468–475.

Krippner, S., & Ullman, M. (1970). Telepathy and dreams: A controlled experiment with electroencephalogram-electro-oculogram monitoring. *Journal of Nervous and Mental Disease, 151,* 394–403.

Krippner, S., Ullman, M., & Honorton, C. (1971). A precognitive dream study with a single subject. *Journal of the American Society for Psychical Research, 65,* 192–203.

Lowry, R. (1981). Apparent PK effect on computer-generated random digit series. *Journal of the American Society for Psychical Research, 75,* 209–220.

Marks, D., & Kammann, R. (1980). *The psychology of the psychic.* Buffalo, NY: Prometheus.

Mosteller, F., & Bush, R. R. (1954). Selected quantitative techniques. In G. Lindzey (Ed.), *Handbook of social psychology* (Vol. 1, pp. 289–334). Cambridge, MA: Addison-Wesley.

Neher, A. (1980). *The psychology of transcendence.* Englewood Cliffs, NJ: Prentice-Hall.

Puthoff, H. E., & Targ, R. (1976). A perceptual channel for information transfer over kilometer distances: Historical perspective and recent research. *Proceedings of the Institute of Electrical and Electronic Engineers, 64,* 329–354.

Radin, D. I. (1982). Experimental attempts to influence pseudo-random number sequences. *Journal of the American Society for Psychical Research, 76,* 359–374.

Rechtschaffen, A. (1970). Sleep and dream states: An experimental design. In R. Cavanna (Ed.), *Psi favorable states of consciousness* (pp. 87–120). New York: Parapsychology Foundation.

Romm, E. G. (1977). When you give a closet occultist a Ph.D., what kind of research can you expect? *The Humanist, 37*(3), 12–15.

Rosenthal, R. (1984). *Meta-analytic procedures for social research.* Beverly Hills, CA: Sage.

Strauch, I. (1970). Dreams and psi in the laboratory. In R. Cavanna (Ed.), *Psi favorable states of consciousness* (pp. 46–54). New York: Parapsychology Foundation.

Ullman, M. (1969). Telepathy and dreams. *Experimental Medicine & Surgery, 27,* 19–38.

Ullman, M., & Krippner, S. (1969). A laboratory approach to the nocturnal dimension of paranormal experience: Report of a confirmatory study using the REM monitoring technique. *Biological Psychiatry, 1,* 259–270.

Ullman, M., & Krippner, S. (1978). Experimental dream studies. In M. Ebon (Ed.), *The Signet handbook of parapsychology* (pp. 409–422). New York: New American Library.

Ullman, M., Krippner, S., & Feldstein, S. (1966). Experimentally induced telepathic dreams: Two studies using EEG-REM monitoring technique. *International Journal of Neuropsychiatry, 2,* 420–437.

Ullman, M., Krippner, S., with Vaughan, A. (1973). *Dream telepathy.* New York: Macmillan.

Van de Castle, R. L. (1971). The study of GESP in a group setting by means of dreams. *Journal of Parapsychology, 35,* 312.

Wagner, M. W., & Monnet, M. (1979). Attitudes of college professors toward extra-sensory perception. *Zetetic Scholar,* no. 5, 7–16.

Wolman, B. B. (Ed.). (1977). *Handbook of parapsychology.* New York: Van Nostrand Reinhold.

Zusne, L., & Jones, W. H. (1982). *Anomalistic psychology: A study of extraordinary phenomena of behavior and experience.* Hillsdale, NJ: Erlbaum.

Appendix C

Argyris, C. (1968). Some unintended consequences of rigorous research. *Psychological Bulletin, 70,* 185–197.

Belvedere, E., & Foulkes, D. (1971). Telepathy and dreams: A failure to replicate. *Perceptual and Motor Skills, 33,* 783–789.

Child, I. L. (1985). Psychology and anomalous observations: The question of ESP in dreams. *American Psychologist, 40,* 1219–1230.

Hall, C. (1967). Experimente zur telepathischen Beeinflussung von Träumen. [Experiments on telepathically influenced dreams] *Zeitschrift für Parapsychologie und Grenzgebiete Psychologie, 10,* 18–47.

Hansel, C. E. M. (1980). *ESP and parapsychology: A critical re-evaluation.* Buffalo, NY: Prometheus.

Murphy, G. (1971). Introductory address. In D. Dean (Ed.), *Technique and status of modern parapsychology: AAAS Symposium* (pp. 3–4). Newark, NJ: Newark College of Engineering Press.

Rechtschaffen, A. (1970). Sleep and dream states: An experimental design. In R. Cavanna (Ed.), *Psi favorable states of consciousness* (pp. 87–120). New York: Parapsychology Foundation.

Reed, H. (1985). *Getting help from your dreams.* Virginia Beach, VA: Inner Vision Publishing.

Rhine, J. B. (1964). Special motivation in some exceptional ESP performances. *Journal of Parapsychology, 28,* 42–50.

Ullman, M., Krippner, S., with Vaughan, A. (1973). *Dream telepathy.* New York: Macmillan.

Ullman, M., & Krippner, S. (1970). *Dream studies and telepathy: An experimental approach.* New York: Parapsychology Foundation.

Van de Castle, R. L. (1977). Sleep and dreams. In B. Wolman (Ed.), *Handbook of Parapsychology* (pp. 473–499). New York: Van Nostrand Reinhold.

Van de Castle, R. L. (1971a). *Psychology of dreaming.* Morristown, NJ: General Learning Press.

Van de Castle, R. L. (1971b). The study of GESP in a group setting by means of dreams. *Journal of Parapsychology, 35,* 312.

Appendix D

Owen, I. M., with Sparrow, M. (1976). *Conjuring up Philip: An adventure in psychokinesis.* New York: Harper & Row.

Ullman, M. (1969). Dreaming as metaphor in motion. *Archives of General Psychiatry, 21,* 698–703.

Ullman, M. (1973). A theory of vigilance and dreaming. In V. Zikmund (Ed.), *The oculomotor system and brain functions: Proceedings of the International Colloquium held at Smolenice 19–11 October 1970* (pp. 455–466). London: Butterworths.

Ullman, M. (1979). Psi communication through dream sharing. In B. Shapin & L. Coly (Eds.), *Communication and parapsychology* (pp. 202–227). New York: Parapsychology Foundation.

Ullman, M. (1984). Dream, metaphor and psi. In R. A. White & R. Broughton (Eds.), *Research in parapsychology 1983* (pp. 138–152). Metuchen, NJ: Scarecrow Press.

Ullman, M., Krippner, S., with Vaughan, A. (1973). *Dream telepathy: Scientific experiments in nocturnal ESP.* New York: Macmillan.

Vaughan, C. J. (1966). The development and use of an operant technique to provide evidence for the visual imagery in rhesus monkeys under "sensory deprivation." *Dissertation Abstracts, 26,* 619.

Index

Adler, Alfred 26
Advice to a Young Artist (Daumier) 95
Age of Reason, denounced dream
  interpretation 6
Agent, role of 163
Agent-subject, rapport of 163–165
Aggressiveness, as dream theme 93, 112
Alcock, James 203–204, 205
Alcoholic cat 38
Alexander the Great 5
American Society for Psychical Research
  (ASPR) 29, 36, 45, 119
Analysts, responsibilities of 40
Animal neuroses 38
Animals (Tamayo) 75, 112
Anomalistic Psychology (Zusne and Jones)
  205
Apple Thiefs (Goya) 98
Apples and Oranges (Cézanne) 89
Archetypes 26
Aristander 5
Aristotle 5
Artemidorus of Daldis 5, 6
Asclepius (healing god) 5
Aserinsky, Eugene 58
Association for Research and Enlighten-
  ment 167
"Association theory" 46, 50
Attic Footrace (vase) 99, 100
Augustus 7

Balint, Michael 24
Barany, Robert 24
The Barrel Organ (Daumier) 91
Bauhaus Stairway (Schlemmer) 80

Beckman (artist) 93
Bedtime (Keane) 85
The Beer Drinkers (Daumier) 125
Belligerence, patient 40
Bellows (artist) 83, 92, 128
Beloff, John 168
Berger, Hans 58, 64
Bessent, Malcolm 131, 133, 135, 138,
  143–144, 161, 165, 166
Bible, dreams recorded in 4–5
Bichitir 16, 92
Bijin by a Waterfall (Harunobu) 122
Bisexuality 71–72
Biting, as dream theme 112, 113
Bohr, Neils 173
Boller (artist) 98
Bonnard (artist) 151
Booth, Gothard 29
Boston University School of Medicine
  167–168
Both Members of This Club (Bellows) 92,
  128
Braud, William 169
Brown, Harvey 14
Bruce, Walter 12–13, 14
Bruegel (artist) 154
Burne-Jones (artist) 124

Caesar 7
Capobianco, Michael 90
Carington, Whatley 46, 57, 68–69;
  association theory of 50, 70, 125
Carlson, Chester F. 119–120
Carlson, Dorris 119–120
Carrington, Hereward 69

Cayce, Edgar 6, 167
Cayce, Hugh Lynn 6
Cellini (artist) 116, 123
Cézanne (artist) 89, 114
Chagall (artist) 81, 85, 88, 101, 123, 125, 183
Chance: as factor in paranormal dreams 11, 23, 29, 50, 73, 117, 118, 145; in precognition experiments 144
Character defenses 176
Chester F. Carlson Research Laboratory 119
Child, Irvin 168, 209
Childbirth, as dream theme 134
Christ, as dream theme 86, 125, 129, 150-151
Church at Auvers (Van Gogh) 126
Churchill, Winston 94
Cicero, Marcus Tullius 3, 7-8, 28, 57
Clairvoyance 18, 57, 67, 121, 122, 123, 124, 142
Coincidence, of dreams 5
Collective consciousness 34
College of Psychic Studies (London) 128, 132
Color, in dreams 61, 162
Communication, use of telepathy for 40-41
Conflict resolution 175
Consciousness, altered states of 162
Content Analysis of Dreams (Hall and Van de Castle) 126, 139
Corn Poppies (Monet) 126
Correspondences in telepathic dreams 50, 53, 76-78, 79, 81, 82, 86, 89, 91, 92, 96, 111, 126, 150; chance in 73; interplay of 150
Crisis dreams 48-49
Crisis telepathy 49
The Crucifixion (Sutherland) 116

Dale, Laura A. 45; dreams of 45ff; precognition experiences 46
Dalí, Salvador 86, 88, 109, 146, 152
Danger, as dream theme 133
Daniel (in Bible) 4, 5
Daumier (artist) 91, 95, 122, 125, 163
Davidson, Richard 126, 131
Dean, E. Douglas 67, 70
Death, as dream theme 10, 11, 13, 20, 79, 113, 138
de Chirico 79, 98, 99, 114, 120, 127

Deflected ESP dreaming 150
Degas (artist) 88
Dement, William 168
Dempsey and Firpo (Bellows) 83
Departure, as dream theme 81, 127
Departure (Beckmann) 81
Departure of a Friend (de Chirico) 127
Descartes, René 173-174
Descent from the Cross (Beckmann) 93
Destructiveness, as dream theme 93
Detachment, analyst's 40
Dickens, Charles 6
Disaster, as dream theme 18-19, 20, 138
Discovery of America by Christopher Columbus (Dalí) 109
Distrust, patient 40
Downpour at Shono (Hiroshige) 91
Dream analysts, interaction of, with patient 34
Dream books, commercial success of 5
Dream creativity 179
Dream experiments 67-73, 74, 85-96, 97ff, 139ff; evaluation procedures of 76-78, 79, 87, 88, 89-90, 91, 93, 95, 98, 99, 136, 140-141; subject selection 75
Dream incubation 5
Dream interpretation 5; in ancient Rome 7; denounced during Age of Reason 6
Dream Laboratory, Maimonides 10, 74, 92, 97, 106, 107, 131, 138, 165, 166, 167, 169, 171, 192, 207, 209, 210
Dream Telepathy (Ullman, Krippner, Vaughan) 210
Dream themes: aggressiveness 93, 112; biting 112, 113; childbirth 134; Christ 86, 125, 129, 150-151; danger 138; death 10, 11, 13, 20, 79, 113, 138; departure 81, 127; destructiveness 93; disaster 18-19, 20, 138; drinking 101; emotions 20, 26; fighting 101; karate 113; lighting candle 79; Medusa 123, 124; murder 112; Perseus 123; pets 51; rain 92; religion 87, 88, 131, 162; schizophrenia 132; sex 30, 51-52, 70, 71, 72, 162; soldiers 93; stock market 6; strangling 113; suicide 111, 112; swimming 79; violence 92, 93, 104; water 79
Dreams (and see Dreams, telepathic following): "accommodating," by patients 30, 37-38; of analysts, by patients 27; ancient's use of, in diagnosing illness

5; archetypal 25, 30; of Biblical
Pharaoh 4; clairvoyant (*see* Clairvoyance); in color 61, 162; content of,
influenced by telepathy 85; as conveyor of ESP 19; correspondences, in
50, 53, 76–78, 79, 81, 82, 86, 89, 91,
92, 96, 111, 126, 150; crisis 49; difficulty in remembering 18; element of
chance in 11, 23, 29, 50, 73, 117, 118,
145; Freudian—interpretation of
26–27; Freudian—symbolism in 75; of
great men, lack of documentation for
5; as heightened state of vigilance 176;
inability to recall 61; induced 14–15;
influencing content of 30, 62–64, 70–
71; information arrangements of 173;
intrinsic properties of 175–176; latent
content of 70; manifest content 70; as
metaphors 177, 218–219, 220–222;
non-REM 64; occurrence of ESP in
65; outside stimulus 62–64; paranormal 9–10, 18, 73 (Freud on 22–23);
perception of the external world in 64;
physiology of 59–60; posthypnotic suggestions in 63; precognitive 18, 38,
136, 138, 144 (element of chance in experiments of 144; experimentally controlled 141); psychoanalytically interpreted 23; reasons for 60, recall of 61,
174; recorded in Bible 4–5; reflect
emotionally laden anxieties 26; REM
activity during 58–59, 64, 147–149;
simultaneous 3, 14, 48; stimulation for
62; symbolic content of 20, 30, 70,
94–95 (phallic 114); time acceleration
in 61–62; training to remember 61
Dreams, telepathic (*and see* Dreams *preceding*) 18–19, 37–38; advantage of
psychoanalytic situation for discovering 42; art prints used for 75–84, 85–
95, 97–105, 109–117, 120, 128, 131–136;
"building up" effect 159–160; coincidental events in 10–11; correspondences in
50, 53, 76–78, 79, 81, 82, 86, 89, 91,
92, 96, 111, 126, 150; definition of 57;
element of chance in 11, 23, 50, 73,
117, 118, 145; elements of, traced 23;
experiments 67–73, 74ff, 85–96, 97,
106– 107, 109–118, 139–144; increasing
scientific interest in 3; induced by
experimental means 15–17; monitoring
of 219; patients, use of, to communicate 40–41; psychology of 97;
rarity of 11; setting the stage for 42;
spontaneous

4, 8–20, 164; symbolism in 105; trivial
14; use of by patients to communicate
40–41
"Dreams and Telepathy" (Freud) 23
The Drinker (Chagall) 101, 125
Drinking, as dream theme 101
The Duelers (Goya) 101

Edison, Thomas 121
EEG *see* Electroencephalograph
Ehrenwald, Jan 5, 29, 30, 31, 32, 42,
130
Eisenbud, Jule 24, 28, 29, 32, 33, 42,
47; contributions of, to parapsycho-
logical literature 30; on telepathic pro-
cess 42
Electroencephalograph (EEG) 58, 67,
80, 85; new findings about 177
Ellis, Albert 28, 29, 30
Emotional bonds 20
Emotions, as dream theme 20, 26
The Engineer Heartfield (Grosz) 148
The Enigma of Fate (de Chirico) 114
Ermacora, G. B. 15, 16, 17; experiments
of 15–16, 17
Erwin, William 76, 85–96, 125, 166,
183, 199; dream reports of 183–190
ESP *see* Extrasensory perception
ESP: A Scientific Evaluation (Hansel)
201–203
Evasiveness, patient 40
Evergood (artist) 146
Extrasensory perception (ESP) 19, 24,
26, 38, 135, 137, 213; dreams as con-
veyors of 20, 177; experimental testing
of schizophrenics for 42; occurrence
of, in dreams 65; professional controversy over 28; as secondary communication system 42; spatial or temporal 25; spontaneous experiences of
23, 131, 132; synchronous 145

Fabergé (artist) 83
Fast, Howard 67, 68
Feldstein, Sol 74, 75ff, 82, 97, 100, 123,
125, 166; success of, as agent 82ff
Ferenczi, Sandor 24
Fielding, Jean Eleanora 14
Fighting, as dream theme 101
Fischer, Stuart 122

Fodor, Nandor 24, 28
Football Players (Rousseau) 80
Foulkes, David 160, 163, 165, 169, 202, 216
Foundation for Mind Research 130
Franz, M. L. von 26
Freiburg University Institute for Border Areas of Psychology 107, 145
Freud, Sigmund 22, 24; on analyst's responsibility 40; contribution of, to parapsychology 24; on occult phenomena 23, 24; on paranormal dreams 22-23; rejects precognition 24, 25; on telepathic stimulus 159, 161; traces telepathic elements of dreams 23

Gangster Funeral (Levine) 115
"Ganzfeld" theory 171
Garrett, Eileen 51, 66ff, 129, 138
Gauguin (artist) 79, 97
Girl Before the Mirror 110, 111
Globus, Gordon 167
Goya (artist) 98, 101
The Grateful Dead 134
Grayeb, Theresa 97-100, 166
Great Sphinx of Gizeh 4
Green, Elmer 65
Green Violinist (Chagall) 81, 123
Griffith, Mrs. Morris 11, 12
Grosz (artist) 148
Gurney, Edmund 10

Hall, Calvin 106, 107, 209, 210
Hansel, C. E. M. 201
Hanukkah Candelabrum (Boller) 98
Haraldsson, Erlander 167
Harris, Robert 126, 145ff
Harunobu (artist) 122
The Harvesters (Bruegel) 154
Hitler, Adolf 151
Homosexuality 71-72
Honorton, Charles 138, 141, 142, 154, 161, 167, 169, 170, 171, 172, 193
Hormakhu 4
Hospital Corridor at St. Rémy (Van Gogh) 140
Houston, Jean 130, 131
Howe, Elias 173
Human Personality (Myers) 17, 22
The Humanist (Romm) 204, 205

Hypnagogic imagery 169-170
Hypnopompic imagery 169-170
Hypnotic suggestion 62-63, 168

Incubation, dream 5
Institute for Dream Research 106, 209
Interior of the Synagogue (Katz) 95
International Psychoanalytic Congress 23
The Interpretation of Dreams (Freud) 22

Jackson, M. P. 139
James, William 15
The Jesters (Rousseau) 127
Johnson, Douglas 128-129, 131, 132, 134, 138
Johnson, Martin 167
Jones, Warren H. 200, 206, 207
Joseph (in book of Genesis) 4
Judging 76-78, 83-84, 89-90, 91
Jung, Carl G. 24-26, 29; on archetypes 26; on synchronicity 161

"K-object" (Carington) 46
Kammann, Richard 203
Karate, as dream theme 113
Kathak Dancing Girls 113
Katz (artist) 95
Keane, Walter 85
Kekulé, Friedrich 174
Keller, Helen 60-61
Kennedy, Robert 145
Kinder, Margaret 108, 109, 110
Kleitman, Nathaniel 58
Knight on Horseback (bronze aquamanale) 152
Krippner, Stanley 74, 83, 85, 102, 113, 122, 128, 129, 130, 140, 145, 171, 193

Laidlaw, Robert 29
Leger (artist) 152
Less-differentiated people 60
Levine (artist) 115
Lidsky, Barbara 108, 113, 114, 115
Lighting candle 79
Lily and the Sparrows (Evergood) 146

Love Song (de Chirico) 98
Luncheon (Bonnard) 151

Maimonides Dream Laboratory 10, 74, 97, 106, 107, 131, 138, 166, 167, 169, 171, 192, 207, 209, 210
Malamud, Judith 169
Man with Arrows and Companion (Bichitir) 116
Man with Violin (Picasso) 154
Manzini, Maria 15
Marks, David 203
Markwick, Betty 168
The Mask of Apollo (Renault) 95
Masserman, Jules 38
Masters, R. E. L. 130, 131
Maury, Alfred 61, 62
Medusa, as dream theme 123, 124
Meerloo, Joost 29, 50
Memories, subliminal 18
Menninger Foundation 65
Merry Jesters (Rousseau) 97
Mind Science Foundation (San Antonio TX) 169
Miree, Gayle 122, 128, 132, 145, 146, 150, 155
Mitchell, Edgar 137
Monet (artist) 126
The Moon and the Earth (Gauguin) 79, 97
More-differentiated people 60
Morris, Robert L. 143n, 144
Moss, Thelma 130
Mother and Child (Daumier) 122
Multisensory material 90
Murder, as dream theme 112
Murphy, Gardner 29, 45, 51, 172, 209, 210
"Mutual resonance" 159–160
Myers, Frederic W. H. 10, 17, 18, 22
Mystic Night (Sheets) 83
Myths 5

The Naval Barracks (de Chirico) 120
Nebuchadnezzar, dream of 4, 5
Neher, Andrew 203
Nelson, Robert 123
Neuroses, animal 38
New Dimensions of Deep Analysis (Ehrenwald) 30
New York Academy of Medicine 38
Numinousity 33

Occult phenomena, Freud on 23, 24
"On Divination" (Cicero) 7
Oneiromancy 4, 5
Oriental Warrior 97
Orozco 76
Osis, Karlis 67
"Out-of-the-body" experiences 168

Paranormal dreaming 10, 21, 73; Freud on 22–23
Parapsychology 9–10; critics of 97; Freud's contribution to 24; research at Maimonides Dream Laboratory 74
Parapsychology Foundation 51, 166; pilot experiments at 72
Paris Through a Window (Chagall) 88, 183
Parise, Felicia 127, 135, 136, 145, 152ff
Parker, Adrian 172
Pederson-Krag, Geraldine 27, 28, 29; on telepathic dreams 27
Penile erections 59
Penis envy 27
Percipient, qualities for 164–167
Perry, Norman 142
Perseus, as dream theme 123
The Perseus (Cellini) 116, 123
Perseus and the Graiae (Burne-Jones) 124
Persinger, Michael 171
The Persistence of Memory (Dalí) 88
Pets, as dream theme 51
Phallic symbolism 70, 114
Phantasms of the Living 10, 12, 14
Pharaoh (in book of Genesis) 4
Picasso, Pablo 81, 154
Plosky, Joyce 74, 80–81, 123
Podmore, Frank 10
The Pork Butcher (Daumier) 163
Portrait of Gala (Dalí) 146
Portrait of Jahangir as a Young Prince (Bichitir) 92
Posin, Robyn 83, 100–105, 120, 125
Posthypnotic suggestions 63
Powell, Dick 95
Prasad, Jamuna 164
Pratt, J. G. 19
Precognition 18, 38, 46, 57, 128; problems in designing experiments for 141; rejected by Freud 25; spontaneous 141
Precognitive dreams 18, 38, 136, 138, 144; experimentally controlled 142; element of chance in 144
Proceedings (of Society for Psychical Research) 19

Pseudo-paranormal experiences 22
Psi (psychic phenomena): patient
  response to 31; "psi vigilance" 178, 179;
  role played by, in psychodynamic in-
  teractions 72
Psi and Psychoanalysis (Eisenbud) 33
Psilocybin 147
Psychedelic drugs 135, 147
Psychical Research, Society for 10, 11
Psychoanalysis 22
"Psychoanalysis and Telepathy" (Freud)
  23
Psychokinetic phenomena 24
The Psychology of Transcendence (Neher)
  203
Psychology of the Psychic (Marks and
  Kammann) 203
Psychopathology of Everyday Life (Freud) 22
Psychophysical Research Laboratory 172

Rain, as dream theme 92
Rama, Swami 65
Rapid Eye Movements (REM) 58, 59,
  64, 117; controversies about 58–59;
  dreams and non-REM 64, 147–148;
  experimental discovery of 174; mental
  activity during 64; perception of exter-
  nal world during 64–65; physiological
  changes during 177
Rating scale in dream experiments 89
"Reanalysis of an Alleged Telepathic
  Dream" (Ellis) 29
Recall, dream 61, 174
Rechtschaffen, Alan 168, 211
Reed (artist) 147
Reed, Henry 168
"Regularly Occurring Periods of Eye
  Motility . . ." (Aserinsky and Kleitman)
  58
Religio-Philosophical Journal 12
Religion, as dream theme 87, 88, 131,
  162
REM *see* Rapid Eye Movements
REM-EEG dream monitoring technique
  61, 65, 66
Renault (artist) 95
The Repast of the Lion (Rousseau) 111
Resolution conflict 175
Rhine, J. B. 211
Richards, Betsy 52
Rivista di Studi Psichici (journal) 15
Robbins, Bernie 53

Rock Crystal Easter Egg (Fabergé) 83
Rome, superstition in ancient 8
Romm, Ethe l Grodzins 204, 205
Rorschach tests 111
Rousseau (artist) 79, 80, 97, 111, 127
Ryback, David 171

Sacrament of the Last Supper (Dalí) 86
The Sacred Fish (de Chirico) 79
Scanning activity 59
Schizophrenia 41, 53; as dream theme
  132
Schlemmer (artist) 80
Schmeidler, Gertrude 50, 51, 72, 150,
  165
Schneider, Diane 123, 126
School of the Dance (Degas) 88
Schwarz, Berthold E. 121
Science (journal) 58
Science and Psychical Phenomena (Tyrrell) 18
Scoring 76–78, 82n, 83–84, 89–90, 96
Scralian (artist) 135, 136
Sensory bombardment 130, 139; long-
  distance 134–135, 136
Servadio, Emilio 34
The Seven Spinal Chakras (Scralian) 135,
  136
Sex, as dream theme 30, 51–52, 70, 71,
  72, 162
"Sheep-goat" hypothesis (Schmeidler) 72
Sheets (artist) 83
Simultaneous dreams 14, 47
Skepticism 7
Sleep: as favorable state for telepathy 23;
  mental activity during 64; responding
  to outside stimuli during 64; stages of
  59
Sleep and Dream Laboratory (Univer-
  sity of Virginia) 106
The Sleeping Gypsy (Rousseau) 79
Sleeping Peasants (Picasso) 81
Smoot, Don 97–98
Snow Mountain (Chang Shu-Chi) 128, 151
Society for Psychical Research (SPR) 10,
  11
Soldiers, as dream theme 93
Sondow, Nancy 171
Spartacus (Fast) 67–68
Spontaneous telepathic dreams 4, 20,
  164
Stanford, Rex 171, 178
Starry Night (Van Gogh) 80, 81

States of Mind (Parker) 172
Steenburgh, Sally Van 83
Stevenson, Ian 19–20
Still Life with Three Puppies (Gauguin) 79
Stimulus, telepathic 64, 159–160
Stock market: crash 6; as dream theme 6–7
Stoyva, Johann 62
Strangling, as dream theme 113
Strauch, Inge 167
Stubbing, Mrs. 13
Subliminal memories 18
Suicide: as dream theme 111, 112; prevention by telepathy 53–54
Superstition 8
Sutherland (artist) 116
Swimming, as dream theme 79
Symbolism of dreams 26, 30, 54, 70, 94–95, 105; phallic 70, 114
Synchronicity 25, 26, 29, 161
"Synchronicity: An Acausal Connecting Principle" (Jung) 25
Synchronous ESP 145

Tabori, Cornelius 23
Tamayo (artist) 75, 112
Taranow, Myron 122
Tart, Charles 63, 81–82
Telepathic contagion 42
Telepathic dreams *see* Dreams, telepathic
Telepathic stimulus 159
Telepathy (Garrett) 66, 69
Telepathy 23, 29, 57; crisis 49; definition 10; dream (*see* Dreams, telepathic); Eisenbud on 42; influences dream content 82; patient-doctor relationships conducive of 43; sleep as favorable state for 23; use of, in communicating 39
Telepathy and Medical Psychology (Ehrenwald) 30
Themes, dream *see* Dream themes
Thompson, William 127, 132, 152
Thought Transference (Carington) 46
Three Musicians (Leger) 152
Thutmes IV, Pharaoh 4
Time, accelerated in dreams 61–62
"The Time Sense in Psychiatry" (Meerloo) 50
Trees and Horses (Cézanne) 114
Trivial dreams 14

Tyre 5
Tyrrell, G. N. M. 18

Ullman, Montague 29, 35, 45, 46, 66, 74, 106, 107, 108, 112, 171, 178, 179, 193, 209; begins dream exploration 66ff; case histories of telepathic patients 37ff; experimental goal of 70; work on paranormal dreams 36ff
Uncertainty of the Poet (de Chirico) 99
United States National Institute of Mental Health 170
University of California, Davis 63
University of California, Los Angeles 106, 130
University of Chicago 58, 62
University of Leningrad 9
University of Virginia 106, 163
University of Wyoming 201, 202, 211, 214, 216

Van de Castle, Robert 106, 107, 108, 109–118, 160, 162, 163, 164, 166, 167, 177–178
Van Delft (artist) 110
Van Gogh (artist) 80, 81, 126, 140
Vase, attic 99, 100
Vasiliev, Leonid L. 9, 10, 58
Vaughan, Alan 21, 124, 132–133, 141, 142–145, 147, 166, 172; and telepathic dream of Kurt Vonnegut, Jr. 3, 21
Vaughan, Iris 124, 127, 132–133, 142, 152ff
Violence, as dream theme 92, 93, 104
Virginia Wesleyan University 168
Vogel, Gerald 170
Vonnegut, Kurt, Jr. 3, 21

Walker, Dudley 18
Washburn, Brian 133
Washington, George 147
Washington and Lafayette at the Battle of Yorktown (Reed) 147
Water, as dream theme 79
Webster, Donald C. 138
West, Mae 40
White, Rhea 169
Wine Taster (Van Delft) 110

Withdrawal, patient 40
Witkin, Herman A. 60

The Yellow Rabbi (Chagall) 85
Young, Arthur 121, 138

Zapatistas (Orozco) 76
Zoroastrianism 87
Zusne, Leonard 200, 205, 206, 207